CO-ATX-280

An Essay on Names and Truth

'Hinzen attacks directly what some see as the greatest question hovering over linguistics in the past century: does structure itself contribute to meaning? He argues with sophistication and passion that syntax itself has meaning: it is not just a vehicle for another level of semantics. Hinzen's argument ranges over modern theoretical biology and developmental psychology, and utilizes the essence of minimalist grammar. The "interface" between syntax and semantics can be, essentially, an "identity". This is one of the most profound claims about mental structure and the notion of 'truth' that has been offered since Bertrand Russell sought to ground 'truth' in an external reality. Hinzen's claims cover a number of classic philosophical puzzles, but remain intuitive and provocative. The book marks a signal step in the evolution of generative grammar and the unification of mind and brain. It should command the attention of linguists, philosophers, psychologists and the field of cognitive science.'

Tom Roeper, University of Massachusetts, Amherst.

'In *Minimal Mind Design*, Wolfram Hinzen laid out the philosophical foundations of a minimalist naturalization of meaning. Most philosophers would have been satisfied with that important contribution; Hinzen took it as a mere first step. In this sequel, he embarks on a far-reaching program, aiming at rethinking the old chestnuts of concepts, names and truth within a radically Chomskyan paradigm. I simply do not know of any other work of this scope and profoundness that is as well-versed on current syntactic theorizing.'

Juan Uriagereka, University of Maryland at College Park.

'In this finely crafted essay Hinzen argues that quintessentially semantic notions like Truth and Reference are in fact deeply grounded in natural language syntax. This is nothing less than the beginning of a Copernican revolution in philosophy of language and mind. It should be on everyone's required reading list.'

Cedric Boeckx, Harvard.

Also by WOLFRAM HINZEN
Mind Design and Minimal Syntax

An Essay on Names and Truth

WOLFRAM HINZEN

OXFORD
UNIVERSITY PRESS

Great Clarendon Street, Oxford OX2 6DP

Oxford University Press is a department of the University of Oxford.
It furthers the University's objective of excellence in research, scholarship,
and education by publishing worldwide in

Oxford New York

Auckland Cape Town Dar es Salaam Hong Kong Karachi
Kuala Lumpur Madrid Melbourne Mexico City Nairobi
New Delhi Shanghai Taipei Toronto

With offices in

Argentina Austria Brazil Chile Czech Republic France Greece
Guatemala Hungary Italy Japan Poland Portugal Singapore
South Korea Switzerland Thailand Turkey Ukraine Vietnam

Published in the United States
by Oxford University Press Inc., New York

First published 2007 by Oxford University Press

British Library Cataloguing in Publication Data
Data available

Library of Congress Cataloging in Publication Data
Data available

Typeset by SPI Publisher Services, Pondicherry, India
Printed in Great Britain
on acid-free paper by
Biddles Ltd., King's Lynn, Norfolk

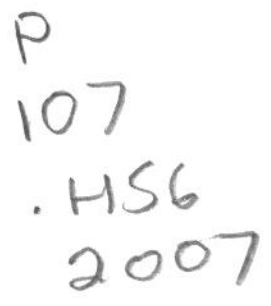

ISBN 978–019–927442–0 HB
978–019–922652–8 PB

1 3 5 7 9 10 8 6 4 2

Contents

Acknowledgements

The largest intellectual debt of this book is to Juan Uriagereka. I have been, in both my earlier book on *Mind Design* and here, merely trying to follow up some few of his ideas and to translate them into a philosophical programme: my effort to bridge a huge disciplinary gap between my own academic field and others with which it has been historically united has continued. This was not to the detriment of my career: hence I particularly wish to thank all those who have been supportive and good-willed about my enterprise, such as my departments at the Universiteit van Amsterdam and Durham University. That said, I was tempted to dedicate this book to all those who have a serious concern with pursuing the project of 'naturalizing philosophy' that Galileo and Descartes started. If I am right, much of twentieth-century philosophy has been a backwards movement in this regard, and it seems to me that the scope of this enterprise, and the changes for the nature of the discipline of philosophy that this perspective implies, are not seen. Institutional change does not occur, and interdisciplinarity remains a buzzword with little meaning. I also wish to express my dear thanks to numerous people with whom I have had enormously enjoyable and fruitful discussions over the past three years (in no particular order): Martin Stokhof, Cedric Boeckx, Robert Chametzky, Michiel van Lambalgen, Umberto Ansaldo, Peter M. Molenaar, Henry P. Stapp, Machiel Keestra, Enoch Aboh, Noam Chomsky, Massimo Piattelli-Palmarini, Brendan McGonigle, and Andrea Moro. Last but not least I wish to express my heartfelt gratitude to John Davey, my editor, who has been continuously in the background of my endeavour, a source to rely on at all times.

Therefore thinking and that by reason of which thought exists are one and the same thing, for thou wilt not find thinking without the being from which it receives its name.

Poem of Parmenides : On nature
(trans. A. Fairbanks)

Prologue

An earlier book of mine on mind design (Hinzen 2006a, henceforth referred to as MMD, for 'Minimal Mind Design') was dedicated to the pursuit of the naturalization of semantics on a novel, 'internalist' course. It consisted in reversing the traditional strategy that this naturalization enterprise had taken ever since the work of W. V. O. Quine and B. F. Skinner. That latter tradition aims to account for the semantic in terms of the non-semantic, and in particular in terms of *external relations* between expressions (or neurological configurations), on the one hand, and mind-external things in the world that pass the filter of metaphysical 'physicalism', on the other (where physicalism is the doctrine that only what is physical is real). In a thoroughly non-reductive spirit, by contrast, the internalist stance I defended in MMD grounded semantics in mental structures in our organism that, while formally described, provide a necessary structural skeleton for linguistic meaning to emerge in these structures. Put differently, the syntax of natural language expressions is intrinsic to their semantics.

The appeal to 'mental structures' might seem to give up on the naturalization project, yet I argued, following Chomsky (2000), that this conclusion arises from the confusion of an incontrovertible *methodological* naturalism with a highly contentious *metaphysical* naturalism (namely, physicalism). The former pursues naturalistic inquiry to whatever metaphysical conclusion it leads, whereas the latter premises such inquiry by certain metaphysical assumptions. Physicalism will in particular exclude the mental or semantic from nature on *a priori* grounds, rather than letting the methodological schemes of modern science decide over what is real. From the perspective of methodological naturalism pursued here, by contrast, the existence of the semantic should not be more controversial than the existence of gravitation. Newton could not explain the latter in more fundamental terms, and it even seemed somewhat bizarre how it could possibly relate to or emerge from matter. But Newton did not make the gravitational force's reality or existence dependent on their metaphysical 'reduction' to (or 'supervenience' on) matter. Arguably, modern science has followed this metaphysically open course: unlike Descartes it does not stipulate which properties the real is bound to have.

The present book explores the limits to the MMD-position on the structural origins of meaning, and the extent to which it is feasible and may prove to have some fruits as a programme of research. In fact, the position is subject to one very obvious attack: if semantics is to be grounded in structure (syntax), what would it have to say about the semantics of expressions that have *no* relevant structure to speak of? A paradigmatic example for such expressions is *names* (assuming their structure is not that of a description). What is worse, these are said to be the very paradigm of a *referential* expression; hence an externalist approach to their semantics would seem mandatory. Today such an approach is largely entertained in the field, whose discourse still sets out with the old Millian or Russellian idea of reducing the meaning of a word to a relation between a physical (and as such meaningless) *symbol* and an external physical *object*, with which the symbol's meaning is literally identified. Thus, a typical undergraduate discussion (for example, Lycan (2000) or Read (1994)), might begin with the notion that a proper name is no more than a 'label' attached to a thing: its entire meaning derives from what external thing it is (arbitrarily) associated to, hence it becomes meaning*less* if there is no such external object to which it refers (the so-called 'problem of non-existents'). The discussion might then proceed to show how this paradigm can be extended to all kinds of complex expressions, and consider the various theories that explain the meaning of, for example, sentences. These theories usually associate some meaning-determining relation to external objects for every sentential constituent ('properties' like wisdom for predicates like 'wise', individuals like Socrates for singular terms like 'Socrates', and a mystery referent for the copula 'is'), while the sentence *Socrates is wise* itself is regarded as some sort of 'mirror' of yet another external object, a 'state of affairs' or 'fact'. All such 'associations' are rated as either 'causal' or 'conventional'.

It is a commitment of both the earlier book and this one that the external relations in questions are non-explanatory if they exist at all. I claim that the question of their existence and nature, to the extent that the question is clear, is entirely empirical. No doubt mentally represented (non-acoustic) properties of linguistic expressions stand in various causal relations with external physical patterns in the environment (and in fact by and large necessarily adaptive ones). But these causal relations make as such virtually no contribution to the explanation of forms of intentionality we find in humans specifically, as opposed to creatures with another kind of mind. As things stand, we are the only creature on Earth that intentionally refers, which clearly is a function of our internal mental organization—the kind of mind we have. So, my claim here will be that the causal relations in which an organism comes to stand are (among other things) a function of its mental structures. The stance taken is that there is no 'mirror', and that predication (for example) exists because our minds happen to exhibit it: *externalizing* these structures does not further our understanding of them and explains nothing.

The basic externalist direction of explanation pursued in contemporary philosophy may be a residue of the old empiricist conception of 'ideas' or 'concepts'—the meanings of words—as being like little 'pictures' in the mind that 'mirror' and 'resemble' external objects. But as pointed out in MMD, it is a major insight of the eighteenth century, to whose thinkers this empiricism is often strangely ascribed, that ideas are modes of thought that do strikingly *not* resemble the objects to which they apply, and that their relation to these objects is *not* a causal one. Our idea of a city, say, or of a person are both radically unlike the objects referred to, if viewed from a physical or mind-independent perspective. Under the perspective of physics these objects essentially reflect light, say, have a colour, exert gravitation, consist of physical particles or waves, are penetrable by radiation, etc., properties all quite irrelevant to the way in which we think about cities and persons and the way these concepts function in human language. Moreover, major traditions in the study of cognition have long since moved away from the idea of the mind as a sort of 'theatre' of 'subjective' ideas accessible to introspection which can be modelled as 'representatives' or 'representations' of external objects. Such mental structures can be more abstract and algebraic, organizing experience in rational ways which experience does not suggest.

This book specifically aims to reconsider the contemporary debate on the nature of truth by these internalist lights. The old idea that truth is correspondence to reality again assumes that declarative sentences get their meaning from their relation to a mind-external fact (or 'truth-maker') whose structure somehow mirrors that of the sentence or the proposition expressed by it. Again, the structure of the truth-maker is an externalization of the kinds of structures we know sentences to have—subjects and predicates, in particular, which are said to 'correspond to' objects and properties, respectively, with predication corresponding to a posited external relation of predication or 'instantiation', often assumed to be a part of the mind-external world. The correspondence theory has by now been largely replaced by a 'deflationism' or 'minimalism' about truth, which discards external relations to 'facts' as explanatory for what the truth of a sentence or proposition consists in. But an actual internalist research programme, which would attempt to explain by appeal to inherent structures of the human mind what the origin of our specifically human ways of relating to the world is, has not so far been entertained. It is thus interesting to see where we arrive if we approach putative paradigmatically externalist dimensions of the mind, such as reference and truth, from an internalist perspective—perhaps not unlike the way in which Kant approached the topic of causality. In short, this book set out from the idea that placing contemporary debates on truth and reference in an internalist or 'biolinguistic' setting (Lenneberg 1967; Jenkins 2000; Uriagereka 1998) might engender entirely novel perspectives on what these things are.

Truth is a particularly interesting issue also with respect to twentieth-century attempts to vindicate a physicalist metaphysics: truth never quite found a place in this metaphysics. An interesting episode in this history can be found in Skinner (1957): his system disallows truth being referenced at all, and leads to problems with the analysis of a sentence like *All swans are white.* An utterance of this sentence is said to be controlled by an external stimulus (like every other utterance, on Skinner's view), and to be equivalent to the statement *Swans are white,* with swans as the external stimuli and *all* modifying this whole sentence, equivalent to *always,* or *always it is possible to say.* But as Chomsky (1959, section X) notes, *Swans are white* is just as general an expression, and moreover it is just as 'possible to say' that *Swans are green.* So the intended analysis of the expression presumably is that *All swans are white* means: *that X is white [as opposed to green] is* **true**, *for each swan X.* This analysis however involves a reference to truth. For all it seems, talk about 'stimulus control' of the utterance in question cannot but be a misleading paraphrase of the traditional truth-locution.

The same question of the 'legitimacy' of truth is raised in Tarski's seminal work on truth (Tarski 1944). Tarski attempted an *eliminative definition* of truth that translated all semantic terms into logical, syntactic, set-theoretic, or physical notions. Whether Tarski succeeded in this is subject to a large debate (see e.g. Field 1972; Etchemendy 1988). Yet, the one commitment that is least frequently questioned in contemporary analytic philosophy and the philosophy of truth is physicalism itself. Truth is also the prime *persona non grata* on the stage of eliminative materialism (Churchland 1995), where propositional forms of thought tied to 'linguo-formal' means of description are regarded as philosophical myths. Not unrelatedly, contemporary neo-pragmatism renounces 'belief in truth', which Richard Rorty (2001) in particular suggests replacing with a belief in the benefits of prosperity. The present work not only considers physicalism as incoherent but also replies to pragmatism and eliminative materialism that truth as a cognitive universal is an empirical given. The existence of propositional structures of thought is an empirical matter again, which a general metaphysical theory of cognition or 'mind' cannot prejudge.

Contemporary 'deflationist' discussions on truth somewhat grudgingly acknowledge the apparently ineliminable role of a truth predicate in generalizations such as the one concerning swans above, suggesting that the role of truth in generalization is the crucial obstacle to a 'nihilism' about truth, in the sense of Ramsey (1927), who suggests the redundancy of truth. The whole and only point of truth is now said to be to allow us to express infinite conjunctions such as *swan-1 is white*, *swan-2 is white*, etc., in each conjunct of which there is no talk about sentences being true, but just about swans. Thus, truth is made non-existent again and 'objective reference' to particular swans (as opposed to a reference to linguistic forms of expression) is restored. As Quine would put this conclusion, talk about the truth of a sentence is (almost) entirely a *circumlocution*, an 'indirect' and (virtually) unnecessary way of talking about reality:

> language is not the point. In speaking of the truth of a given sentence there is only indirection; we do better to simply say the sentence and so speak not about language but about the world (Quine 1968: 10–11).

By and large, thinking about truth over the last forty years seems never to have fundamentally questioned either Skinner's externalism or his physicalist metaphysics. The approach to truth in this book *is* a syntactic one, like Tarski's, not however in the sense of the logical syntax that Tarski knew but in the sense of the generative grammar that post-dated his work, and without the reductionism and eliminativism that was a part of his project, including the external relations of reference or satisfaction that he posited. The syntactic structures in question are universal structures of language interpreted as universal structures of the human mind. My perspective is in this sense thoroughly 'psychologistic'—although the underlying picture of the mind is very different from the one that underlies the 'anti-psychologistic stance'.

Predicating truth does not in my view mean adding any novel substantive content to the predication entailed by the sentential structure to which the truth-predicate attaches (in our example, the predication of whiteness to swans): conceptually, a proposition changes no more its content when we call it true than an object changes its nature when we judge it to exist. Nonetheless, when a predication of truth is added to the simple predication contained in the sentence to which it attaches, it changes the intentional structure of a statement in which that expression figures in structural and quantificational respects. For these reasons, truth *is* intrinsically linked to the generative structures underlying human language—language *is* the point, *pace* Quine—and it seems we can learn little about the origins of these structures from looking at the physical world or at what simple predications like 'this swan is white' are about.

Overall, then, this book has a simple message: truth has an internalist explanation; the origin of our human sense of truth lies at least in part in the structures that happen to characterize our kind of mind. Its external and adaptive aspects, if such there are, follow once truth is there; they are not its origin. All this is meant as a contribution to the study of an aspect of human nature: we are creatures pondering, seeking, valuing, avoiding, and denying—the truth. I am not saying this is our 'essence', it is simply that our sense of truth is a rather surprising and unexplained feature of our mental life, presumably a cognitive universal, and, as I will assume, a contingent fact of our natural history (as opposed to a logical necessity) that requires reconstruction and naturalistic inquiry.

Nothing in that reconstruction will tell us much about our capacity to 'find the truth'. But maybe it reveals that the question of whether we do is misdirected. We happen to have minds that creatively produce thoughts, virtually incessantly. Although we never run out of thoughts, sometimes thought 'stops', as when we look at a white sheet of paper, lacking an inspiration. All we can then hope for is that the generative engine of thought starts again, and gives us something useful; but there are no real techniques for 'having thoughts', or inspirations. They come, or they do not. Some of these thoughts, in a further thinking effort, we also come to evaluate and mark as 'true', although we know that in marking them this way, their elevated status will remain fluid, subject to disturbances at all times. Thus in particular the outside world will not support maintaining many such assessments for long, and as a consequence of that, what we judge to be the truth will not ultimately be out of tune with the real. Still, the coming of thoughts, their assessment as true, and their dismissal as false, are, for all that the social and the external environment contribute, ultimately part of a dialogue of the mind with itself, which exploits structural resources inherent to the mind perhaps found nowhere in nature but there.

The book consists of one large opening chapter providing some stage setting and laying out some background concerning the framework of theoretical linguistics used, two intermediate chapters fleshing out a stance taken here on 'concepts' and their initial structuring in a syntactic derivation ('conceptual structures'), and two final chapters proposing a syntax for truth and for reference, respectively ('intentional structures'). The theoretical framework of generative grammar introduced in Chapter 1 is that of recent minimalist syntax, in particular a derivational, level-free system with a 'single-cycle' generation architecture in the sense of Chomsky (2006). It is here introduced with the specific tint argued for in MMD, which particularly affects assumptions as to what explanatory role the interfaces of the linguistic system with other cognitive systems play. The basic commitment here is that propositional thought and language are deeply entangled, to the extent even of being non-distinguishable. Chapter 2 begins the internalist reconstruction of meaning from where meaning itself is here argued to begin, namely concepts that are 'atomic' in the sense of lacking any internal semantic structure. The essential point here is that meaning begins from concepts, literally: hence, in particular it does not begin from reference, which is an intentional relation built up in human acts of language use in which concepts *figure*. Put differently, how we refer is a function of what concepts we possess, as human beings, rather than vice versa. Also Chapter 3 does not delve into intentional reference or truth as yet, depicting instead initial conceptual structures as something where acts of intentional reference (affecting our relations to the world in quantificational and scopal respects) are not yet structurally supported. The final two chapters provide internalist accounts of this intentional aspect of expressions for the case of declarative sentences and names, respectively.

1

Roots of the Intentional

1.1 Truth as a human universal and as explanandum

'True' is a word of English that has a sound and a meaning. Its meaning is what I shall call a 'concept': a concept is the meaning of a word, whatever that meaning is. Other, probably all, languages have words with different sounds expressing, closely enough, the same concept, which I presume every human being has. Pilate famously asked, jestingly, 'What is truth?', and I will not answer that question in this book any more than he did. What matters here is that even to understand this very question, we must have the concept of truth. Even if we do not know how to tell what truth is, we know what we are talking about when asking what it is: we are talking about *truth*. Surely enough, the philosophical tradition has provided us with a staggering number of tomes on the nature of truth. But this should not distract from the fact that in another sense, truth is something rather mundane and known to everybody. To know what truth is, in this mundane sense, is to have the concept of truth, and to *use* the relevant word in a particular way. Using it in that familiar way does not mean that we would know how to tell what truth is, or what is in fact true; it means to evaluate things as true or false, to make judgements which distinguish the true from the false. Descartes regarded this capacity as the most common human possession, the 'best distributed thing in the world':

'Le bon sens est la chose du monde la mieux partagée; car chacun pense en être si bien pourvu que ceux même qui sont les plus difficiles à contenter en toute autre chose n'ont point coutume d'en désirer plus qu'ils en ont. En quoi il n'est pas vraisemblable que tous se trompent: mais plutôt cela témoigne que la puissance de bien juger et distinguer le vrai d'avec le faux, qui est proprement ce qu'on nomme le bon sens ou la raison, est naturellement égale en tous les hommes' (Descartes 1637).[1]

[1] 'Good sense is, of all things among men, the most equally distributed; for every one thinks himself so abundantly provided with it, that those even who are the most difficult to satisfy in everything else, do not usually desire a larger measure of this quality than they already possess. And in this it is not likely that all are mistaken the conviction is rather to be held as testifying that the power of judging aright and of distinguishing truth from error, which is properly what is called good sense or reason, is

Truth, that is, is part of our general faculty of judgement. Different people *use* that faculty differently, but the faculty as such does not therefore differ too. Some people extend their faculty to things they should not judge about, and thus they make mistakes; others do not exercise their sense of the truth to a great extent. Yet, in principle, everyone can make a judgement of truth about anything: if we ask a person what she thinks of something, she will either find herself thinking something about it, and proceed to make an assertion, or else abstain from judgement, as she realizes she should undertake no commitment on the truth in this matter. Truth is in this way perspicuously unrestricted to any particular ontological domain: we make judgements of truth about virtually everything. This *domain-generality* of truth is perhaps surprising given the high degree of specialization and 'modularity' that we observe in cognition, action, and brain anatomy at large. Yet, nobody would restrict his capacity for truth to the domain, say, of the chemical. Truth is everywhere, in any domain where judgements are made.

The faculty in question is not only limitless; it also cannot be taken away from a human being without effectively depriving him or her of personhood, as in torture. In this sense, our sense of the truth is absolute: there is nothing to restrict our capacity to say no to something that someone else asks us to agree with. If we find ourselves disagreeing, there is nothing in principle that could make us say yes, except our own decision to reverse our opinion. Our sense of the true is therefore also a source of power: anyone lecturing to an audience will have to subdue to its sense of truth and truthfulness, and we predict that as the truthfulness and substance of the message decreases, the use of rhetoric, insecurity, demagogy, and deception will increase. Again, that absolute power which resides in our sense of the true is not necessarily exercised greatly, as that takes effort, freedom from external control, and passion. Yet, there are striking cases where we see it developing to its full extent, as in cases of political dissent where truth may count for more than life.

Abstracting from individual differences, then, we are talking about a common human possession, in the same way that language is. Language as well is used differently by different people, from poetry to sharing information to upholding social relations or deception, but a linguist interested in the architecture of the human language faculty would abstract from such differences: they leave a basic abstract structure intact. Language shares many aspects of our sense of truth and is plausibly correlated with it: in

by nature equal in all men (...).' (Translation from the online Gutenberg edition, see http://www.literature.org/authors/descartes-rene/reason-discourse/index.html.)

particular, it is as limitless in extension and as domain-general as truth is. There is nothing that we *have* to talk about at any given moment, and the ability to talk about non-existents, abstract objects, or objects arbitrarily remote in space and time is part of the essence of language. There is no stimulus that cannot trigger language use, be it a noise of a passing car, an odd feeling in one's stomach, or an enthusiasm about the latest recording of Bach—leading in all cases to a linguistic response that is creative in the sense of not being stimulus-controlled, yet not random. It never fails to be appropriate to the circumstance. Moreover, language can *access* any domain of information, as long as we are looking for a 'rational' sort of access, in which the question of truth arises: we can describe music as much as emotions or indeed anything else in language, even if often only imperfectly; by contrast, we cannot make much use of music or emotion to convey the articulated and propositional messages that language conveys.

Consciousness is not the point in any of this. When consciously deliberating about what judgement of truth to make in some particular issue we are not essentially conscious of any of the mechanisms underlying the thought processes involved. We *judge* the truth rather than being consciously aware of it somehow, or seeing it. We are simply not aware of how the concept of truth is lexically selected, how it enters complex predications in the context of a phrase or sentence, and how it is applied on an occasion. There is no *phenomenology* associated with any of these mental processes—or, to the extent that there is, it may well relate to the phonetic form (the internal sound representation) of the expression involved, alone. In this sense, in the realm of truth we are mentally moving around in a fundamentally *abstract* dimension. Moreover, we essentially *find* ourselves thinking certain thoughts, or being convinced by certain arguments and opposed to others; hunches as to what the truth might be with respect to a particular issue essentially *occur* in us. 'Being creative' is a euphemism for the attitude of attentively waiting for such a process to happen.

Despite this remoteness of our propositional mental life from consciousness and the phenomenology of experience there is a kind of *evidence* to truth. Someone calling George W. Bush a 'liar' usually has no qualms about what truth is. What truth is, and what deception is, is often essentially obvious to us. Again, that evidence disappears the moment we theorize about what it is. Common-sense explanations of what truth is tend to take on a circular flavour: 'truth' is when something 'is the case'; truth is 'what can be asserted, without any mistake', etc. In any such explanations a possession of the concept of truth is not only presupposed; the explanation given is only adequate if the notion itself or a close synonym occurs in it. The latter we see when testing putative explanations in which no such close synonym occurs, for example explanations in terms of the notions of correspondence or assertion. On the view of truth as correspondence with reality, if we are asked *what* relation correspondence is, and *what* thing it is that a true proposition corresponds to, the answer is that it is a thing that stands in such a relation to the proposition in question that it makes that proposition *true*. No other relation, and no other thing, will do. But these depend on an understanding of what truth is rather than explicating it. As for assertion, commonsensically it is clear that assertion is not truth. Nothing is true because it is asserted, by us or others, so we think. The contention that in academia assertions become true if only one re-asserts them often enough, is just cynical. In making this contention we in essence know it is false (or else confuse something's being taken to be true with its being true). Moreover, nothing is asserted because it is true (though it is asserted because it is *meant* to be). So, while there is a connection between the notions of assertion and of truth—assertion is the predication of truth—there is simply no question that one would reduce to the other (Hinzen 2000).

The most immediate explanation for this absence of non-circular characterizations of truth may be that there simply is no such thing as a definition or theory of the ordinary notion of truth. To ask for a theory of truth may be like asking for a theory of houses or people. We know what houses or people are, but we do not theorize about them. To be sure, we *can* theorize at least about what people are, say in a neuroscientific investigation. But such an inquiry will presuppose that concept, and analyse only one dimension of it. Moreover, it will typically no more aim at giving a definition of our concept of a person than a physical inquiry into light would aim for a definition of our ordinary concept of light. Ordinary concepts in general not only seem to lack (non-circular) definitions, natural science is also not the endeavour of defining them. Explanations in naturalistic inquiry do not proceed by a conceptual analysis of the domain of inquiry, and they do not presuppose one (except for the fact that the concepts in question will have to be sufficiently clear in order to delineate the area of inquiry). Moreover, as the theory matures, the intuitive contents of the notions delineating the relevant area are typically abandoned.

Our inquiry here, which is a naturalistic one, will similarly not be one into the definition or nature of truth. Nor is one such analysis presupposed here. All that is presupposed is that I and you, the reader, plainly share the concept of truth, which figures (more or less centrally, given individual differences, as noted) in our respective mental lives. The inquiry is about the *phenomenon* of truth, not the concept, much as a physical inquiry into time is about the phenomenon not the concept. A naturalistic inquiry into truth is possible, because, like persons, matter, or time, human truth has aspects that lend themselves, under the appropriate idealizations, to naturalistic inquiry.

In particular, truth figures in judgements of the truth of propositions such as 'That the Earth is round is true'. Even looking superficially at this human phenomenon, we should be rather puzzled by it. If nothing we ever think or see is conclusive evidence for the truth in some particular matter, and no assertion ever as such entails truth, our concept of truth is the concept of something that we judge despite the ultimate lack of a basis for these judgements in our experience. This is as in other cases, such as the discrete infinity of the natural number concept, to which we generalize as well, even though neither our factual experience nor our factual thought processes, both of which are finite, could provide evidence for it. Truth in this way becomes an evolutionary puzzle, as language (and mathematics) are (or other categorial structures entering human and perhaps animal cognition, like the notion of a *cause*).

While there is an evolutionary necessity for *adaptation*—for associating the right response to a given stimulus, for having sensorimotor mechanisms to cope with external pressure—none of this predicts or necessitates the propositional forms of thought that we associate with language and truth. There is no functional necessity to either truth or language (of the human kind)—most organisms get along without either, even if they have sophisticated systems of communication, all of which are radically different from human language in both their structure and content.

There may be no *logical* necessity for truth either. Although truth is a fundamental concept of logic, the necessity for logic to revolve around it may be disputed.[2] If that necessity in turn is granted, the question will shift to the status of logic itself, as something that exploits truth rather than explains it. If logic is not a contingent product of our natural history (perhaps an evolutionary offshoot of language, from which it is abstracted), and is transhistorically and transculturally necessary, this will aggravate the problem of the origins of truth: it will now seem as if it is virtually written into the fabric of the universe, and an immutable aspect of it. If it is a contingent product and at least partially related to the evolved architecture of the human mind/brain, it will need a naturalistic explanation.

This is what we pursue here, via an analysis of what can perhaps be subjected to such an explanation, the structures of the human judgements

[2] See Koslow (1992).

in which truth occurs, even if we are only learning to make the first beginnings with the relevant explanatory schemes.

1.2 An internalist approach to the origin of human truth

I will study truth as a semantic primitive in human thought, as a category that corresponds to the meanings of particular kinds of expressions, in first approximation sentences as opposed to words or sub-sentential phrases such as Noun Phrases (NPs). As such it has formed the foundation for most formal semantic theories. The assumption here, at a most basic level, is that human thought exhibits semantic properties: thought is *intentional*. In the philosophical discourse of the last fifty years, intentionality is broadly speaking taken to invoke *a relation that thought has to the world*. At that level of generality, this is not very illuminating. Of course, all animal cognition is bound to be *adaptive* in one way or another: it will tend to subserve the organism's survival, which depends on its dealing with its environment in ways that enhance its life prospects. Presumably, this is the very root of the intuition that cognition and intentionality have a relational character: they are determined or constrained from 'without' rather than 'within'. However, intentionality in human thought may be crucially different in character from adaptive behaviour in general.[3] Much human thought is not really directed at the external world, involving abstract objects instead that have no direct perceptual dimensions to them, such as fairness, joy, social progress, numbers, or truth. Ordinary human thought is also not about the physical world in any direct sense: that is, the molecules, waves, fields and quantum potentials that surround us and that, ultimately, we are ourselves. It is rather directed to such 'things' as love, wars, fame, cities, and people. It is about a specific *Umwelt*, which the concepts with which we think themselves help to

[3] Dretske (2006) distinguishes merely adaptive behaviour from behaviour that has a minimal rationality to it. The latter is behaviour that is explained by what the organism in question 'thinks'. This is not the distinction I have in mind here. In Dretske's view, animal behaviour is by and large bound to be 'rational' in the sense of consistently serving the organism's fitness. But, Dretske argues, *thought* need not be involved for that to be so, even if, if it was involved, it would cause the same behaviour. Thus, it is surely rational to blink upon sudden movements towards the eye, in the sense that I don't want your finger in my eye, and I believe that closing my eye in the right moment is a way to achieve this. In other words, in a rational decision analysis, blinking is the right thing to do. But that sort of thought process is irrelevant for the production of the behaviour, which does not exhibit minimal rationality in Dretske's sense. His distinction, it seems to me, makes good conceptual sense as long as we do not ask what is meant by 'thought'. In particular, it seems to me that abstract thought and judgement can be reflex-like as well, and will not be less rational for that reason; moreover, it can be characterized structurally or algebraically, as opposed to merely by an appeal to the maximization of the efficient pursuit of goals. My point in the text is that thought may be distinct from biological adaptation not conceptually or on normative grounds, but empirically and structurally.

constitute. Although there is a sense in which ordinary thought and talk is about the external world—we talk about Popes, zebras, and traffic lights, all of which are external to ourselves—reacting to the world linguistically by means of propositionally structured thoughts is very different from simply reacting adaptively to it. A propositional form of thought, containing a subject and a predicate, is capable of 'objectifying' a stimulus. Reacting to an alarm signal ringing, or the smell of food, is not such a form, or at least need not be. Ordinary ways of responding to an environment, like drinking beer in a pub or evading an approaching car, need not be propositional either. Objectification requires taking a distance from the *Umwelt* in which we are immersed, to lose the grip that the environmental stimulus has on us. Possession of a concept of truth entails that we distinguish appearance from reality, that we *judge* the appearances as opposed to being stuck in them. A mere process of adaptation neither predicts nor demands such a capability (although it is of course consistent with them).

As I will argue in Section 2.3, moreover, there is no such relation between a word and a thing as what is commonly called 'reference' in philosophy. Intentionality does not depend on or start from such a relation. The very point of *human* intentionality, at least, is that it is not under the control of the stimulus or the referent.[4] Human reference is *intentional* reference; it cannot, for all we know, be characterized in non-intentional terms: terms not employing the range of human concepts and perspectives that underlie human acts of reference. Explaining the intentional as a relation to the environment is thus uninformative. The question is where these relations *come from*. They are *premised* by human intentionality, but do not explain it. No *causal* specification of the relations in question helps.

Human concepts, this book will contend, are not referring as such, but only when *used* on an occasion where they enter into an *act* of intentional reference. Intentionality, as I will understand it here, is strictly a phenomenon of language *use*: concepts, as such, do not exhibit it. To put this differently, there could be a creature that only had concepts, but did not use them to make judgements or to intentionally refer to things. The basis for this claim will be that, empirically speaking, the structural principles responsible for concepts and for compositionally interpreted conceptual structures are both distinct and independent of the structural principles we find to be relevant in

[4] Cognition and mental representation in *non*-human animals *may* be characterizable in terms of a relation of reference specifiable in non-intentional terms (see Gallistel 1990).

structures underlying intentional acts of reference and truth. It may in fact be that most species have concepts, yet only one uses them to intentionally refer (see further Chapter 2). The challenge is thus to explain how concepts are put to use on an occasion. On the story told here, this depends firstly on the evolution of a lexicon which *lexicalizes* concepts through words, each of which consists in the pairing of a phonetic label with a concept or meaning. Secondly, it depends on embedding them in hierarchical structural patterns correlating with specific semantic capacities. Particular kinds of patterns enable particular acts of intentional language use. The ideal is to see semantic complexity track syntactic complexity.

This perspective on the origin of truth implies an 'internalist' turn, as noted. So let me begin by characterizing the *externalist* conception of cognition and semantics that has characterized recent philosophical discourse throughout, starting from Frege in the late nineteenth century, via its reception and development through the great fathers of analytic philosophy, Bertrand Russell, and Willard van Orman Quine, essentially up to the present day. I will be telling a story to illustrate this conception, which runs under the name of 'Plato's Beard' and revolves around negative existential propositions such as (1):

(1) King Lear/Satan/the King of France does not exist.

The story forms an inherent part of virtually any undergraduate course on the philosophy of language or philosophical logic (see e.g. Read 1994: 122ff.). Its formative influence for the history of twentieth-century philosophy can hardly be overestimated: it gave rise to the theory of descriptions in analytic philosophy, which became a part of the theory of names and lies at the beginning of a whole philosophical movement based on the foundational assumption that there is a parting of ways between 'grammatical' and 'logical' form. Consider, then, the following reasoning:

(i) the meaning of a referential expression (noun phrase) is (identical to) the external object it stands for or 'refers' to (e.g. the meaning of *Socrates* is the philosopher Socrates, a physical object, and the meaning of 'wise' is an external property, wisdom).
(ii) So-called 'empty names' such as 'King Lear' or 'Satan' stand for no such object.
(iii) Although seemingly referential, they are therefore meaningless (by (i) and (ii)).
(iv) Compositionality holds: the meaning of a complex expression is composed of the meanings of its parts plus their mode of combination.

(e.g. a proposition like 'Socrates is wise' is literally composed out of Socrates himself and wisdom.)

(v) A sentence composed of a meaningless part is itself meaningless.

(vi) If truth requires meaningfulness, sentences containing empty names cannot be true (or express true propositions) (from (iii)–(v)).

(vii) But it seems that a sentence like 'King Lear did not exist' *is* meaningful, and in fact perfectly true.

(viii) Contradiction (from (vi) and (vii)).

The externalism and relational conception of meaning that lies at the heart of this reasoning comes out clearly in (i). Perspicuously, meaning as conceived in (i) does not depend on the mind. There is a word/symbol, and there is a physical object, and there is a physical or conventional relation between them. The mental does not figure anywhere in this conception of meaning: the mind does not enter.

The context of the above reasoning and the reason why Quine called it 'Plato's Beard' is that Plato played with it in his dialogue *Parmenides*. Parmenides had argued that being equates with thinking. Thought is the measure of existence, since what does not exist cannot be thought or talked about at all. Accordingly, all we can think about and ascribe a property to—be it Satan, Lear, or a mountain of pure gold—must in some sense *be*. Russell thought this militated against a 'robust sense of reality'. Not thought but 'reality' itself must be the measure of existence and being. Accordingly, a way must be found to make negative existential propositions come out as either meaningless or false. Yet, a contradiction arises from this assumption, as we have seen.

To resolve this contradiction Russell took a step that consisted in what appears as a deliberate distortion of reality: a speaker uttering 'King Lear went mad' or 'Satan/King Lear/Hamlet does not exist', he argued, is not *referring* to any object at all. He cannot be, as reference is a relation to something physical. Linguistic form, the conclusion is, leads us to wrongly suspect a referential act in cases such as (1), which seem to contain a singular term, and a singular term on Russell's view is inherently referential. Linguistic form systematically misleads us. The *logical* analysis of the expression must reveal that there is no name or singular term here at all, blatant as that fact may seem. Appearances notwithstanding, there is a *description* involved here, which is a *complex quantified* expression of the sort we can express in English by forms such as 'the rival of God according to the Christian tradition', 'the hero of Shakespeare's play "King Lear"', etc. These complex descriptions are analysed according to first-order predicate logic as in (2), where '∃' is a second-order symbol added to the formal representation language, depicting a second-order property. This quantifier in (2) predicates existence of the first-order property of being the hero of 'King Lear' which has gone mad. In plain English, (2) says that this very property has an instance:

(2) ∃x (x is the unique hero of 'King Lear' & x went mad)

Assertions of the type in (1) do not then have to be meaningless, because they can simply be *false*, which Russell suggests is the natural semantic evaluation of (2). A referentialist model of meaning is kept, which indeed was the point of the exercise: it can be kept, because (1) analysed as (2) is not thought to refer at all.

Russell's analysis of non-referring descriptions and of names as false quantificational expressions inaugurated the programme of 'philosophical logic', the attempt to lay down rational structures of thought viewed as being systematically out of tune with what empirical evidence their linguistic expression may provide for them. Rather than studying human forms of expressions and their rational stucture empirically, the move is to externalize these forms of thought and to encode them in an artificial medium, a constructed and conventional 'formal language'. On a standard view, for us to understand a sentence S is to stand in an external relation to a 'proposition' that has a 'logical form' written in such a formal language and to know that S expresses that proposition. The contents that our mind can think are not now intrinsically the contents of this mind any more. Propositions by definition are language- and mind-independent. Our mind, as a subject matter for philosophy at least, becomes a device for 'representing' or 'grasping' them.

As MMD (Hinzen 2006a) argues, the move is a defining feature of modern philosophy and an instance of an inherently *functional* characterization of mind, as opposed to a characterization of the mind as a natural object. Both 'representing' and 'grasping' are two essentially mysterious notions by comparison to the entirely naturalistic proposal in MMD or generative this book, that provides syntax an empirical account for *how propositional meanings are actually derived* in a constructive computational process internal to the human faculty of language. This suggestion does not appeal to processes of 'grasping' in an explanatory role. It naturalizes them by appeal to the mental processes that explain certain meanings from the structures that encode them.

Russell was consequential enough to conclude that *no* English name really is a name. For, a name is only a name if its reference is *guaranteed*, but that is never the case. Natural language has no 'logically proper names'. Or rather, for Russell it has them only in the form of what we ordinarily never think of as proper names, namely demonstratives such as 'this' or 'here', which, Russell said, refer to the immediate data of experience, and cannot fail in reference. But this, of course, is unintuitive: we do not strictly speaking refer to anything when we say 'here'. That would be like saying that there are 'heres' to which we can refer. It rather seems that if we use the indexical 'here' to refer to anything, this is humanly possible only if we refer *under a description* to whatever it is we are referring to, that is if we use a descriptive term to characterize *what* we are referring to: we are referring to this *place*, this *room*, this *universe*, etc. There is no such thing as a human referential act carried out in terms of *this*, *the*, *here*, *now*, without these items being implicitly understood as attached to a descriptive noun: *this man*, *the place here*, *the time now*, etc. These expressions are not *lexically* referential at all, then, but *become* referential once they are part of a context in which they occur within a syntactically *complex* expression.

It also remains unintuitive that a person referring to *the golden mountain* or *the highest prime number* would not be referring to anything (hence that these are not 'referential expressions'), and that any positive assertion about these things must be necessarily false. Even if we judge them not to exist, there is a fairly obvious sense in which they are *referenced* in the acts in question, in disregard to physical constraints on existence. In this sense, Parmenides was right. Accordingly, one might suspect that the existence of some *external* object is not *necessary* for a referential act to occur. The result we need is that an act of reference does not entail a judgement of existence, nor existence as such.

It is true as well that expressions of the forms *God's rival*, or *the author of King Lear*, etc., are fundamentally different formally from expressions of the forms *Satan* or *Shakespeare*. Evidently, the former expressions are *structured* in a way the latter are not; in particular, they exhibit a compositional semantics. It would be rather surprising therefore that they meant the same, hence that the difference in structure would be semantically irrelevant or redundant (see further Section 5.1). Of course, the description may be associated purely *semantically* to the name, that is, not as a function of its linguistic form. But a radically arbitrary or non-transparent mapping from syntax to semantics should, all else being equal, be avoided. The familiar objection that reference can be 'rigid', hence does not proceed via a mode of presentation or description (see Chapter 5), remains too.

One thing I will effectively suggest, then, in this book, is that Russell's 'rectification' of language has things backwards, and that what he calls 'logic' and sets *against* natural language does not bring us closer to analysing the inherent rationality of the human mind. As Pietroski has pointed out, the gap between language and logic is probably much smaller (Pietroski 2002; and see Hornstein 1984). The Russellian turn is based on a wrong externalist premise, that meaning is constrained by physical existence, which has not been abandoned since.

Frege had, of course, already enriched Russell's externalist and reference-based picture by assuming names had a 'sense' as well as a reference, where the sense roughly speaking corresponds to a Russellian definite description of a referent. That is, the meaning of a name is not only the object referred to but also the mode under which it is presented to a thinker, or a way in which he recognizes or identifies it. In this way, an assertion about Lear or Satan can be meaningful (at the level of sense), yet lack a truth value (at the level of reference). But a sense for Frege is as mind-external as a physical referent: an externalism is maintained. One can trace the same externalism to the uneasiness in analytic philosophy to grant truth-aptness to domains of discourse without clear physical correlates, such as moral or aesthetic discourse. These are areas in which there are rational debates and ordinary people unproblematically apply their concept of truth. Nor are ordinary applications of this concept necessarily sensitive to whether we have a fictional context or not, whether we are talking about abstract objects like justice or numbers, or material entities like stones.

None of this is to imply that Plato or Parmenides were right to grant existence to unicorns and golden mountains. But it is highly doubtful whether this *ontological* rendering of their views is the right one. A more reasonable view in itself, and certainly a more reasonable interpretation, is that 'golden mountain', say, is a (complex) *concept*, and is *as such* meaningful and a potential meaningful *constituent* of complex expressions with a compositional semantics and possibly a use for purposes of reference on an occasion. As a complex concept, its formation is free and unconstrained by issues of existence. Similarly, 'unicorn' is, to start with, a concept, and can come on occasion to be used to *refer* to a concrete object—for example to an object I consider a unicorn, to a picture of a unicorn, or to a former girlfriend: our concepts as encoded in words or phrases in language will not determine to what the speaker will finally use them to refer. For the word 'unicorn' to be meaningful is for it to express a concept, not for there to be some mysterious relation of reference between it and some such external object. Neither is it for me to use it as part of a predication to assert the existence of any such object. Again, I *may* find evidence such as (3), and with that I would have a basis for asserting (4), a judgement of existence:

(3) Myrtha is a unicorn.
(4) Unicorns exist.

In such a case, I have intentionally referred to an instance of the concept of a unicorn (an object viewed as a unicorn), and then asserted that concept's existence. But there is nothing in our *concept* of a unicorn as such that speaks for or against existence, and hence implicates an ontology or would support either (3) or (4). Merely contemplating a concept of something, be it the concept of unicorns, of Fred, or the universe, leaves the question of its existence open. *Thinking* about unicorns does not mean or suggest there is one. That question is an empirical and *a posteriori* matter entirely. It is only by engaging in *judgements* such as (5), which by Kantian standards are *synthetic*, that the question of the existence of individuals arises, and we can conclude (6):

(5) This is Fred/a unicorn/the universe.
(6) Fred/unicorns/this universe exists.

No judgement of existence is implicit in simply using a concept as a constituent of a thought, or at the level of what I call conceptual structure: a *concept* does not have that much internal structure: it is not a *judgement*. Nothing external is entailed by it qua lexical item, or assumed to be entailed by a speaker. A subject S of a predication (7) has no such internal structure, and in particular contains no predication itself, in the way that (8) suggests:

(7) S is P.
(8) [S exists] (and) is P.

It is the very grammatical form of (5) or (7) that leads to this conclusion, for nothing in these expressions suggests anything of the form in (8). We don't have to wait for logic to correct grammar in this case. Intentionality and reference are issues simply not arising either at the level of unstructured concepts or even structured concepts like *blue house* or *golden mountain* that mean what they do independently of whether they are judged to have an instance or are used to refer to one.

Both the idea of a purely conceptual mode of thought, where intentional properties relating to judgements are not yet involved, and the asymmetric dependence of the judgements on the conceptual specification of the proposition judged, will turn out to be fundamental in the present work. The combination of these ideas allows, on the one hand, for Parmenides to be right, in the sense that there is a form of being that we cannot logically fall short of as long as we merely think; but, on the other hand, it also allows for Kant, Frege, and Russell to be right in their second-order analysis of the predicate of existence, because that former form of being which we cannot fall short of leaves the question of existence open, as a matter for judgement as opposed to conceptual understanding. As Kant noted in his analysis of existence, once an object of thought is conceptualized, predicating existence of it will not make it a *conceptually different* object any more. The predication adds nothing to the object's conceptual specification. Relational and intentional properties of our thoughts are in another dimension entirely than their conceptual ones: concepts enter into a judgement, hence judgements presuppose them, but logically, concepts are independent of judgements that specify their referential impact.

I will thus be trying to put externalist modes of thought upside down and to argue that meaning begins within, from a concept, not without, from a referent. It is because we are creatures with a species-specific range of concepts that we can refer to numbers, phrase structures, or moral qualities in the first place. Describing the physical world in non-intentional terms (terms not employing human concepts that provide specific perspectives on things) reveals and predicts essentially nothing about the contents of our thoughts, both in conceptual structures and their intentional uses. Nothing external explains why we refer to the world in the way we do, as possibly the only creature on Earth, as the current comparative literature on reference suggests (Terrace 2005; Hauser *et al.* 2002). As I will argue later on, following Chomsky, Hobbes, and Hume, there are no independently specifiable external physical objects that correspond to referential expressions we use. Both positing putative external objects called 'properties' as somehow corresponding to predicates and positing mind-external objects as referents for singular terms should be regarded as making empirical claims that are subject to naturalistic inquiry (see Chapter 2).

As for whole sentences and phrases, the entire combinatorial process which gives rise to novel complex meanings productively once singular terms and predicates are recursively combined does not seem to involve the external world. It is a process not taking place in the world but in a mind that is equipped with the relevant combinatorial operations. That mind organizes our thoughts such that their meaning follows lawfully from their parts and the nature of their construction. Nothing external enters this construction process ('narrow syntax'), and nothing external 'corresponds' to it. I will argue that the entire presumption of a structural complexity in the outside world that somehow directly 'mirrors' the complexity of the thoughts that we think and use to make sense of the world is a step that is empirically unargued for, and apparently theoretically redundant. A thought expressed by a clausal structure, for example, contains a predication. But predications do not occur in the outside physical world. Much research shows they have a very specific structural basis (Bowers 1993; Moro 2000; den Dikken 2006) and are different from mere function–argument relations in an abstract algebraic or logical sense. Hence there is little *a priori* reason to regard them as very widespread in the animal realm, let alone the physical world out there. Postulating an ontology of 'states of affairs' out there that somehow corresponds to the propositional structures that are the result of these predications does not make us better understand why predications exist and how they work.

Let us now illustrate this internalist line of thought for a concrete case of a sentential meaning. Let us assume that there is a mechanism of lexical selection that together with a basic recursive combinatorial operation, commonly called Merge, yields the complex thought:

(9) Charles I died on the scaffold.

Once we have generated this thought (our mind has operated), this thought apparently acquires a relational property, namely truth or falsehood, which, for all it seems, is *not* due to our thought but is ultimately due to something that is fully outside or external to it, namely the existence of a particular historical event three centuries ago. We can think or hope or believe what we want, our thought, merely by virtue of its meaning, has that relational property. In this way, the conclusion might be, truth as well as meaning (which determines truth, together with the world) is relational and external. No amount of inspecting my thought, no intrinsic quality of it, will make it true, if it is not, or make it false, if it is true. Truth is a *relational* quality of thoughts, not an *intrinsic* one (cf. Russell 1912: 18).

This externalist intuition has fuelled thinking about truth for millennia. What could one possibly say against it? Well, to make a first start in criticizing this intuition, the world out there doesn't simply 'contain historical events'. As for the ontological category of an event as such, see Chapter 3: it seems to be an open question to what extent this ontological category contains language-specific elements. But as regards *historical events*, these are not like objects deposited somewhere outside or 'in the past'; we cannot simply hit upon them. If we were to embark on an empirical search for historical events of emperors dying on scaffolds, there would be no way to identify our target except by essentially re-using the complex linguistic expression in question. It is because of the mind—its capacity for language and a particular brand of memory—that there is something like 'history' in the first place. As for events such as deaths of emperors, specifically, there is little reason to believe that these can be described in non-intentional terms either.

None of this takes away the obvious fact that the intentional description of the world in terms of historical events, executions, and other such human perspectives involves plenty of mind-external aspects of the world. Denying that would be like denying, equally pointlessly, that a bronze of Charles I contains metal. But the external aspects of meaning *need* no denying: the question is what they *explain*, and whether, in particular, they explain the meanings human expressions carry. I here argue they do not—they do not do it any more than the metal in the bronze of Charles I explains the form of the figure. By contrast, relational aspects are not so hard to explain. They are too obviously required to be there: they begin where adaptation begins, and adaptation is a condition for life. But adaptation as such does not explain the specific forms of thoughts that I am calling propositional here, as noted. The power to recursively combine words into arbitrarily many and arbitrarily complex thoughts, exploiting a range of specific human concepts, involves a process of autonomizing from the environment, of taking a distance from it, rather than mirroring its structure or being immersed in it. The constraints of adaptation will require that we *use* our forms of thought to some extent, and from this we can predict that our truth-judgements will by and large not be counter-adaptive. But for this to be the case we need not posit propositions out there, or 'facts' as external objects that mirror our forms of thought as these transpire in language.

Once we question a basic externalist direction of explanation in semantics with respect to facts such as (9), we can question it for so-called 'referential expressions' like *Charles I* too. Indeed, once we naively ask what such an expression 'refers to', puzzlement ensues. It seems as obvious as anything that *Charles I* refers to Charles I. But this is merely a *disquotational* account of (lexical) meaning, which is as uncontentious as it is unilluminating with respect to what the content of our concept of Charles I is, and what it means: understanding the statement (10) requires *understanding* the expression *Charles I*, or knowing what concept it expresses:

(10) 'Charles I' means/refers to Charles I.

But every meaning explanation going beyond the unilluminating (10) becomes questionable immediately. If we are asked what object Charles I, the putative referent of *Charles I*, is, we essentially become clueless. If a current day user of *Charles I* is said to refer to a physical object that once existed but now does not exist any more, we have to look at this as an empirical claim. As such, it is the claim that there is a relevant relation connecting my thought about Charles I or my use of his name to some physical object of the past. Do such relations of reference exist? Am I connected causally or physically to a certain object of the past when I am thinking a thought about Charles I? The suggestion seems rather peculiar. What are objects of the past in the first place? We should not, I suppose, imagine them like furniture stored in a warehouse. So, in what sense is Charles I, as a physical object, *there* for me to refer to him? There is a suggestion that there is a *causal chain* running from my utterance of the noise 'Charles I' to an earlier person's use of the same noise, to an earlier person's use still, and so on, until the very point that we reach the person using that noise for the first time to refer to Charles I (although in the shape of a baby, one should note: this is not how we today think of the referent of our name 'Charles I'). This, in turn, on this view, is a physical object, and the primordial act of naming it is again just a physically specifiable (causal) relation between one organism and another. But the person involved in that act had a *concept* of what she *intended* to *name*: not, in particular, the skin of the object in question, its physical shape as a baby, its colour, its screams, or its nose, all of which were physically present on the occasion as well as salient in it. Nothing rules these other objects of reference out *except* the intention of the baptizer not to refer to them. The concept in question was that of a person, not a body, a skin making up its topological surface, or its nose. Even for this first act of naming to succeed, that is, it seems one has to presuppose what the physicalist account was meant to explain, the existence of individual concepts: concepts of individuals that are essentially persons as opposed to, say, topological surfaces. From this point of view, what happened in the act of naming is that a new phonetic label got linked to a pre-existing concept.

If Charles I now lived, the suggestion that he, as a referent of human acts of naming, is a certain physical object having a certain space–time position with blood running through its vessels, etc., might seem to make more sense. Yet it is unclear with what space–time slice exactly we would identify him. Would he be a point in time? A slice associated to the time of a life? More than that, since an essential part of this organism, its genes, predate it? These questions are as puzzling as they seem pointless from a semantic point of view. We are not talking about *such* an object when we use the name 'Charles I', but about a *person*, something that we conceptually distinguish from a functioning organism or a position in space–time. This is particularly clear once persons stop having a functioning organism but keep being referred to. All that is left of Charles I now is in fact the *person* that we still refer to (in principle we *could* be talking about bones in a tomb when talking about Charles I, but it is certainly not necessary for us to do so, or a requirement for the name to be meaningful). Even humans in the time of Charles I's life did not refer to a physical object or functioning organism, however, it seems, since they will have conceptually distinguished a person from the physical features of his body as well. So upholding a physicalist conception of reference is not to offer a theory of reference, but a suggestion for viewing it differently, or for suggesting that humans are mistaken in what they think they are referring to when using proper names.

Some would argue that the neurosciences have shown that persons are just physical objects. But this observation, even if correct, does not speak to the problem, for scientific advance leaves the structure of human reference virtually untouched. Humans may mostly believe that reincarnation is scientifically impossible, but that does not mean that humans do not refer to reincarnated people as such when having relevant thoughts: their conceptual capacity to intentionally refer to things which are distinct from their bodies (hence can change them) is untouched by the assumed scientific advance. It is the structure of intentional reference that is in question here, and this structure is not clarified by a theory that entails the non-existence of the phenomenon in question.

The irrelevance of the revision of beliefs through scientific advance for the analysis of ordinary human intentional reference and conceptual understanding is also attested by the fact that the same observations just reviewed hold for children. If personal proper names referred to physical objects, few children's stories would even be intelligible. Thus, we hear about sorcerers telling cats that they are so powerful as to transform themselves into roaring lions. Witnessing this stunt, the cat in question requests a transformation into a mouse, to see full proof of the sorcerer's powers. Upon accomplishing this second transformation, he is eaten and his life ends. Cognitively, this is very telling, not only because it shows that in a child's mind persons are not individuated by their physical features, or because of how clear it makes it that no amount of physical information could provide evidence for the concept of a person for someone who completely lacked that notion. The story is also telling because of the transformation apparently *dis*allowed if personal identity is to be kept: a person whose physical dimension is such that it moves as a mass-like object through a cat's digestive system ceases to be a person. The process of becoming a formless mass, apparently, is not reversible (sometimes persons are swallowed as whole pieces, but this is a different sort of case).

If we move from the intentional properties of names to those of complex noun phrases (NPs), we notice that just as a fictional name can be used to refer in an entirely standard way, even if it has no physical referent, and a sentential expression means what it does even if it is false, so a complex NP too means whatever it does, even if it picks out nothing in the real world. Thus, the phrase *my dinner* precisely means *my dinner*—this is what I am referring to—even if I don't have one. If, for example, I ponder what my dinner would be like if I had somebody else cook it, the question of real-world reference of the phrase *my dinner* seems irrelevant to the question of what *my dinner* means. I am referring precisely to my dinner, not yours, or tomorrow's breakfast. Reference is resistant against the vagaries of existence. If the Eiffel Tower was decomposed yesterday, reference of the NP 'the Eiffel Tower' remains one to *the Eiffel Tower*: its meaning-specification is ultimately bound to be essentially disquotational, hence circular. When using *this book* to refer to a book on the table, and it turns out to be a box with nothing inside it, or a solid block that looks like a book, my expression will still have meant what it did, namely *this book*. It just so happens that at that moment, there was no book there, something that is a historical accident irrelevant to my intentional act. Even in the case of God, if I use the word *God* with the meaning it has, that is to refer to God, I will have used it with that meaning, hence to refer to God, even if I come to believe that God does not exist. The word *God* in the sentence *God does not exist* would not simply start to mean something else because of the new context in which it occurs: if I change my mind on His existence today, I cannot detect any change in the *meaning* of my *concept* of God between yesterday and today. 'God' means *God*, quite simply, not Pluto, potatoes, or Schwarzenegger.

So, just as in the case of truth, there is an external aspect to our acts of reference, and the world makes itself noticeable in potentially unexpected ways—emperors turn out to have died in beds, people become atheists, books can turn out to be solid blocks—but our referential acts *retain* the semantic or intentional properties that seem to be intrinsic to them. In this way, our thought exhibits properties of *intentional stability* that do crucially not covary with environmental or external parameters. Intentional aspects of thought and language are due to the intrinsic combinatorics of the mind, which have no equivalent or causes in the external world, but rather *make* that world an object of reference in a way it could not be otherwise. Human intentional reference is what it is because of the concepts that configure these acts of reference, and the structures that embed them. It is not, or so at least it appears, that the concepts are what they are because of what causal or physical relationship we take up to an environment. It is exactly the other way around, a reversal of expectations that I have called an 'explanatory inversion'.

Some current approaches to human intentionality do not generally appeal to an externalistically conceived relation of reference in explaining the intentional. Instead they involve social-normative notions like that of a *commitment* incurred by a speaker in making an assertion (Brandom 1994). Here the externalism of the approach consists in the fact that the content of the assertion is meant to follow from or to be explained by the socially regulated commitment in question. But if commitments are to be rational as opposed to enforced or externally controlled behavioural responses, undertaking a commitment will have to *depend* on understanding the meaning of the expressions or thoughts involved. We commit to what we commit to in part because we understand what it is. It is not that we act as physical objects or machines first, and a content or meaning accrues to the machine because other machines punish or reward us depending on what we say. No amount of punishing us *could* provide us with a rational motivation for accepting a norm: normative force cannot be due to what others want us to do. It is due to the force that meanings exert on us when we understand them. Thus, for example, children born to Pidgin-speaking parents do not acquire or replicate the dialect of their peers. They develop intuitions that have a normative force for them (intuitions on how expressions are to pattern structurally), not because they are socially enforced but because of the structure of their minds. No amount of social enforcing could make such behaviour rational, if the children's minds by themselves did not provide the motivation and validation for speaking in the way they do. If they did not, their behaviour could not be any more rationally endorsed than we could rationally accept a system of arithmetic where 2 + 2 is stipulated to be 5, and which we adopt because we happen to be born into a community that has banned all reference to the number 4.

All that said, could it really be that thoughts come with whatever structure they have and it *simply so happens* that they *also* acquire some external function with respect to the external world? That is, could our mind really be a sort of generative engine that creatively produces thoughts with determinate structures, and that the intentional properties that these structures have are entirely due to *these structures*, with adaptation merely providing constraints on their external significance? MMD is an attempt to tackle this question, and to explore a positive answer to it. It views linguistic meaning as a natural necessity, the outcome of a natural structure-building process inside the human faculty of language that has an *external significance* in being expressible and thereby physically manifest and shareable, but has no externalist rationale. Language viewed as a natural object even lacks an external existence: there are external linguistic productions, but they are physical and ephemeral representatives of a process virtually all of which is internal. The essence of the system lies in its dynamics, in its never being a completed whole or a set of expressions. Unless the move was forced by empirical evidence, it would be a mistake to reify expressions, which are abstractions from this dynamics, into external objects with stable sorts of 'referents'. As Humboldt put it, language is *energeia*, not *ergon*: it *consists* in the derivations that it produces, not in a completed physical product or effect (see Chomsky 1966). A derivation's last line is an interface representation where a structure built by narrow syntax is handed over to external systems for further processing, in particular the sensorimotor systems of speech articulation that externalize language. This combinatorial machinery of syntax—the computational system of language—and the capacity for externalization describes the specific forms of a mind of a certain type. This mind grows from within, like other organic systems in our body.

But for all that, reference and truth were left largely untackled in MMD. The present book's message is to deny the externalist contention even in these cases. If we turn to scrutinize our human sense of truth empirically, our method of study turns out to be internalist as in much of the rest of the biolinguistic programme. Reference and truth, as specific and contingent forms of intentionality, if anything *have* a crucial structural basis in the specific format of language (this is argued specifically in Chapters 3 to 5). I am hoping for a reader who will think: what if *not* the relations to the environment in which we stand would explain why our thoughts have the reference-theoretic and truth-theoretic properties that they have? If either one or both of these properties are due to the internal structure of the mind, and their external aspect is more a consequence of them than a cause, this whole expectation crumbles. In turn, the general internalist perspective is strengthened, as is the whole idea of the need to re-conceptualize the study of human nature as the study of intrinsic aspects as opposed to the relational character of the human mind. This is what MMD calls the question of 'mind design': the question of the architecture of mind, not functionally conceived, but as an object in nature.

One of our prime foci here will have to be the reference–truth *distinction*. Not all meaning-bearing structures relate to the world in the way of being truth-evaluable. For example, *this book* is not true, although you may find that *what it says* is. Similarly, there clearly seems to be something wrong with (11):

(11) a. *My dinner* is true
(11) b. *the Eiffel Tower* is true
(11) c. *the Earth's surface* is true
(11) d. *John* is true
(11) e. *God* is true

This suggests that there is a fundamental semantic distinction between reference and truth, corresponding rather directly to a *syntactic* distinction between NPs and sentences. The intuition would be that an act of reference to my dinner by means of the NP *my dinner* of its nature does not involve any potential for truth. An act of reference carried out by means of an NP may *fail* or not, but there is a sense in which it is not *true or false*. At least a predication needs to be involved in an expression before evaluating it as true, and to refer to John is not to predicate any property of him (to say something 'about' him), as Kripke (1980) has famously argued.

This contention *would* explain the oddity of (11), but it would do so by making *predication* the crucial presupposition for truth, and predication as such is not unique to sentences, since it may arguably occur within nominal structures as well (see e.g. den Dikken 2006: ch. 5). On the other hand, where it does so occur, it is a plausible suggestion that in these cases the nominal construction actually *is* a clausal one. Moro (2000: 52) argues that the apparent complex NP in (12), prior to the raising of 'books', is in fact a Small Clause (SC) selected by *of*, as indicated in (13), where *of* plays a role somewhat similar to that of the copula:

(12) John read [$_{NP}$ books of this type]
(13) John read [. . . of [$_{SC}$ books [this type]]]

Either the SC-subject or the SC-predicate can then vacate the SC, leaving a trace t, to yield (14) or (15):

(14) John read [books of [$_{SC}$ t [this type]]]
(15) John read [this type of [$_{SC}$ books t]]

In other words, even if propositional structures did not require either verbs or tenses, they may still be intrinsically predicational as well as clausal. In this sense, the truth–reference distinction *may* mirror the sentence (clause) vs. NP distinction, and is possibly a consequence of it. This is Carstairs-McCarthy's (1999) intuition, who argued that the semantic distinction in question cannot be made in language- and syntax-independent terms at all.

Were a semanticist to develop an artificial formal language for efficient use in communication, he might in fact want to abolish a truth–reference distinction as a part of the design of its semantics, which confirms that the origin of the distinction is probably not semantic. Using a generalized semantic notion such as 'satisfaction' or 'applicability', for example, the semantic engineer might suggest that the sentence 'The present king of France is bold' and the NP 'the bold present king of France' share the same semantic property, that they are 'non-applicable' to the world. That outcome would imply the loss of a distinction (or discarding of an intuition), but if we were to design a language from scratch, it is not clear that we would miss it, instead of priding ourselves for having simplified the system (see further Hinzen 2006c).

That the contingent structural format of syntax is the cause of certain crucial semantic distinctions, rather than mirroring either these distinctions or the world viewed as independently given, is the claim explored in this book. The general Humboldtian vision of language as the creative expression of human thought rather than an externally or functionally driven instrument of communication does not make this claim at all unlikely.

1.3 Child truth, animal truth

What is it about certain structural forms in human language that deprives them of a certain semantic potential such as truth (recall (11))? More fundamentally: why does syntax matter to how we relate to the world in the first place? Few philosophical books on intentionality even mention syntax as one explanatory factor. This is even initially surprising for the following reason. Part of the so-called 'creative aspect of language use' is that we can endlessly combine and recombine words so as to generate new thoughts that we can apply appropriately on novel occasions.[5] This creative aspect of language entails that we must make a categorical distinction between *complex* and *simple* linguistic expressions—expressions that have proper constituents (parts), and that lack them. In a system such as language where there is such a distinction, it seems plausible to expect both that complex expressions do not have the meanings of simple ones, and that the meanings of the complex ones would not exist in the *absence* of the combinatorial operations of the system in question, that is syntax.

One could, of course, invent new *words* for complex expressions, so that *John loves Mary* would be a lexical item *pling*, *Mary loves John* would be *plong*, etc., so that a language would be simply a (very long) list. But although this is possible for a finite number of complex expressions (not for their full infinite range), it seems that even in those cases, *pling* and *plong* would be mere placeholders (names) for what is in fact an intrinsically complex thought encoded in them. Thus, understanding the expression *John loves Mary* is inherently *structural*: it involves grasping, not just a specific relation between John and Mary, but an abstract algebraic relation between variables, hence an infinity of expressions in which these variables take on different values.

[5] The number of distinct thoughts we can produce at any moment far exceeds, as it is often put, the number of particles in the universe; it may even exceed the number of natural numbers (hence not be denumerably infinite), although this is an open question (Langendoen and Postal 1984).

The expression *Mary loves John*, for example, is therefore systematically related to the former, not merely contingently. The idea of coding these complex expressions in words would obscure these relations. Similarly, we could code the sentence in (16), which can either mean (17a) or (17b), as the sentences (18a) and (18b):

(16) Everyone loves someone
(17) a. For everyone, x, there is someone, y, that x loves
(17) b. There is someone, y, that everyone, x, loves
(18) a. x plings y
(18) b. y plongs x

But this is not a natural language. The scope relations that (17a) and (17b) bring out are an intrinsic aspect of the expressions involved. Moreover, (17a) and (17b) share exactly the same conceptual structure: in both cases we speak of an event of loving, with x being the subject/Agent and y the object/Patient. There is in this way a common conceptual core to them, which leaves their intentional/quantificational/scope properties open, as something to be mapped *from* the conceptual structure, in the course of the further derivation. Again, reducing these expressions to lexical items is to miss these facts.

In short, the syntactic structure of a complex expressions is intrinsic to it and its meaning. The structural complexity of an expression is not a feature of it that it could have lacked, so that it, and in particular its meaning, would have existed also if the structure had been absent. It is logically possible, perhaps, that meanings of complex expressions are somehow God-given in a Fregean 'third realm', and a structurally radically different format could in principle be found to express them. Evidence for that would be languages other than English which would express quantificational scope in some way different from how we assume English does it in (17). An argument that this logical possibility does not exist, however, is that the very structural format of (17) which we use to analyse it (in technical terms, its LF/SEM) appears to *define* what the logical structure of the thought in question is. The structure is the thought's essence, something the thought cannot lack. Why is this? Well, one might express the content of a propositional thought in both musical and pictorial terms, for example. Then, its musical expression would be no more a defining property of it than its pictorial one. In both cases, there would be logically possible worlds in which the thought lacked the relevant representations. However, its *logical* properties cannot in this way vary from world to world. This is not to say that we are necessarily *right* in the specific syntactic format that we use to describe the logicality of natural language expressions. After all, LF-syntax is an empirical account of the logical properties of expressions. But it is to say that *the properties themselves that we target* in our theory of LF could not be different from what they are. The claim is: we have no *conception* of a thought that lacked them but was the same thought. If God were to think these thoughts, they would have to have the same structure. By virtue of the combinatorial system of language new meanings come into existence that, since their complex structure is essential to them, would not exist otherwise. In this sense, syntax opens up new spaces of thought. As I will argue in Section 3.3, this does not just apply to LF-syntax, but possibly also to conceptual structures in language, from which LF syntax is mapped.

At a most basic level, what allows this stupendous potential of language to generate new meanings is *recursion.* In the case of the natural numbers, recursion means that each element is generated from another that in turn is generated in the very same way. That is, we do not just know that 95 is a member of the same set as 94, and that there are many more such members. We know that 94 and 95 are generated in the very same way, except that in the latter case we have applied the relevant generative principle one more time, resulting in a new discrete object with distinctive properties, yet of the same type. This understanding yields an infinite set, since it entails that there is no largest number. If there was one, we could apply the successor operation to it, thereby proving it was not the largest number. Language exhibits this feature too. Every natural language expression belongs to a generated set. We know that, once we have generated one member, we can apply the very operation that constructed it to itself, so as to obtain a new object of the very same type. Hence, also, there isn't a longest sentence. For, if there was, we could apply the very operations that constructed it to obtain a longer one, thereby proving it has not been the longest sentence (merging 'I deny that . . .' with the sentence in question would be an easy way to do this).

Prima facie, the availability of the relevant operation (successor in arithmetic, Merge in language) follows from nothing in experience or external: nothing in our sensory experience could cause or provide a rationale for the infinite combinatorics that we witness in mathematics and language. No finite number of applications of this principle as we might witness it in experience could either. Since the generative principles in question are of an essentially mathematical nature, it is even unclear which features of the *physical* world at large could be the cause for it. At least standardly, it is not concluded from this that infinitary structures do not exist, or cannot be grasped by our minds. They do exist, and we have access to them. Here we are simply hitting upon the general mystery of how it happens that we are capable of mathematical thought, and how and why mathematics fits into the natural world (Steiner

1998; Penrose 1994), about which I have nothing more to say, except for noting that if anything is distinctive about human minds, it is this recursive ability. It may well be that it is unique to humans.[6]

The consequences of this ability are not merely semantic but existential. The ability to freely and limitlessly combine a number of primitive elements (in the case of arithmetic, a single initial element of the set of natural numbers, in the case of language, a finite number of words or morphemes from a lexicon) into complex recursive structures frees our mind. The moment we have that recursive ability, we need not respond to whatever is present, as we can *make present* (literally 'think up' or construct) whatever we *want* to be present in our mind. We can *make* whole worlds, rather than responding to this one. If anything is a characteristic property of humans, it is that they are not overly impressed by what is real: humans tend to be more intrigued by what *should* be. In an important sense, with recursion *thought itself*, as opposed to merely adaptation, begins. Non-human animals might share some of the primitives of the human conceptual system, although this remains unknown. But without the ability to freely combine them so as to produce infinitely more (complex) concepts, they remain stuck in the here and now, as they by and large seem to be.[7] Dennett nicely formulates this predicament:

> Getting it right, not making mistakes, matters to [organisms]—indeed nothing matters more—but they don't, as a rule, appreciate this. They are the beneficiaries of equipment exquisitely designed to get what matters right, but when their equipment malfunctions and gets matters wrong, they have no resources, as a rule, for noticing this, let alone deploring it. They soldier on, unwittingly. The difference between how things seem and how things really are is just as fatal a gap for them as it can be for us, but they are largely oblivious of it.... Is there enough food laid by for winter? Have I miscalculated? Is it safe to enter this cave? Other creatures are often visibly agitated by their own uncertainties about just such questions, but because they cannot actually *ask themselves questions*, they cannot articulate their predicaments for themselves or take steps to improve their grip on the truth. They are stuck in a world of appearances, seldom if ever worrying about whether how things seem is how they truly are. (Dennett 2003)

[6] The present state of the art in comparative cognition seems to suggest that it is. Thus, recent claims to the contrary for the case of starlings by Gentner *et al.* (2006) suffer from the drawback that they do not distinguish cognitive architectures equivalent to the class of finite state machines from those equivalent to context-free grammars. The experimental evidence in question is not evidence for the latter architecture.

[7] Since recursion is nothing that can evolve gradually (you have it, or you don't), moreover, this difference in combinatorial power is not a variance on a continuous scale. Freedom may evolve, to use Dennett's (2003) term, but that evolution must leave room for leaps as well.

With the ability to freely combine and recombine the primitives of thought, the appearances recede: it is a grasp of *alternatives* that makes us question the real. Free combinatoriality in this way lies at the heart of an appearance–reality distinction, at the heart, in short, of a *concept* of reality and truth, and a faculty of judgement that assesses them. That nothing which *seems* true *needs* to be, is of the essence of our human concept of truth. Whatever the appearances, we judge, things could be otherwise. No disposition we might have to think one thought rather than another will make it true. This insight boosts thought, as it will never be committed to what it factually does: my thinking P will never make it *true* that P. Assessing whether it is will forever require *more* thought, as there is nothing that thought cannot question (except itself, as Descartes pointed out). Once thought is externalized through language, the same aspect is found in discursive communication: nothing a person says is thereby true, no matter what the person is or what it is the person says. Assertion is *evidence* for truth, but nothing becomes true by being asserted. Reality (in the sense of what is merely factual, like what assertions are being made) is not truth; and something is truth only if we notice it has an opposite. As has often been assumed in the psychological literature, the real test for understanding *belief* is the understanding of *false* belief. That is, we do not have a full-blown and explicit concept of truth before we have a concept of *falsehood*.[8] When is that?

There is a saying that animals and small children never lie. They always tell the truth, which is why one should not lie to a child. Susan Carey notes (p.c.) that an eighteenth-month-old child might consider it a hilarious joke if a spoon is called a fork. I take this to mean that they simply cannot make sense of the fact that anyone would intentionally want not to speak the truth (hence they must be making fun). Two-year-old children, in turn, might react to the assertion that a bear is a dog by saying 'No!', and if the assertion is repeated, get angry (if they think it isn't a joke), and say 'No, no, no!!', perhaps feeling some sort of insult to their sense of truth. While this is anecdotal evidence, there is some interesting experimental work on the dawning of truth in infant cognition that I will try to briefly survey. Perner (1991) provides evidence that by the age of 24 months at the latest, infants recognize the *realis* force of a statement and can assess its truth value. Correlatively with that, they appreciate pretend scenarios and jokes, as noted, and hence grasp statement with *irrealis* force. However, although the truth–falsehood distinction is appreciated, the insight that something can be false (by their own lights), although it

[8] Already Parmenides' 'ascent to truth', one of the earliest explicit conceptualizations of truth, followed a path to truth that went through the realm of falsehood.

is asserted in *realis* mode by someone else ('perspectival relativity') is not explicitly understood before four years of age. For example, a child may be given a story such as (19), and be asked (20):

(19) Mom said she bought apples, but look, she really bought oranges.
(20) What did Mom say she bought?

A three-year-old child will answer 'oranges'—it will stick to the truth—while a four-year-old will answer 'apples'. As J. de Villiers (2005: 188) notes, it is as if the former child still has to realize the structural fact that in (21),

(21) Mom said she bought apples

there is an embedded clause ('she bought apples') which can be false even if, at the same time, the matrix clause ('Mom said...') is true. More precisely, it must become clear to the child that in the question (20), the question operator *what* is actually the direct object of *bought*, and that sub-clause has to be kept in memory while processing the matrix-clause which embeds it. If this structural fact is decisive, it seems that although syntax of a specific kind has no implications for what is true, it may well have to do with the concept of truth as such, and with how it matures in childhood.

This suggestion raises the question of *pre-propositional* forms of thought on this path of maturation, some residual forms of which may still be alive in adult language. The existence of these might lend more credibility to the claim that alethic competence grows as sentential structures do. Thus, at the bottom of a hierarchy of pre-propositional forms of thought we might have the simplest type of self-standing utterances, exclamatives, as in (22):

(22) a. Fire!
(22) b. Idiot!

Slightly more sophisticated are complex expressions that juxtapose two predicates in a pseudo- or pre-clausal fashion that Potts and Roeper (2006) call *Expressive Small Clauses* (ESCs). These have a characteristic intonation pattern and crucially have an *expressive* content (as opposed to a declarative and truth-evaluable one). They are also linked to a momentary attitude, and are grammatical only as root clauses (they cannot occur embedded):

(23) a. Me idiot!
(23) b. You idiot!

These, as Potts and Roeper argue, contrast semantically with sentential constructions, such as *I am an idiot*, which are neither expressive nor linked to a situation-specific attitude, and need not be root-clauses. Slightly closer to declaratives would be incredulity-type adjunctive SCs as in (24), below, which retain the essentially expressive content of ESCs, as well as non-expressive constructions of an 'appelative' type, exemplified in (25), which do not involve the self-disapprobation typical for ESCs. None of these structures project any sentential syntax either, and they are again only grammatical as root clauses:

(24) a. Me, laugh?
(24) b. You, tall?
(25) Me, serial killer

In (25) I am evoking (referring to) me twice, first as 'me', then as 'serial killer', but in both cases it is as if I am merely naming me, as in attaching a label to something. This is very different from (26), where functional structure enters the SC so as to change its intentional structure, even though a verbal element is still missing:

(26) (I consider) [me (as) [a serial killer]]

The SC in (26) *qualifies* an object of reference (me), as opposed to merely referring a second time to it. It introduces a specific *perspective* on that object, which becomes even more perspicuous upon adding *as*. Example (25) has the reference of its predicate not anchored in that of the subject in the way of (26). It is only with (26) and SC-predications as in (27) that the intentional structure of a clause shifts, and it is only here that we may be witnessing the dawning of declaratives and truth:

(27) a. I consider [$_{SC}$ you (as) John]
(27) b. I consider [$_{SC}$ you [*(an) idiot]]

Unlike (23)–(25), which cannot be selected and hence are necessarily unembedded, SCs of the type in (27) crucially are *not* grammatical as root clauses. Like the expressive and appelative ones, they are still verbless. But insofar as they express a predication, they obligatorily contain functional material (27b): the determiner 'a(n)', which (25) in the intended reading necessarily lacks. Example (27a) does not; but arguably as a consequence of that, it exhibits a peculiar 'identificational' semantics, which allows for no asymmetry in the subject and predicate: (27a) is possible along with (28) (and compare (29a, 29b)); by contrast, the predicate-second rule for (27b) is strict (see (30)):

(28) I consider [$_{SC}$ John you]
(29) a. I consider [$_{SC}$ Dr Jekyll Mr Hyde]
(29) b. I consider [$_{SC}$ Mr Hyde Dr Jekyll]
(30) *I consider [$_{SC}$ an idiot you]

As verbs enter, the intentional potential of the structures in question change again:

(31) a. I heard [$_{SC}$ dogs bark]
(31) b. I saw [$_{SC}$ John run]

Clearly, the relevant propositional event depicted by the SC in (31a, 31b) is not merely *named* twice (as in 25); it is also not merely qualified (as in 26); nor does it invoke an identificational semantics among two referential expressions. In (31b), in particular, we do not merely have, say, an event depicted that is a running and John, but an event that is a running *of John* (an event of *John's* running). John is now being anchored referentially to *running*, and is intrinsically an event-participant as opposed to a predicate merely holding of it or externally added to it. In short, the SC-subject becomes a *part(icipant)* of the event described by the verb. The projection of a verbal phrase precisely corresponds to this shift in the intentional structure of the predicational expressions. At this stage, we have reached the beginnings of the human verbal phrase (VP) and its extended projection, the sentence.

Pott's and Roeper's (2006) view is that adult SCs retain a certain similarity to child SCs in the two-word stage, and are kept in adult speech as self-standing utterances only in the rare case where no sentential expression could express what they do: the case of ESCs like (23), which *remain* root clauses, verbless, and predicate-second even in adult speech. On this view, they are first highly ambiguous, and the process of maturation of a full-blown sentence-syntax with extended and functional projections can be described as one of gradual semantic disambiguation. To cite Potts and Roeper:

> The general trend [in acquisition] is toward a one-to-one mapping from structures into meanings. The more structures one has at one's disposal, the closer one can come to this ideal. Thus, increased syntactic sophistication correlates with decreased semantic ambiguity. (Potts and Roeper 2006: 193)

But it seems an unwarranted aspect of this view that the meanings to be expressed are assumed to be simply available independently of the structures that express them. Taking their view literally, the acquisition is like a march to one grand expressive 'ideal': full propositional competence. As more adequate functional projections become available, the productions 'match' the propositional structures to be expressed better, and the original SCs do not survive, unless they express a content that no adult clause can express. For example, (32a) can no longer express the content of (32b):

(32) a. Mommy milk
(32) b. Mommy drank milk

But adopting this line of reasoning is to simply assume that the propositional structures are there from the start, and that expressions are gradually designed so as to match them. Maybe, however, (32a) simply does not compete with (32b) for expressing the content of (32b), because the content of (32b) is not available, or does not exist, at the time of (32a). At that time, there is no such a thing around as the fully propositional meaning of (32b), for (32a) to 'ambiguously denote' it. This is the line I pursue here: that propositional and alethic competence matures *as the syntactic structures* do that code them; they cannot be disconnected from these structures. Potts and Roeper may still be right, on this view, in their central claim that as clauses with extended projections become available, early root clauses lose their functionality, and survive only where no full sentence matches them in content. But early propositional syntax will not 'ambiguously denote' the contents later expressed by more sophisticated structures.[9]

So, on the present view, as we gradually go up the clausal skeleton, from small-clausal to standard head-complement constructions, and as we add head-movement, A-movement, and A′-movement, we are on the path to a structure that arises only at the end: a structure that can encode a judgement of truth. To get there, we will first modify a VP aspectually and create a *v*P, which then embeds within a projection encoding finite Tense, which localizes the event

[9] The authors also discuss the interesting case of

(i) Ali in Nepal, [as written under a photograph]

which clearly means something different from what a full sentence can express, e.g. in (ii):

(ii) Ali is/was/photographed in Nepal.

But it is puzzling, on their view, why (i) should still exist, even though (iii) does not:

(iii) Mommy milk

Why doesn't (i) give way to a sentential structure in the way that (iii) does? If the answer is that (iii) is already meant to carry the content that a structure like (29) will later express, hence is in essence fully propositional already, that propositionality is simply presupposed. The view is circular, as it disambiguates (iii) with respect to meanings expressed by other structures only later. On the view contemplated here, there is no propositional ideal available at the two-word stage that could explain why (iii) disappears but not (i).

representation encoded in the *v*P in time—a conceptually plausible presupposition for evaluating propositional truth (as truths hold at a time). Only when we have a full hierarchical structure assembled, we can add a last predication that completes our task to generate a full judgement in the formal shape of a complete CP, which in particular includes a specification of assertoric force (or the 'presentation' of a proposition as true, as I will put it in Chapter 4). The point to emphasize is that predications of truth, which as it were close off this construction process, come *last*, or *after* a great amount of structure is already in place: this is one way of saying that truth is an *inherently structural* phenomenon, as opposed to a non-structural or purely 'conceptual' one (assuming the above distinction between conceptual and intentional information).

Consistent with this proposal, MMD notes the architectural point that in the history of generative grammar, the level of semantic representation (originally called 'Deep Structure') has been consistently moved, from being an input to the computational system of language, to being the latter's *outputs* (in their various incarnations as S-structures, LFs, or SEMs). Hence a meaning is something *computed in a derivation*; it is not what is *fed into* it. As we boost up the computational resources and formal complexity of the system, new meanings ensue; and the more we see specific semantic effects tightly correlating with specific syntactic configurations or operations—predicate composition with adjunction (Chomsky 2004), say, small clauses with predication (Moro 2000), event structure with verbal and nominal argument structure, head-movements with lexical entailment patterns (see Chaper 3), A-movement with the configuration of propositional representations in time, A-bar movement with quantification, etc.—the more we see syntax and semantics closely intertwined, as well as 'language' and 'thought' (on the relation of which see further Section 1.5, below).

What the line of thought in this section adds to this general architectural consideration is the more specific one that a mind asking for, asserting, and pondering the truth is very *late* on a scale of structural complexity generated in narrow syntax. The suggestion is that the 'origin of truth' is in this sense at least in part a *syntactic* one. At the root of the intentional lies—not alone, but as an essential ingredient—syntax, or form, as opposed to content, or semantics. Standard conceptualizations of 'mind' make such a result, I think, not even conceivably true, based as they are on a strict distinction between form (syntax) and content (semantics), with either an arbitrary mapping between them, or else the contention that syntax is a 'mirror' of semantics, a disambiguation device, a way of coding externally and independently given 'semantic contents' or mind-external 'propositions'. Before I return to the language–thought relation, I wish, in the light of the potential unfamiliarity of all this, to comment a bit more in the following section on the sense in which we talk of 'mind' here.

1.4 On 'mind' and its architecture

By and large, the mind is nowadays interpreted 'from without': it is an instrument for representing the environment or mind-external propositional 'contents', for negotiating commitments in discourse, for coordinating action. In direct opposition to that, the viewpoint of MMD is that mind is a structure in nature, a system of forms to which brains find access, or, perhaps, which brains have a way of causing, by some unknown principles. These structures, like those of arithmetic, are simply the ones they are, they are not specifically good 'for' anything, although they do prove functional—functional enough to be maintained on the evolutionary scene.

The viewpoint is developed in MMD on the model of pre-Darwinian biology and some of its revitalizations in structural and formalist biology today (see Newman *et al.* 2006; Müller and Newman 2005, for some paradigmatic examples of an internalist move in theoretical biology today). Characteristic to the Darwinian and neo-Darwinian ('New Synthesis') perspective on organisms is a *relational* viewpoint on them: organisms are characterized by their relational properties, in particular by reference to their genealogy and adaptive history. Species are not natural kinds described by some intrinsic properties, but temporally extended populations consisting of individuals whose sole unifying feature is their origin or descent from a common ancestor. Some pre-Darwinian biologists, the 'rational morphologists', by contrast, did not take relational properties of the organism as a starting point, be it adaptation or origin, but the intrinsic features of organic form. The latter, as opposed to the facts of adaptation, were regarded as biology's prime explanandum. A phenomenon of nature in its own right (as opposed to its being the consequence of something else, like the law of adaptation), organic form was thought to fall into a small number of universal 'types'. Types or *Baupläne* are basic arrangements of form and function that are highly preserved in evolution, across wide differences in the conditions of existence under which organisms survive. They are posited for explanatory reasons, with observable variance being something that would have to be 'derived' from the underlying types by a number of primitive transformations.

This research programme is structurally analogous, MMD points out, to that in generative grammar, where UG is nothing other than a putative *Bauplan* of language, of which particular languages are possible modifications.

Types in rational morphology become significant and explanatory the moment we see apparent *restrictions* on permissible variance: in short, variance is seen as non-arbitrary. Parallel to the assumption that there are formally impossible organisms, the basic premise of any theory of UG is that there are (biologically) impossible languages.

Rational morphology as a research programme has been derided and marginalized throughout much of the Neo-Darwinian synthesis (Gould 2002), and to this day it is called by many bad names such as 'essentialism', 'Platonism', 'anti-evolutionism', and even 'racism', all of which arise from a total misunderstanding, as MMD argues. Even early rational morphologists such as Geoffroy de St. Hilaire were not anti-evolutionary, for example, quite in contrast to their functionalist colleagues, such as George Cuvier (Amundson 1998). Types were, moreover, not *essences* of particular species, in some Aristotelian sense, precisely because they were meant to be more general and to *cut across* species boundaries: in the limit, types even implied the non-existence of species as biologically significant entities. They are also not otherworldly 'Platonic' entities. On the contrary, the study of organic form and its structuring principles was an empirical research programme which was meant to operate at a much less inferential (i.e. more directly empirical) level of description (Amundson and Lauder 1994). Nor does the whole perspective imply any denial of processes of adaptation. Adaptation, rather, arises where laws of form have pathed a way; what is naturally selected must first exist, and it does not come into existence or originate from natural selection. In this sense, adaptation is indeed secondary; it is not a *creative force* in evolution, but a consequence of the evolutionary process (indeed a necessary consequence).

MMD transfers this general viewpoint to the study of what we call 'mind'. What would this mean? It means taking the intrinsic forms of mind as primary, as opposed to beginning from certain assumptions on the 'functions' of mind, and deriving hypotheses of structure from there. That has certain consequences for the language-thought relation (see also Section 1.5). On a functionalist viewpoint, 'thought' is for representing the world, and 'language' is for expressing or communicating it. Thought is assumed to be somehow independently given, and developing or evolving a language consists in mapping these thoughts to a linguistic form (a 'medium') which consists of phonology and syntax: sound and structure. Syntax thus enters *after* a semantic content is already there and, in standard terminology, 'grasped' by our mind, as the so-called (mind-external) 'content' of the thinker's so-called 'propositional attitudes'. This viewpoint is the reason why even today, in classes on philosophy of language, the syntax (and phonology) of natural language is essentially ignored, as if it didn't belong to language. Few if any introductions to the philosophy of language contain introductions to syntax (or highly misleading ones, such as Devitt and Sterelny (1999); see MMD for discussion). Most of the kinds of complexities of human language that linguists spend their time analyzing are ignored, as a matter of methodological principle: languages are deficient, they are ambiguous, they contain non-referring expressions, expressions mean different things in different contexts if they contain indexicals, two different sentences in two different languages can express the same propositional content, and so on. These are not features that a properly regimented medium of communication should have. Hence the focus of the philosophy of logic and language, it is argued, must be not *sentences* but 'what is said', with the notion of proposition reifying this presumed non-linguistic content of assertions. Since these notions are not natural objects or subjects of naturalistic inquiry, the path is cleared for a project that is bound to be normative instead, being the study of the 'pure form' of thought—thought as 'regimented', or as purified from the distortions that intrude through their linguistic manifestation.

The view finds its origin in times that predate the 'second' cognitive revolution inaugurated by Chomsky (see Chomsky 1966), say Frege's and Russell's, but it seems hard to defend when naturalistic inquiry into the nature of language is taken into account. What we notice when taking it into account is that a premise of Russell's argument for propositions is the assumption that linguistic expressions are 'signs', individuated in terms of their physical properties alone. That they are not signs in this sense is one of the founding claims of modern linguistics. What supports this claim is that, to distinguish utterances of linguistic creatures from mere noise or movements of the air described in terms of physical acoustics, we have to refer to non-physical properties of them, such as phonological, syntactic, and semantic ones. These are as real as anything for a creature that has a mind like ours, although they are non-existent for a scrubjay or hamster. What we have learned about these abstract properties of expressions includes that they exhibit rational or logical features. Languages arguably do not differ in their logical-semantic aspects, as they should not, since languages are learned from phonetic-acoustic data and variance in meaning could not easily be evidenced in linguistic experience. It therefore simply does not follow, from the observation that two different sentences from two different languages can have the same meaning, that this meaning is something non-linguistic, or that it is a 'mind-external proposition'. Such properties are due to the non-physical aspects of language as processed by a mind like ours. Nor does it follow from the fact that the sentence 'I am tired' receives different interpretations depending on whether

Peter utters it or Joe, that we may have one linguistic expression but two interpretations, and that we therefore, from a philosophical point of view, have to focus on 'what is said' as opposed to the expression itself. The conclusion simply makes the same faulty assumption that an 'expression' as such is to be analysed in *non-semantic terms*, rather than as a sound–meaning pair (Chomsky 1995, 2000). As a sound–meaning pair, there is a sense in which 'I am tired' is a different expression depending on who utters it.

In sum, the Russellian invocation of propositions as entities, dominant in philosophy to this day, is based on an empiricist and externalist conception of language, for which language is what is overtly there: it is its outer aspects alone (and, on later views, if there are inner aspects, they are neurological ones that can be functionally characterized, for example through a notion of 'mental representation'). If it has aspects that are not physically overt, they are stipulated to be external (abstract) objects that are referenced by internal 'mental representations'. Somehow, the rather natural view that these abstract aspects of expressions may reflect the inherent structures of the human mind rather than what it externally refers to, does not enter any serious consideration.[10]

It also seems, now, that once the presuppositions of what I call the 'Russellian' paradigm are questioned, it is not clear any more whether the opposition between what is 'thought' and what is 'language' is conceptually maintainable. Suppose semantics is not external to language. Why then abstract a new cognitive domain, propositional 'thought', from the forms of language with which we denote, identify, and encode such thoughts? Surely, one *can* study the mind abstracting from the empirically overt forms of language, and code propositional contents through various non-linguistic constructs such as an algebra of possible worlds—but if the goal is to *explain* their existence and origin, how would these tools help? What are these intermediate shadowy entities that the Russellian position posits *between* what we can empirically study—the structures and forms of the linguistic mind—and the physical world out there? As we saw in the previous section, the moment we inquire empirically what propositions are, we find that numerous *very different* linguistic constructions are 'propositional' in some sense: from VPs with full argument structure to Expressive Small Clauses (ESCs), normal Small Clauses, non-finite TPs, finite TPs, CPs, or even complex DPs. Is the term 'proposition' thus likely to capture a natural kind? Does it not acquire specificity and empirical content the moment we talk about one of these *syntactic categories* and their associated interpretations?

[10] Of course, the alternative assumption so fundamentally clashes with the metaphysical presuppositions of the paradigm that this is maybe not so surprising.

That form or syntax not only speaks to content and intentionality, but is even the root of them and the engine of thoughts that wouldn't be there without it, is essentially a Kantian line of thought: all contents that appear in our minds are conditioned by certain forms that are inherent to that mind. The duality between the thought or proposition expressed by an expression, and the structure of that expression at a semantic level of representation, becomes here opaque. Again, one could, if one wanted, define a mapping from LF-structures to mind-external propositions. However, if the semantic phenomenon one wishes to explain is structurally determined by linguistic form at all, then the structure of the object onto which one maps the relevant LF must be isomorphic to that of the LF; in which case the danger is to simply reproduce, in one's 'semantics', what the syntax delivers already; if it is not isomorphic, it is not clear what it can explain, as a new mapping will have to be defined that maps the LF-structures to the distinct semantic ones, and it is not clear what this mapping can follow from (see MMD, section 5.6). Thus, I argue that as a regulative idea, we should strive for there being no more to the (linguistic) semantics of an expression than we can see it having at the interfaces of the language faculty with language-external systems that access its products and use them (Figure 1.1).

In Figure 1.1, 'semantic systems' are 'use' or 'performance' systems that access the linguistic products delivered to the interface and process them further, for whatever purposes of referring, joking, deceiving, etc., we happen to use the expressions in question for, taking instructions from their respective LFs. But, as seems to be well accepted now, it is not even clear that the level of LF is needed, in its traditional conception as a level of representation on which representational conditions of well-formedness are imposed (a sieve that lets only the good structures through). The alternative is to dissolve LF as a

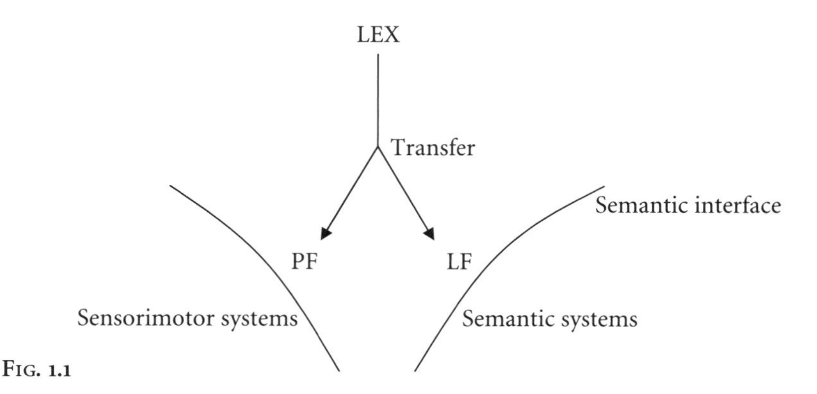

FIG. 1.1

unified structure within the linguistic system that has to satisfy certain conditions, and to rather make the more minimal assumption that there is only the semantic interface SEM itself, which is reached or accessed as often in a derivation as principles of computational efficiency and interface constraints demand. In other words, 'Transfer' occurs several times: each chunk of structure (constructed during one 'phase' of the derivation) is delivered to the external systems at the end of each of the phases, each of which have their own distinctive phonetic and semantic interpretations. LF thus gives way to a mere interface representation, SEM, which now has only virtual existence, as it never exists as a unified object in the way that LF did (Figure 1.2).

If, moreover, operations within phases and Transfer operations apply not optionally but necessarily, if they can apply at all, we see a semantic representation SEM arising as a natural necessity in narrow syntax (NS). What meanings there are is a consequence of the sheer workings and architecture of the system. Conventional (and in this sense 'non-natural') aspects of meaning enter at the level of the arbitrary sound–meaning pairings in the lexicon that are fed into the derivations, as well as in how we make use of SEMs and employ them in discourse and for wider purposes of thought.

While much of this is at least consistent with mainstream Minimalism—in particular, Chomsky's position from 2000 until today—Chomsky (2006) notes that MMD goes beyond this standard position in one crucial respect. The standard view of SEM, the semantic interface, is that the structures NS delivers at that interface are a significant consequence of what expressive conditions the semantic systems *impose* on the syntax. But notice that to say, for example, that the structures have to lend themselves to propositional

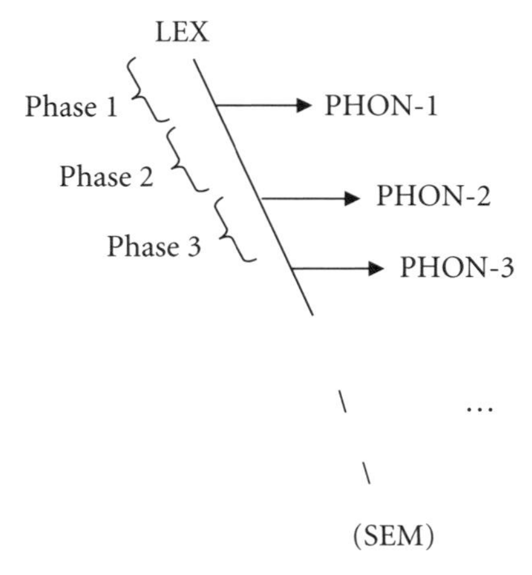

FIG. 1.2

interpretations (be truth-evaluable) is to simply *assume* that the semantic systems have a vocabulary, as it were, in which such notions as 'propositionality' can be formulated. If by 'proposition' we mean the fully projected structure of the sentence (for concreteness, a CP) or its interpretive correlate, I take this assumption likely—almost certainly—to be false. The semantic ('conceptual-intentional', C-I) systems are by definition non- or pre-linguistic (in particular, pre-syntactic) ones. However much one wants to dismiss the formative influence of language on thought, and however generously one wants to credit non-human animal thought with compositional and hierarchical structures, one will have to stop at some point. In the presence of significant doubts on the presence of even much simpler structures in the animal mind, interpretations associated to at least the higher functional portions of the clause (or later 'cycles' of the derivation) will simply not be there. It is a logical consequence of this that to *some* extent, for sure, syntax will have to *condition itself*, instead of being *conditioned from the outside*. The view that NS as a whole—or even to a significant extent—is 'determined by interface conditions' is clearly in need of empirical grounding.

A case in point is the so-called 'duality of semantic interpretation', which distinguishes argument structure from structures expressing 'discourse properties' (quantification, scope, focus, force, etc.), and which has been evoked by Chomsky (2004, 2005a, 2006) as an explanation of the duality of external and internal Merge in syntax from interface conditions imposed on it. But there is no empirical evidence for the language-independence of this duality, to my knowledge. Even weaker statements, such as that the C-I-system 'permits interpretation of quantification in some manner', and that, therefore, 'language should provide such a device if expressive potential is to be adequately utilized' (Chomsky 2006: 8), strike me as unwarranted, even conceptually. Consider, in particular, that even if there was evidence from comparative cognition for some semantic condition, there is no reason to assume that 'expressive potential' must be fully utilized. Partially meeting expressive conditions may be a more optimal solution. So even if there are expressive conditions (an assumption that can only be partially true, as noted), syntax does not need to meet them. It only has to meet conditions on *usability*, a weaker demand.[11]

But suppose we accept some such principle as full utilization of expressive potential, and the syntax does answer this condition. Then the fact that

[11] So the reply to the assertion that because 'C-I permits interpretation of quantification', 'language must generate expressions that yield such interpretation' (Chomsky 2006: 17) should be: no, there is no such necessity.

quantificational power is already assumed on the non-linguistic side of the interface requires the existence of some computational machinery to implement it on that semantic side of the interface. In that case, the syntax need not re-invent new resources to meet the expressive demands in question. We should instead envisage a direct mapping from thought to PF. If it did invent such resources, they would reduplicate structures already there. If in turn the structures are not yet there on the semantic side, the question is how quantification can be.

It may well be that the machinery for syntax to match the expressive needs is easy enough to accomplish: the duality of external and internal Merge can and should be employed to the purpose, and maybe this is easily enough to engineer. Still, note that the internal application of Merge makes new demands on the systemic memory of the system, as Uriagereka (2007: ch. 7) notes, which need not exist once (external) Merge exists, an operation that is simpler both computationally and in terms of memory demands. A more radical reorganization of the system thus appears to be required, if it is to have the mechanism—and the associated semantic benefits—of internal Merge. It is unclear how this structural change could be triggered by the external systems in question.

An alternative line of thought that I therefore suggested in MMD was one that makes empirical properties of thought contents *derive* from the structures generated in the faculty of language, which provides the forms of these thoughts. As noted above, this view *must* be true at least to *some* extent, for all minimalist parties involved: this is the extent to which language is *productive* for certain forms of thought, that is, does not merely 'answer' expressive conditions imposed on it from the outside. As Chomsky (2006) describes the resulting view, 'the primacy of C-I is reduced', and 'the concept of principled explanation . . . simplified'. He objects that C-I conditions 'cannot be entirely eliminated', though, for:

> C-I must have some range of resources that can exploit the properties of generated expressions, along with whatever is involved in use of language to reason, refer, seek to communicate perspicuously, and other mental acts. (Chomsky 2006: 11)

In other words, the external systems must at least be structurally rich enough if the productions of the computational system are to be usable. However, again, it is an empirical question entirely, and a widely open one, to what extent the faculty of language, upon generating expressions, has also *reorganized* the external systems, as opposed to being shaped by them. I see no *a priori* reason to assume, with Chomsky in the quote above, that the preferred choice of explanatory direction (from the outside systems to the computational system's internal organization) is somehow primary. It seems entirely possible at this stage that we will have to re-conceptualize today's commonly held vision of the 'interfaces', and impose a weaker demand on the architecture of the system: not that its generated expressions must meet pre-given semantic demands, nor that they meet conditions of very richly structured external systems, but that, more modestly, they be (at least partially) *usable*. This amounts to a 'use theory of meaning' of sorts. Conceptually necessary is that language is used, not that there is an 'interface' of the kind that current mainstream Minimalist theorizing imposes on the architecture of the linguistic system.

1.5 On 'language' and 'thought'

Non-human animals have structured mental representations of various types and perform computational operations over them using innate systems of natural geometry and spatial representation that, in the case of, for example, insects, are congenial to human capacities or even exceed them (Gallistel 1998). It is also well known that infants and indeed a much wider range of vertebrates have early-developing systems for representing objects as spatio-temporally continuous bodies. These systems centre on constraints of cohesion, continuity, and contact that structure our intuitive physics (Spelke 2003). Potentially, *no* such systems of 'core' knowledge—relating to such domains as space, time, and number—are humanly unique. Animal 'thought' and reasoning even appear to be 'systematic' in the classical sense of Fodor and Pylyshyn (1988), as manifested by the capacity of monkeys to master transitive inference and hierarchical classification tasks under suitable conditions of training (McGonigle and Chalmers 2006). But for that very reason, or the more impressive and human-like we discover the performance of non-human animals to be, the less such capabilities will explain what makes us *different* from them, and another source of what is special to our minds must be brought in, language being one plausible candidate.

Moreover, ascribing 'propositional' thoughts and logicality to animals on the basis of passing certain behavioural tests leaves the specific format of their thoughts rather open: it does not predict the specific structure of the human clause, for example, as far as I can see. Potentially, even, there is a *logical* problem in the attempt to sharpen our account of this format in the non-human case: if described in standard human linguistic terms, the animal mind is *bound* to come out as similar to ours—but describing the non-human mind in terms of human linguistic conceptualizations is not evidence for these conceptualizations. Povinelli and Vonk (2004) point to another such logical difficulty: they ask whether currently available experimental paradigms could *possibly* enforce the conclusion, for example, that experimental subjects reason about unobservable mental states in addition to observable behaviour, as opposed to about behaviour alone. Is behavioural evidence conceivable that would strictly rule a behaviourist interpretation out? There may be a problem here with the inscrutability of meaning and mind that is principled, hence can be overcome only where an entirely different form of access to mental reality is employed, which standard scientific experimentation tends to disallow: introspection. Not being available in the case of other minds (and being unreliable in our own), it may be that the problem of whether other minds reason about non-observable mental states may not possibly be overcome. Similarly for the *structures* of non-human 'thoughts': if these are not human-linguistic ones, it is quite possible that we do not know what we are talking about any more.

A sad consequence of this is that the scope of the comparative method in the study of language evolution (Hauser and Fitch 2003) may be more limited in principle than often assumed. The same would hold for the minimalist set-up in the study of language evolution (Hauser *et al.* 2002) at large: for it is *based* on figuring out the structure of the supposedly 'non-linguistic' C-I systems. Again, the same, perhaps principled, methodological problems arise. The problem of studying 'thought' independently of language—to extract or disentangle thought from its link with language—is a hard and familiar one, whose solutions will likely tend to be partial. But note that even if not, and we solved the problem of the inscrutability of other minds, this would not be evidence that we have 'thought' before—hence independently of—'language'. That contention would be valid only if we thought of language as something like English, a socially regulated communication system. But we may and should think of language also in structural terms, as a system of computations that may be what it is irrespective of whether it becomes externalized or not. Understood as such a computational system, 'language' can be *shared* across species barriers, and hence structured thought in non-humans is not evidence *against* the language-dependence of thought (that is, its dependence on syntax). Indeed, if we describe structured thought processes in monkeys, we seem to primarily use the notation and syntax of universal logic, which may well be abstracted from the syntax of natural language: the apparatus of predicates, arguments, and quantifiers.

On the other hand, if recursion is of the essence of human syntax, and recursion is lacking in non-human animal thought, the dissociation of human and non-human animal thought is again principled, and it is again unlikely that non-humans have thoughts that can impose any interesting conditions on thought in a linguistic creature. To whatever extent there will be a residue of thought that is inherently linguistically structured, and that available mechanisms in non-humans cannot generate, linguistic mechanisms will have to be generative for it. That residue in fact seems to begin not just with complex recursive structures, but with human concept use in the simplest instances of intentional reference and use of words, to be reviewed in Chapter 2. It continues with other types of thoughts of which syntax is a plausible source, such as thoughts about truth and existence, or, more generally, stimulus-unbound thought that transcends the here and now. The more we saw different types of thoughts correlating with specific structures of language, the more the conceptual distinction between them and 'language' would become opaque. Again, in a combinatorial and recursive system it *must* be that its structure is intrinsic to a complex thought; the way it is generated is the thought's rationale for existence. By consequence, an expression in the linguistic sense of say Chomsky (1995), being a sound–meaning pair whose meaning is intrinsic to it, would not be the one it is without meaning what it does *in virtue of the structure it has.* If we wish to analyse the inferential properties of the expression, for example, we cannot but turn to its internal structural properties, as these are what explains the inferential properties, to the extent that these *are* determined by linguistic form (as opposed to contextual or pragmatic factors). Just as one would not abstract some mind-external, non-phonological structure called 'sound' from a phonetic structure represented in the mind/brain to let it figure in relations of rhyme and assonance, one need not abstract an external 'meaning-entity', a 'proposition' or 'thought', to explain rational inference. Naturally, such propositions and their entailment relations can be *modelled* as non-linguistically structured entities (e.g. as sets of possible worlds), and of course such models may be useful to descriptively analyse their entailment patterns. But my question has been what such modelling could explain. If we ask *why* we map particular expressions to particular sets of possible worlds, the answer is still the meaning that the expression has. But it has this meaning because of what expression it is—hence what structure it has.

Suppose we study the logical, referential, and inferential properties of thoughts, and explain these properties by positing certain abstract structures internal to these thoughts—structures that intrinsically belong to them, making them the thoughts they are. What would then tell us whether these structures were 'linguistic' or 'non-linguistic'? Structures do not come labelled with a sign saying they are 'linguistic' ones. Once we have abandoned the view that language is of its essence externalized as a communication system (Chomsky 2006), the conceptual and empirical difference between structures of 'thought' explaining their logical and inferential properties, on the one hand, and 'linguistic' (LF/SEM) properties of corresponding expressions, on the other, becomes undefined. The formal and internalist study of language effectively becomes the study of structured and propositional thought. There is every temptation to regard language as the external 'cloth' in which inner thought is 'wrapped'; but while the phonetic side of language may justly be regarded as a way of 'dressing up' (and indeed partially obscuring) the logical and semantic structure of an expression, it is not clear what the syntactic/semantic structure of a thought as uncovered in a structural analysis of an expression should in turn be obscuring. Or, if it still obscured the structure of thought, we would be making thought ineffable, as something that is in principle different from its possible manifestations in what we can empirically study, pronounce, or describe.[12]

Related remarks hold for the suggestion to separate the 'language of thought' that we study in *linguistic* terms and associate with a 'linguo-semantics' from some unknown and non-linguistic language of thought in the technical Fodorian sense (the LOT, *sensu* Fodor 1990), with its associated 'psycho-semantics'. According to this suggestion, thought is encoded in a symbolic medium functionally defined as a carrier of semantic interpretation. So an expression, E, of a natural language is not a <PHON, SEM> pair, as assumed here, but has no meaning/SEM in itself, which only 'thoughts' have, which are distinct. But in that case, rules are needed by means of which E is mapped to a relevant region in this system of 'thought', acquiring its semantics there, as Chomsky (2000: 176–7) points out. However, there already *are* substantive theories about the computational processes that *make an expression have* its respective SEM, whereas these are unknown in the case of the LOT, if it exists. This makes it hard to accept that the former conception should be traded for the latter. We are offered a new level of representation in the brain, but without an account of how universal properties of meaning (and of sound, if E, above, is deprived of a phonology as well) are expressed in the structures that receive semantic interpretation there. The move under discussion *adds* complexity, and we will have to ask how intricate properties of semantic interpretation, for which we so far have assumed explanations internal to the faculty of language, are encoded in the LOT. The explanatory benefit is unclear.

Methodologically, it seems to me that the defender of the LOT should criticize the explanatory mechanisms that are being offered for particular meaning-theoretic phenomena in generative grammar: say, to give a very concrete example, the explanation of Anderson and Lightfoot (2002) for

[12] Perhaps this was Wittgenstein's position in the *Tractatus* (Wittgenstein 1984).

why the phrase *John's portrait* can denote a portrait with John on it, a portrait painted by John, or a portrait owned by him, whereas *the portrait of John's* interestingly lacks the first interpretation. Anderson and Lightfoot (2002: 47–51) explain these facts in syntactic terms, appealing to the structure of the expressions in question. It is not clear what the alternative is.

I will assume, then, in what follows, that the combinatorics and structural principles that we see operative in language are, first, intrinsic to the meanings we can express in it, and, secondly, that they must—at least to some extent—be productive for the meanings in question. They must give us new thoughts to think, as opposed to merely clothing up given thoughts in language that the non-human and non-linguistic mind can think already.

Perhaps the most distinctive feature of this combinatoriality is the *domain-generality* of thought that it entails: the recursive operation Merge that builds phrases recursively is not sensitive to the *conceptual content* of the elements it combines or the domains that they describe. This is sheer luck on our part, as noted in Mukherji (2007, ch. 1), given that progress in the understanding of the content of lexical concepts has been scarce ever since Plato developed the theory of Ideas. In comparison, insight into the combinatorial properties of language has been burgeoning. If the architecture of our mind was such that progress in syntax depended on progress in a 'science of meaning', perhaps our enterprise would be doomed. Assuming the lack of this dependence, what unbounded Merge may have done is not actually to *add concepts* to our inherited primate conceptual system, but to merely *structure* those concepts that, in non-humans, exist encapsulated in particular cognitive domains (Spelke 2003). Language, that is, does not give us new concepts of fairness, colour, substance, or shape, but ways of *combining* them into structures, some of which can now be *true* or *false* in a domain-neutral sense, hence acquire distinctive intentional properties as a consequence of their structure, with associated adaptive benefits.

In a language with a compositional semantics, in which all complex concepts are implicitly mastered when simple ones are, a whole and unbounded conceptual realm will now open up in one big bang. With language, for the first time, knowledge will evolve that makes us *aware* of the domain of the conceptual as such, allowing us to target and structure *it*, rather than the world out there or particular tasks arising in particular adaptive domains. As Spelke (2003: 291) summarizes, 'natural languages provide humans with a unique system for combining flexibly the representations they share with other animals', and her viewpoint is consistent, I think, with the view that some representations and meanings of them are new and humanly specific, in particular those propositional constructs that, if I am right, uniquely exhibit the aspect of truth. This general vision of things is 'Whorfian' given its view on the intimate relation of language and thought. But, as Rob Chametzky points out in personal conversation, this language-dependence of thought does not entail any linguistic relativity. The properties of language in question are universal ones (although this does not preclude parametric variance in the underlying principles of compositional semantics).

'Linguistic determinism'[13] also comes in a more specific variety, largely due to Jill de Villiers, which I would like to discuss in the remainder of this chapter. Her view is that the child is brought to the threshold of mastering a full 'mind-reading' capacity through the grasp of specific syntactic forms of language, in particular finite sentential complements embedded under verbs such as *think* or *believe*. Put in different terms, the *conceptual-intentional* advance in question is to a crucial extent a *syntactic* one, and conceptual maturation patterns alongside syntactic maturation. This view, along with Gleitman's long-standing contention of the causal significance of syntax in the acquisition of verbs (Gleitman *et al.* 2005; and see Fernandez *et al.* 2006), would provide an interesting further confirmation of the need to bring syntax and semantics closer to one another, as suggested here. Specifically, de Villiers (e.g. 2005) claims that the syntax of *say* and *think* forms the very basis for thinking about the mind, that is the imperceptible mental states causally underlying our behaviour. The main sources of evidence for this hypothesis are, first, that the best gauge of mastery of false belief precisely seems to be the comprehension of tensed sentential complements under mental or communication verbs, of the sort mentioned in Section 1.3, repeated here as (33):

(33) Mom said she bought apples.

As noted, understanding (33) requires the appreciation that the complement can describe the representation of reality of a person as something that can be false, although it is adopted by that person in *realis* mode, and although this falsehood leaves the truth value of the matrix clause untouched. A second piece of evidence comes from the study of deaf children who do not learn a sign language natively: their mastery of false belief may be delayed for up to several years. Their mastery of sentential complement comprehension is delayed to the same extent, and *remains* the best predictor of their eventual success. The case of the deaf children is telling because they have age-appropriate non-verbal intelligence and active sociability, allowing us to go some

[13] Possibly a questionable term, as it depends on a conceptual separation between language and thought.

way towards isolating the contribution that the maturation of linguistic competence makes to our cognition (see further, P. de Villiers 2005). A third piece of evidence is that training on no other syntactic construct than sentential complements (not, for example, on relative clauses) helps, or helps to the same extent, in mastering false-belief tasks (Hale and Tager-Flusberg 2003).

One piece of counter-evidence comes from a number of studies apparently showing various levels of false belief understanding in children younger than those mastering sentential complements of *believe* or *think*, as well as in non-human species such as tamarin monkeys (Hauser 1999) or bottlenose dolphins (Tschudin 2006). But the comparative evidence in question makes the mastery in question—as usual—at best equivocal: de Villiers and de Villiers (2003: 368–70) suggest that the mind-reading abilities in question may represent a more procedural and *implicit* theory of belief which does not reach levels of explicit, conscious, or declarative knowledge. Dienes and Perner (1999) call such knowledge 'non-predication explicit': it is not *about* anything, in the same way in which moving a pointing hand to a target (visually guided movement) can be unconscious and fail to involve any explicit predication. Predication-explicit knowledge is accessible in a flexible manner for reasoning and action, and appears to be needed to support explicit pointing as well as evaluating, betting, or choosing; it may well *have* a representational format requiring language.

Perner, Zauner and Sprung (2005) also offer the counterevidence to de Villiers' view that there is a large cross-linguistic *variation* in complement forms, but *no* associated differences in acquiring understanding of a (potentially different) 'point of view', as required for false belief understanding. In particular, in German the complement of 'want' (German *will*) can and must have an overt complementizer and a finite tense in the complement. So, in English, we say (34a), and cannot, according to Perner *et al.*, say (34b):

(34) a. Mom wants Andy to go to bed
(34) b. *Mom wants that Andy goes to bed

But in German, we use (35a) to express the meaning of (34a), and strictly cannot use (35b) to express the same meaning:

(35) a. Mami will, dass Andreas ins Bett geht.
Mom wants that Andy to bed goes
(35) b. *Mami will Andreas ins Bett gehen
Mom wants Andy to bed go

Mandarin and Cantonese exhibit yet other differences to the English paradigm, in particular there is no marking of complementation through 'that' at all. And yet, Chinese like German or English children master verbs of desire (and understand unfulfilled desires) well before epistemic verbs (and false beliefs), suggesting that the difference in the syntax of desire as opposed to belief that exists *in English* cannot be crucial to the conceptual-intentional advance in question. If it was, the same difficulties should, in particular, show up in German children processing verbs of desire such as *wollen*, which is not the case.

However, as de Villiers (2005: 199) notes, this not only leaves unclear *how* the conceptual gap between *want* and *think* is bridged; it also makes the false prediction that the deaf children mentioned above having trouble with syntax should master non-verbal versions of the false-belief task first, before they master verbal forms (since this is by hypothesis a purely conceptual advance). But this is not the case. Perhaps more importantly, Perner *et al.* may too naively take dissimilarities in surface syntax of German and English complements as sufficient evidence for dissimilarities in the underlying structure as well. Thus it is incorrect that in German, as Perner *et al.* (2005: 229) state, desire-type verbs always require finite that-complements, as in (35a). Where the matrix subject controls the interpretation of the subject of the embedded verb, this is not the case, as shown in (36):

(36) a. Andreas will schlafen/ ein Auto
Andy wants to sleep/ a car

(36) b. Andreas will Mami helfen
Andy wants Mom help
'Andy wants to help Mom.'

Nor does English require that-clauses with believe-type verbs: cf. *Peter believes him to be wrong.* All desire-type verbs moreover go with a state of affairs as complement (Andy sleeps, Andy has a car, or Andy helps Mom) that is irredeemably in *irrealis* mood, as de Villiers (2005: 201–3) notes: the embedded proposition is thus not represented as objectively true or false by the speaker. The state of affairs it depicts is represented as merely wanted, whereas with verbs of saying it is represented as factive, as in (37):

(37) Myrtha said Andy doesn't help Mom.

To this Andy may protest with the utterance (38):

(38) (That's wrong:) I do help Mom!

In this case, as noted earlier, he does not realize that embedded complements are not assessed for truth value: complex sentences can only have one truth value. It is the factivity of the complement to which Andy is tuned if he responds with (38). He has to learn that even a proposition in *realis* mood may only be *represented* as being factive, even though the factivity is not endorsed by that representation. Again, recognizing this must be like a dawning of what truth really means, and it is the crucial aspect of de Villiers' structural-syntactic analysis of false belief. Immersed in factivity at first, the child finds out that factivity is only a *take* on things; truth is something that is of its essence *claimed* or *stated*. The putative facts are only *representations*; they need not be facts; the truth *is* not the facts; it is what is *targeted*, by a speaker, who may fail in doing so. Nothing of this insight is hidden in desire-type constructions, in German or any other language, because the complements in that case are never realis. With *say*, as with *think*, they are. That difference will keep *want* and *think* apart in German as in other languages, and indeed it is a *structural* difference. Thus, in German, we have the contrast between the desideratives in examples (39) and (40), which are grammatical, and the truth-related epistemic verbs in example (41), which is not grammatical:

(39)	er	will/	in den Himmel	kommen
	he	wants	in the Heaven	come
	'he wants to come into Heaven'			

(40)	er	hofft/versucht	in den Himmel	zu kommen
	he	hopes/tries	in the Heaven	to come

(41)	*er glaubt/denkt/sagt	in den Himmel	(zu) kommen
	he believes/thinks/says	in the Heaven	(to) come

Consider similar differences in the syntax of volitional and epistemic verbs in passivization. In both German and Dutch, passivizations are possible with *trying* in conjunction with a non-finite, non-factive complement (42–43), but not when a verb like *say* merges with such a non-finite clause (44–45):[14]

[14] Relatedly, it is interesting that in Dutch words of trying or refusing go with an *om . . . te* infinitive with optional *om*, whereas *om* is omitted with words of saying, asserting, thinking, or believing:

(i)	Hij	probeerde/weigerde	(om)	de deur	open	te doen
	he	tried/refused	in order to	the door	open	to make
	'he tried/refused to open the door					

(ii)	Hij	zei/beweerde/dacht/geloofde	(*om)	in de hemel	te komen
	he	said/stated/thought/believed	(*in order to)	into the Heaven	come

In Afrikaans *om* in (i)-type sentences is obligatory, and again forbidden in (ii) equivalents.

(42) German
es wird versucht werden Dir zu helfen
it shall tried be you to help
'it shall be tried to help you'

(43) Dutch
Er zal geprobeerd worden (om) je te helpen
it shall tried be in order you to help
'it shall be tried to help you'

(44) German
*es wird gesagt werden Dir zu helfen
it shall said be you to help

(45) Dutch
*Er werd gezegd worden ziek te zijn
it shall said be sick to be

As a further example, (46), with epistemic verbs, is fine in German, but (47), with volitionals, is not:

(46) a. er sagt/denkt: 'ich komme in den Himmel!'
'he says/thinks: "I come into Heaven!" '

(46) b. er sagt/denkt er kommt in den Himmel
'He says/thinks he comes into Heaven'

(47) a. *er will: 'ich komme in den Himmel!'
'he wants: "I come into Heaven" '

(47) b. *er will er kommt in den Himmel
He wants he comes into Heaven

These grammatical differences correlate with the difference in mood between *wanting/trying*, on the one hand, and *saying/thinking/believing*, on the other. They may be part of the maturation of truth and the notion of belief. It is further interesting that in both English and German 'that' plays similar roles in encoding 'point of view'. Consider that in both languages a transposed CP-complement can go with or without an overt complementizer ('that', 'dass'):

(48) (That) the Earth is flat, I believe.

(49) a. Dass die Erde flach ist, glaube ich.
that the Earth flat is, believe I

(49) b. die Erde ist flach, glaube ich
the Earth is flat, believe I

Interestingly, in both languages, if the complementizer is not overtly there (that is, it is dropped), the pre-posed embedded CP-complement has no declarative force: it is only conjecturally asserted, and one allows the Earth not to be flat. If the complementizer is there, assertoric force is supplied and intonation becomes different: either there is a stress on the epistemic verb, or there is not, in which case the expression is like part of an enumeration of what one believes: *that the Earth is flat I believe, that the Eiffel Tower is in Paris I believe, etc.*, or as in the following list: *this is what I believe: that the Earth is flat, that the Eiffel Tower is in Paris, etc.* In both cases, the Earth's not being flat is ruled out. In both languages, however, it is strictly not possible to drop the complementizer with desideratives or volitionals:

(50) a. *(That) we go to the movies, I want.
(50) b. *(Dass) wir ins Kino gehen, will ich.

Overall, then, it seems to me that de Villiers' view that a full theory of mind implicates a competence to be described in specific structural terms and mirrored in the syntax of sentential complements stands up against counter-evidence provided so far. This is consistent with the assumption that an *implicit* understanding of false belief may be mastered earlier than the time that complement syntax is: in fact, even these implicit competences, when formally characterized, may instantiate or implicate the structural patterns in question. De Villiers' viewpoint is one instance of a general idea that is crucial to the framework of this book, that there is a specific syntax of belief as much as a specific syntax of predication (Bowers 1993; Moro 2000; den Dikken 2006), of reference (Longobardi 2005; Chapter 4), of integral possession (Szabolcsi 1984; Kayne 1994; Uriagereka 2002), or, if I am right, of truth (Chapter 5; or Hinzen 2003). That is, in each of these cases, the syntax of particular phenomena is not merely an arbitrary way of coding independently given semantic phenomena. To rephrase this conclusion, the phenomena in question—semantic phemonena, in a pre-theoretic sense—do not have a life and existence independently of the way that, with the arrival of syntactic patterns on the evolutionary scene, they are linguistically represented.

None of this goes any way towards suggesting that there cannot be thought that is inexpressible: language does not go a long way in conveying complex emotions (say, in marital disputes), for example, and there are numerous occasions where we 'don't know how to put a certain thought'. In such cases I would venture the proposal that the thought will either not be explicit, or not be propositional. The cases in question do not establish that explicit and propositional thought does not co-extend with language.

1.6 Conclusions

Providing a stage-setting and a conceptual framework for what follows, this chapter has summarized some conceptual and empirical assumptions of this book and outlined a research programme in the aitiology of thought. Language use can be described from an internalist or externalist viewpoint. From the former viewpoint, language use is the result of internal causes having to do with the internal organization of the organism in question. In particular, linguistic behaviour is premised by the possession of a language faculty to which we ascribe structure as inquiry proceeds, and which has not been shown to be a function of the organism's encounters with the environment and cannot as of now be described in a physical (as opposed to linguistic or psychological) language either: a phoneme is characterized by its auditory phenomenology, a concept by its meaning. An extreme externalist perspective does away with this internal organization as an independent cause of behaviour, and substitutes a purely physicalist and functionalist account of the behaviour in question, eliminating programmatically all semantic and intentional characterizations of language insofar as they are primitive and irreducible. For example, the behaviour in question may, on this view, be explained by the history of how it came into being (reinforcement, 'learning', 'training', etc.), where this genesis mainly or only involves external pressure exerted on the organism, be it physical pressure or a social one.

I take Chomsky (1959) to have made a still powerful point, not quite against the validity of the externalist programme of a functional analysis as such, but its fruitfulness and internal coherence. This point is vital, as it suggests that there is, at least according to this influential critique, nothing wrong with behaviourism conceptually, or as a 'philosophy of mind'. It is an unobjectionable research programme to aim to characterize the putatively mental aspects of organisms purely functionally and externalistically. It just has not delivered anything that would be of great interest in a science of language. As MMD argues (and see Hinzen and Uriagereka 2006), the follow-up theory of behaviourism, namely functionalism, falls under the same critique and has been an inadequate philosophical foundation for modern generative linguistics (and see Chapter 2 for another argument against functionalism based on the atomicity of concepts). What this leaves us with is a situation in which we have to characterize the mind in an internalist terminology special to it, with no substitute for mentalistic vocabulary anywhere in view. We do not begin to know, for example, how it is that the neural correlate of a particular concept gives rise to that particular concept (with the content it specifically has), as opposed to another. Mind and brain *correlate*, for sure, even lawfully, but this insight, while obviously much enriched in the meantime, was as such available to Descartes, the dualist, who probably even accepted it and developed positive naturalistic proposals on the nature of the correlation.

The position taken in MMD on the metaphysical *nature* of mind is not to *take* such a position. This is not meant to be a perverse statement. Taking a position on the nature of mind implies an ontology: a stance on the nature of a particular object in nature. MMD argues that any such stance should not follow from conceptual reflections alone but be a consequence of naturalistic inquiry. Within such inquiry, we cannot proceed other than by introducing whatever terminology seems needed and useful to descriptive and explanatory purposes. There should not be *a priori* constraints on which vocabulary is permitted. We have made no progress beyond behaviourism if we begin an inquiry into the mind with the assumption that physicalism is true, and therefore only a certain methodology or vocabulary is permitted in its inquiry. It has to be the other way around, that naturalistic inquiry goes first, unprejudiced by ontology, and builds up bodies of theory that may then entail interesting metaphysical conclusions. Put differently, our inquiry is about whatever it is about: unification of one domain with another may come or not, but if it does, it can go in all directions, reduction of one to the other being a rare case in the history of science. So, the biolinguistic programme is, and for now remains, one about the structures of *meaning* and *sound*, characterized as such and in these very terms: meaning and sound are the primitive domains in nature that we subject to empirical study while bracketing the ultimate ontological question of what the entities are that we are characterizing. Naturalistic inquiry does not depend on such a delineation beforehand. Concepts or word meanings as grasped by a speaker are as real as anything else in nature that naturalistic inquiry describes. The empirical question is what the structure of meaning, as a primitive domain in nature, is.

I have argued that linguistic expressions should be viewed as reducing to sound–meaning pairs <PHON, SEM>, where PHON and SEM are interface representations that provide instructions for external systems that use language, while not, on the semantic side, conditioning them. These representations 'correspond' to or are rationalized by nothing external, but they are part of the explanation for why human intentional relations to the world are the ones they are. Complex semantic representations are built around *concepts*, and I have introduced a distinction between the conceptual and the intentional, to which I will often return in this book. The intentional depends on the conceptual, but not vice versa: if we make a judgement of truth, say, or refer to an object, hence engage in intentional acts, these acts will depend on a supply of concepts that feed into a derivation and as such are independent of the intentional act of which they will later form the conceptual constituents. Intentional relations involve or implicate concepts, but are not relations *to* concepts. We do not stand in any intentional relations to the *concepts* we think, we just think them, and use *them* to intentional purposes. Intentional reference to an object—say, a particular person—is possible by accessing and using the concepts that form our species-specific repertoire. Primitive concepts *as such* do not relate to anything external, viewed as independently given: they are internal mental structures, usable in acts of intentional reference. These adaptive relations do not depend on any such fact as that our thoughts are like pictures of external objects, our concepts images of things or representations of them. External correspondents or referents of concepts or SEMs must be argued for on empirical grounds. Where they exist, it has to be asked whether they contribute to the explanation of the internal mental structures in question, or structures of our human understanding. There is no question that there are various causal and adaptive relations between me and the city of London, or between me and George W. Bush. None of this means that London or Bush, qua external and mind-external objects characterized in non-intentional (e.g. causal) terms, could explain why we have concepts of cities and persons. No creature that lacked concepts of persons and cities would acquire them by standing in relations to external objects characterized in non-intentional terms. I return to these claims in Chapter 2.

The *structure* of sounds and meanings generated in a language is essential to them; one could develop (as the philosophical tradition has) a notion of 'proposition' or 'object/content of thought' that forms an equivalence class of a whole number of structured expressions in different languages, equivalent under the relation of 'matching in content'. Structurally different expressions would then be picked out as expressions 'denoting' the one content they all express. But this is not motivation for the independent existence of 'contents' or 'propositions', defined by their 'truth conditions', along with the structured expressions themselves. For a certain complex meaning (and its associated truth condition) to exist in the first place, a certain complex structure has to exist, and if the latter is what syntax derives at the level of LF (or a more recent replacement of the latter), the structure of the meaning in question is universal. The present enterprise is a search for the structured forms by means of which we think, that are intrinsic to our minds as natural objects, and whose maturation in childhood we can track.

Our question more specifically is not only where truth conditions (of specific expressions) come from, but where truth as such comes from, as a putative cognitive universal. We inquire into the structural origins of truth.

Truth is a central—and perhaps the most central—notion in the analysis of human thought and intentionality, along with the notion of reference. Both notions, after a first look in this chapter, are distinct. What makes it interesting to investigate truth on the internalist lines indicated is that it seems so virtually impossible, at least on current philosophical intuitions, that an approach to truth could or should be based on the structural specifics of human mentality, as opposed to the mind's external relations to the world, including the social world. Yet, as noted, a mere exposure to the physical world out there gives us no concepts at all; and while the social world may be crucial for the maturation of the truth concept in ontogeny and the whole idea of a (potentially mistaken) 'point of view' or 'perspective', its significance as an *originator* of truth is unclear.

2

Where Meaning Begins: The Atoms of Thought

2.1 Language as a particulate system in nature

This chapter begins our internalist exploration where the process of meaning construction in language itself begins: with the pristine building blocks of complex meanings, 'atomic' concepts. Meaning has to begin *somewhere*; the structural complexity of meaning *bottoms out* at a point, in a set of simple or atomic meanings. While empiricists have hoped these would be sense data or 'impressions', there is no reason to have such hopes now. The conceptual basis of thought is not confined to sensory concepts, and our basic conceptual repertoire is more abstract. These abstract atoms of thought are what this chapter is about. It is important to see that it is *not* thereby about (proper) *names*. 'Name' as the term will here be used is a category of language *use*: it indicates how a concept attached to a phonetic label *functions* in a given structural and pragmatic context; and using a noun as a name is only one way of using it. That functioning presupposes, if I am right, a conceptual *content* attached to the name: no name without a conceptual content. Conceptual atoms are the building bocks of conceptual contents.

Let us begin with the empirical claim that the human system of concepts that we express in language is a *naturally occurring self-diversifying system* in the sense of Abler (1989). Systems of this kind exhibit an unbounded variety of discrete elements, and sustain this variation over time. All their productions are particulate units formed by a combinatorial operation that is recursive: when the operation has constructed a unit, this very same operation can construct a yet larger unit by applying to the very unit that it built in its first application. All complex synthetic (or 'molecular') units that are formed in this fashion bottom out, when fully analysed, with simple units ('atoms'), which have no structural complexity. The identity of these atoms is unaffected by what compounds they enter into: they are freely *re*combinable, hence preserve their identity when entering a compound. The complex units, equally, like chemical molecules, have a particulate identity, which again is preserved as such when they combine and recombine with yet other simple or complex units. The elements of any such productive system belong to a *generated set*, which is determined by laying down a number of atoms and generative principles that combine the particulate entities of the system (both atomic and molecular) into more complex ones. The successor function in arithmetic is a particularly simple generator of this kind: it generates an unbounded number of discrete units, the natural numbers.

Let me illustrate Abler's notion in an abstract way using Figure 2.1. In (a), a combinatorial operation, +, merges two elements of a system of squares, one black, one white, in a way that the information they contain is averaged into a shade of grey: constituents *blend*, and identities are obliterated as a result. As a consequence of that obliteration we expect variation in such systems to diminish over time. In (b), in contrast, identities are retrievable in the compound formed, and the constituents of the particulate composition in (b) can as such re-occur in other compounds (see in particular (c)).

Temperature and the weather illustrate case (a). Physical chemistry and the system of biological inheritance, by contrast, have a particulate character. It was Mendel's discovery of the particulate character of the units of inheritance—the genes—that saved Darwin's evolutionary theory from an inconsistency. If parents and offspring always combined into an average, evolution by

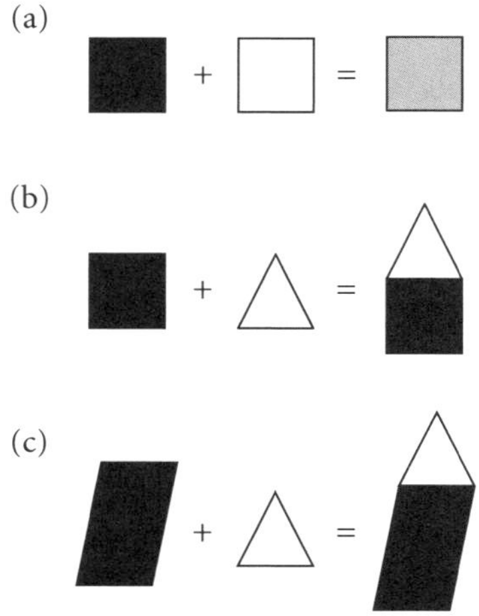

(a) + =

(b) + =

(c) + =

Fig. 2.1

natural selection will have less and less variety to make selections from, and will eventually come to a halt (as Fisher noted in 1930).

Turning to human language as a particulate system, this system is, to start with, widely recognized to be 'discretely infinite', in a sense that is most characteristically exemplified by the natural numbers. As for discreteness, just as each natural number is a discrete unit, each of the unbounded number of elements of a particular language is a discrete unit, which does not blend into any other as complexity builds up. Thus, we can construct an unbounded sequence of expressions, *loves Mary, John loves Mary, thinks John loves Mary, Bill thinks John loves Mary, Bill thinks John loves Mary without regretting it, Jill doubts Bill thinks John loves Mary without regretting it except on Fridays*, and so on, with each expression a discrete unit both syntactically and semantically. It is not the case that for any two sentences, there would be a third sentence 'in between' them, in the sense in which there is an intermediate temperature for every two temperatures. If S is a sentence, 3/4 or 5/7 of S are not necessarily also sentences.

Like other particulate systems, languages *sustain* their variation. They do not, for example, linearly increase or decrease in their structural complexity, be it as a function of the cultural sophistication of their speakers, or because of a general cognitive preference for simpler grammars. The needed notion of 'simplicity' seems to be essentially indefinable. In situations of language contact, languages mix to form new languages, but they do not do so in the way that they become an average of the contact languages involved; or that for every two languages there would be a third one in between them (in which case variation would be continuous, which it is not, as Baker 2001: 82 points out). Rather, new languages are built from the same particulate resources, by *recombining* them (Mufwene 2001).

Language is further *systematic* in the sense of Fodor and Pylyshyn (1988): a relational expression of the form aRb, with a and b syntactic constituents and R a relational head taking them as arguments, necessarily co-exists with an expression of the form bRa. That is, the kind of relation between aRb and bRa is not *statistical*, any more than the relation between x and y in the equation $y = x + 2$ is (Marcus 2001; Jackendoff 2002). Rather, whoever can form an expression of the logico-grammatical form aRb can form an expression of the form bRa—not because he or she happens to 'associate' one with the other, but for *structural* reasons, or as a matter of algebraic law. This is explained if that person's mind is structured in such a way that he or she represents a, R, and b as particulate units of the complex mental representation in question, together with the structural fact that the relation in question holds between *a* in its *first* argument position, and *b* in its *second*. For then, *ipso facto*, an expression can be represented in which *R* holds between *a* in its *second* argument position, and *b* in its first. This requires that *a* and *b* have their respective identities *independently* of which argument position they figure in, and that the argument positions are the ones they are, *independently* of which arguments figure in them. These argument positions are thus *variables*, which take *values*, where crucially the variables do not change in their identity when they take different values, just as the variable 'x' does not change its algebraic role in the equation $y = x + 2$, depending on what number provides its value.[1]

Importantly, the systematicity of language is not limited to the *syntactic* properties of expressions. Languages are systematic not only in the sense that the expression *John loves Mary* can be *syntactically* represented just in case *Mary loves John* can, but also in the sense that the one expression is semantically *understood* when the other is. This *semantic systematicity* is again explained if the same constituents figure in the same argument positions, although in reverse order, where being the 'same' constituent now also entails having the same *meaning*. This very assumption is needed to explain the systematicity of *inference*, since it is the fact that the expression *turtles* has the exact same meaning in the sentences *Rabbits are faster than turtles*, *Ferraris are faster than rabbits*, and *Ferraris are faster than turtles*, that the last of these expressions is a valid deductive consequence of the former two (see Fodor & Pylyshyn 1988).

Note now that a recursive system is not *as such* semantically compositional, in the sense that a meaning is systematically predictable from the part–whole structure of an expression. Recursion is a mathematical property of algebraic entities that implies a self-similarity; the latter may not be accompanied by systematic semantic effects. For example, one could imagine a language whose expressions all arise from merging nouns into noun-compounds recursively:

(1) cat, cat-owner, cat-owner-hater, cat-owner-hater-fighter, cat-owner-hater-fighter-club, etc.

[1] The systematicity of thought and language is a challenge that Fodor and Pylyshyn formulated in 1988 as one against the empiricist connectionist paradigm. Their claim was that as a consequence of this feature, *syntactically structured mental representations* must figure *in a causal role* in the mind, the current lack of neurological evidence for such representations notwithstanding. Hadley (2004) surveys recent attempts to meet this challenge, and argues that it is far from having been met, especially if systematicity in the sense of the following paragraph is taken into account. That said I take it that it is unproblematic to implement a systematic mind in a standard multi-layer perceptron of the general sort characterized by Marcus (2001). The point is that such networks do not predict or explain systematicity.

As it happens, the meanings of these expressions all *are* fully compositional; in particular, a cat-owner-hater-fighter-club simply and straightforwardly refers to a club of people fighting against haters of owners of cats. However, on the face of it, compositionality is no logical necessity; in principle, any of the above noun compounds could have had idiomatic meanings. Their syntactic formation might have been strictly recursive, while on the semantic side all meanings had to be learned one by one, with an ever-increasing memory load. But natural language is not like that. So, it is simply an empirical fact that, although recursion does not entail compositionality, in natural language it does go along with it. This does not mean the latter does not have a principled explanation. As the example just given suggests, in fact, compositionality might be rationalizable as a *principle of cognitive economy*, an idea very welcome from a minimalist perspective.

Consider more concretely this evolutionary story, which I am here putting forward as a speculative one. After recursivity became available in the human lineage and got co-opted into the linguistic system for the combination of lexical concepts, an infinite generative power in the space of meanings arose. Other cognitive systems already in place would cope with this as well as they could. One way to restrict this generative power was to resort to compositionality. Compositionality means that the system will subject infinitary self-similar structures to a part–whole analysis: its productions will be chunked into pieces. These pieces, moreover, which would become the particulate units of the system, would necessarily be of only a few types. Thus the *syntactic categories* arose, effectively a consequence of interface systems restricting the generative power of the system in accordance with memory constraints. We expect the number of the categories to be very limited, as with any larger number the very need to introduce them is contravened, and that indeed is the case.[2]

Note that compositionality, phrase structure, and categoriality are rationalized in this way without any appeal to the functionality of language in communication, the domain where a rationale for compositionality is often sought (see e.g. Smith *et al.* 2003). Moreover, the above line of reasoning suggests that a crucial aspect of syntax may indeed 'follow from interface conditions', although the role of the interface conditions is now a *negative* one: they *restrict* the power of the system rather than imposing expressive constraints on it, deriving from the pre-linguistic structure of

[2] Interestingly, Roeper (2003: 6) cites evidence much in the spirit of this suggestion, namely that 'compositionality *must* apply when Merge of a Noun applies twice': while there are many two-term idioms such as *turncoat*, three-term noun compounds have some systematic compositional analysis: a *turncoat brigade* is a brigade of turncoats.

thought (the line of reasoning I questioned in Section 1.4). The same would then of course be true for the origin of propositionality, and truth: in the process of chunking down the system's complex productions, particulate units with distinctive units arose, and propositional units are simply one of these. What cuts the chunks down to size is sheer economy, plausibly tightly linked to bounds on memory, not the structure of the external world, or what thoughts we want to have expressed (again the line of reasoning again that I argued to be implausible in Section 1.4 in the light of limitations on what structure we can assume is there on the other side of the semantic interface—or in the physical world, for that matter).

The first step on the path to a propositional particulate unit in language is a very mysterious one: the formation of a phrase with a compositional analysis, as opposed to a complex word, or a blend. As we put the lexical items *kill* and *Bill* together, the verb phrase

(2) $[_{VP}$ *kill Bill*],

forms a higher-order unit of linguistic structure. This unit now comes with its own interpretation and referential potential: it is not interpreted as some kind of average of *killing* and *Bill*, but as an *integrated event*. If we refer to a killing of Bill, we refer, to start with, to a killing, which is the notion that anchors our referential act conceptually. Bill is referenced too, but not as an entity in its own right that happens to be associated with the event, adjoined to it, or a modifier of it. Rather, Bill is conceptualized as an intrinsic *part* of the event, an event *participant*, as noted in passing in Section 1.3. Once an event of killing Bill is characterized by a nominal or verbal argument structure, there could not be a killing of Bill without Bill, in the way that there could be a killing of Bill without, say, any pleasure involved. This—a matter of logico-linguistic necessity—is entirely the consequence of the formation of a phrase in the argument structure system, and *follows from nothing external*, as far as I can see: there is absolutely nothing in the external world that distinguishes between mere adjuncts to an event, on the one hand, and event participants, on the other. Any event that is described as a killing of Bill has Bill in it, but no external viewpoint could distinguish between him merely being there (and being killed), and him being a non-dissociable *part* of the event, forming an aspect of its individuation and identity. Of necessity, the event as a whole, moreover, is a function of its inherent participant changing state: namely, becoming dead. There is no such thing, logically speaking, as an event of killing Bill without another event temporally subsequent to it, the event of Bill's being dead. Call this the event's implicational structure: it is inherently *bounded* by the state of Bill's being dead, which is its 'telos'. A killing that ends otherwise can be called by that name only in irony, an observation that points us to what will later be discussed under the label of 'analyticity'. Chapter 3 attempts a structural and internalist explanation for it.

So, what is remarkable about a simple phrase such as (2) is not that it is not analysed (even by children, ever) as a single word like (3):

(3) killBill,

nor is its having a compositional analysis so remarkable. A compositional analysis could *as such* be merely conjunctive (a conjunctive event kill+Bill would be an event that is a killing and is Bill, whatever this would mean); or modificational, with *of Bill* something like a modifier of *kill*; or predicational, with, say, *kill* a predicate of *Bill*. But none of these analyses are adequate. The compositionality of (2) is of a specific type, coming, as we have seen, with *emergent effects* that this particular kind of head–complement structure yields and no adjunct or modificational structure would yield. These effects can no more be predicted from those of *kill* and *Bill* than the properties of H_2O (e.g. its fire extinguishing properties) can be predicted from those of H_2 and O (the latter of which is fire-enhancing), or the properties of a gene can be predicted from the nucleotides that make it up. They are emergent in the sense of being qualitatively different or new properties, not predictable from nor contained *per se* in those of their parts when these are considered in isolation from the structure in which they become structuralized. They do not, in particular, arise from first *thinking* 'kill' and then thinking 'Bill', or from associating, concatenating, or sequencing them (see MacPhail 1998: ch. 5; Fodor 2003).

The VP in question also does not relate to its constituents in the way that the product *6* relates to a possible factorization of it, say the factors *2* and *3*. The latter relation would leave the systematicity of language unexplained: If *kill* and *Bill* were related to the complex event representation [$_{VP}$ *kill Bill*] as *2* and *3* are to *6*, the expressions *Bill killed Hill* and *Hill killed Bill* would not be systematically related to one another. For the above explanation of this relation depended on the fact that *Bill* is a (context-independent, syntactic, and semantic) constituent of these expressions, in the sense that it is necessarily tokened when these complex expressions themselves are, and thus can be a cause (or can explain) their lawful relationship. An element in a possible factorization of *6* is *not* necessarily tokened when *6* is, and does not govern its causal properties. That *6* can be factorized does not make it structurally or syntactically complex in the way that [$_{VP}$ *kill Bill*] is.

The emergent syntactic and semantic effects in question alone speak in favour of the explanatory role of syntax in the genesis of forms of meaning. Why would the interpretive correlates of what the older generative tradition has called 'projection' in head–complement constructions exist in the *absence* of these constructions? Recent versions of minimalist syntax propose that projection is a residue of X′-theory and should not be assumed to exist, since a rich theory of phrase structure of the kind projection entails violates the Strong Minimalist Thesis (SMT). The idea here is that in a head–complement ([H-XP]) construction, H is a lexical item and should, qua Head, be *ipso facto* the label of the construction, the element that determines its status for further computation and provides all the information of it that further computation needs. Hence no projections are independently needed. However, this seems to be a point about notation more than reality. Simply by assuming the very notion 'head', projections are assumed as well. A head is nothing different from a projecting element. Moreover, if projection does yield effects at the interface, its existence is no violation of the SMT.

From this point of view, all that the claim that projections do not exist means is that we do not need an independent notational device for them. Understood in different, more substantive ways, it is hard to see how the claim can be correct. Thus if the result of merging H and XP is simply X (as in (4a)), not to mention the more radically minimalist (4b) (Collins 2002),

(4) a.

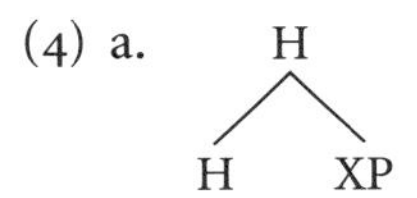

(4) b.

H XP

then the result of Merge is simply one of the Merge partners, and the system erases hierarchical complexity the moment it has erected it, collapsing it into a lexical item again. Put differently, the result of taking a complement would be to reproduce the category we started with, as depicted in (4a), creating a two-segment category as in the case of adjunctions, which H-XP constructions crucially differ from. I will assume that something more has to happen when the system builds a phrase. Its now common depiction as a (perhaps labelled) unordered set, as in (5), does not seem to speak to this question, as, strictly speaking, that depiction eliminates phrases as linguistic objects:

(5) Merge (X,Y) = {X, Y}.

Roeper (2003: 3) formulates the interesting view that 'nodes in a tree are linked to semantic distinctions', a view congenial to the syntax–semantics relation I assume here.[3] Part of his articulation of this view applied to the acquisition process is that recursion, as suggested above, entails compositionality by an economy argument: as the child analyses recursive structures, it submits them to a compositional analysis. Syntactic constituents thus transpire or arise as structures are recursively built: a compositional decision is a hierarchical one. This new object is then not identical to the object *kill*, and it is inherently asymmetric, as the hierarchical decision went for the overall denotation going with *kill*, not *Bill*, making *Bill* a proper part of the resulting phrase, but not *kill* (because the phrase is the projection of *kill*, and *kill* cannot be a proper part of itself). It seems most plausible that there is no such thing as this new object in the lexicon, and that—as a hierarchical object entailing an asymmetry and a compositional decision—it does not exist where the syntactic machinery does not exist that erects it, hence not in the semantic component, as anticipated in Chapter 1. That X is an XP means that upon merging with H, X has become a constituent that is now a new particulate unit. It is not only after Merge has applied that *kill* and *Bill* are constituents, but this is as a consequence of a compositional decision that is forced as a new object different from both *kill* and *Bill* is formed.

It follows that the interface systems either cannot see phrases, lacking the needed machinery, or they can, in which case they must have the machinery. In either case, the (so-called) C-I-systems do not explain the machinery in question, and syntax cannot be motivated from (semantic) interface conditions in the way this claim is usually understood. This is as it should be, if syntax creates something new, as it does: it creates phrases with a compositional analysis.

Once phrases are formed they combine with other phrases, again without blending. If these are separately assembled in another derivation, the Merger in question is a 'generalized transformation'. If they are items taken from the lexicon, we speak of 'external Merge'. If they come from within the phrase marker already generated, we speak of 'internal Merge'. With standard approaches (Chomsky 2004, 2005a, 2005b), I will assume that external Merge necessarily precedes all transformations, and generates phrase-structural hierarchies that cannot be erased by any later transformational operation (a conservation principle that usually goes under the name of 'no tampering'). I return to this, with qualifications, in Chapter 3.

The first result of iterated external Merge is a D-structure-like object that includes structures organized around thematic relations, such as complex

[3] And in conflict with a certain understanding of the 'autonomy of syntax' defended, for example, by Jackendoff (2002).

verbal phrases where all heads have satisfied their thematic requirements, in contradistinction to unaccusatives or passives. Discourse properties of expressions play no role in these structures. Assuming the structure of the verbal phrase is that of a VP introduced by a light verb *v*, hence [*v*-VP], a full verbal argument-structure is conventionally denoted by *v**. To what extent functional projections above *v** belong to the argument-structure system or are an extension or generalization of it is unclear. It is unclear to start with whether there are functional projections at all, hence phrase structure for argument structure as just described for (paradigmatically) nouns and verbs generalizes to the projection of heads such as Agr, T, or C. Chametzky (2003: 214–16) presents an argument for the conclusion that there aren't any functional projections at all, from the premise that the two main proposals for what they are do not work: the first being that a functional head *selects* its complement much as a lexical head does, the second being Grimshaw's (1990) proposal, which is based on a rather plausible rejection of the first, on the grounds that the relationship between a functional category and its complement is very dissimilar from that between an open-class head and its complement (in particular, there is less or no variation with respect to what complements the functional head can take). Grimshaw appeals to the notion of *extended* (lexical) projection instead, as opposed to extending the basic X′-theoretic scheme to the functional layers of the clause. But as Chametzky points out, Grimshaw's proposal is both technically flawed and conceptually inconsistent with the very idea of phrase structure.[4]

D-structure-like objects are the paradigmatic structures where the syntax–semantics is transparently compositional: syntactic constituents are also semantic ones, on the basis of which a complex meaning is built up. This transparency in the syntax–semantics mapping crucially extends to the word-level. This extension of the principle is flatly *violated* in statements such as the following, which implies that word meanings are *structured*:

> In the minimal case, a word is an arbitrary association of a chunk of phonology and a chunk of conceptual structure, stored in speakers' long-term memory (the lexicon). (Pinker and Jackendoff 2005: 212)

In fact, as Fodor and Lepore note, such a mismatch between syntactic and semantic atomicity is widely assumed:

[4] A third proposal on the nature of functional projections, due to Lebeaux (1988), makes the assumption that the functional layers of the clause correspond to a later stage of cognitive maturation in the child's development, with the full clause being a combination of two separate kinds of representations. That proposal may be inconsistent with the projectionless and phrase structure-free framework of standard minimalist syntax, as Chametzky points out.

The idea that quotidian, middle-level concepts typically have internal structure... plays a central role in practically every current approach to cognition. (Fodor and Lepore 1999: 445)

The idea in question is that the apparent structural simplicity of words (and morphemes) misleads us: at a *semantic* level of representation, they are structurally complex too, their overt phonetic forms being added late in the derivation, which begins from semantic primitives (atoms of thought) that are not words or morphemes. When talking about structural complexity in meaning, we might think that phrase-structural complexity is intended (argument-structure or a D-structure-like component in the grammar), but this is no logical necessity: in principle, the conceptual structure of 'thought' that gets encoded into words as opposed to syntactic complexes may be entirely independent of language. What matters is that even in that case the system of human concepts would likely still be a particulate system: the atomic particulate units, though, would not correspond one-to-one or even closely to the meanings of specific words (as assumed by Jackendoff 2002, for example). However, evidence against even such a form of 'lexical decomposition' is significant, and was the major historical reason for the downfall of generative semantics in the early 1970s, which had insisted on studying 'thought' directly, ignoring clues from language as to their structure, such as which meanings are encoded into specific words, and which are not.

Effectively, the grammar model assumed by generative semantics is this:

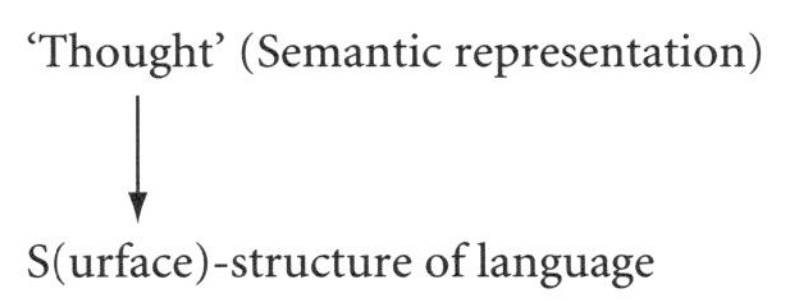

That is, language is mapped from a putative world of 'thoughts' directly. Thought itself is unmediated by language, and a fully structured input for the latter, which is not subject to linguistic constraints. A D-structure level, which was a component of the grammar, is trivialized, as is syntax at large. The negative evidence in question revolves around the fact that whatever structure there is posited internal to lexical concepts does not at all behave like standard syntax does, hence cannot account for it: as is illustrated below, the putative structure internal to lexical concepts is opaque (rather than transparent) to syntax, which does not 'see' (is not sensitive to) it; and the relevant structure-building processes are not productive and systematic in the way that syntactic processes are. This can lead to two theoretical consequences: (i) the recommendation to rather study language in its own right, rather than seeing it as a direct expression of 'thought', and to read off semantic interpretation strictly from the structures that the syntax provides; or (ii) to assume an independent generative system of thought, from which the computational system of language will be radically separated, so that a radical duality of syntax and semantics ensues. The latter view, which is in radical conflict with the one of this book, was effectively the one to remain among those like Jackendoff (2002) who pursued generative semantics further, even if not under its original name.

To review one of the most famous cases supporting Transparency in lexical semantics, consider the decomposition of the meaning of the verb *kill* into the 'conceptual structure' in (6) or even (7):

(6) CAUSE TO DIE
(7) CAUSE TO BECOME DEAD

These decompositions of the relevant lexical item of course look very much like standard syntagmatic phrases or *v*Ps, and seem relevantly isomorphic to them (in particular, it seems the way to bracket these complex structures would have to be the same as in the case of the linguistic expressions *cause to die* and *cause to become dead*). This makes us suspect immediately that the meaning of the putative conceptual structure in question will in fact more or less directly correspond to the meaning of those *phrases*, and not of the word it is alleged to analyse. Transparency predicts that (6) and (7) are compositionally interpreted, and their syntactic constituents map into semantic ones. This should be impossible for *kill*, which lacks such syntactic constituents as much as the number *6* lacks a constituent *3*. In turn, if (6)–(7) *did* behave like the English word *kill* rather than the phrases in question, it would be unclear what work the decomposition is doing in the first place, and what the semantic significance of its constituent structure really is. Capitalizing its constituents (which are not supposed to be words, hence somewhat strangely do not have the meanings of the words we use to depict them), in particular, will not tell us what they mean.

The above suspicion is born out. As is well known, whereas Bill could at noon *cause Hill to die* at midnight (say by tampering with his telephone at noon and having someone give him a ring at midnight, causing an explosion), we could not felicitously comment on this by saying Bill *killed Hill* at noon. And whereas, if Bill *caused Hill to die* by pulling the trigger of his pistol, *his* could back-refer to either Bill or Hill, it is the case that, if Bill *killed* Hill by pulling the trigger of his pistol, the latter possibility is of necessity excluded as a permissible interpretation of the expression in question. This is evidence that a word like *kill* is not only syntactically but also semantically *simple*—it is an atom—contrary to a phrase like *cause to die*, which *does* exhibit syntactic and semantic structure. The same fact shows up in derivationally complex words that unlike *kill* wear their derivational complexity on their sleeves: *privat-ize*, for example, which again behaves differently from *cause to become private*. If the derivational process that gives rise to complex word units of this sort was like that of standard syntax—the internal structure of a complex word would be like that of a phrase—we would not expect, in particular, that such items have to be learned one by one, like lexical items. But they have to: although attaching the causative morpheme *-ize* is a modestly productive process, it is *unsystematic* in a way syntax is not. We can *rational-ize* a proposal, but not *brilliant-ize* it, *endanger* a species but not *un-danger* it, although we can *un-lock* a bike. This is not what we find in standard phrasal syntax; nor do we find that deriving a word leads to a meaning that is unstable with respect to that of the stem we start from: *revolving* is rather different from *revol-ution*, both semantically (we have to learn what the latter means, and cannot predict it from its morphemes) and because of the change of semantic category, which we do not find in syntax-driven inflectional morphology.

None of this is to deny in any way that there is a *necessary* relation between killing and causing death, but only to deny that this relation is a *structural*, *conceptual*, or *semantic* one. The necessity is *not* a structural one, and it does not follow from the content of the concept involved. Nor should any atomist want to deny that we cannot *elucidate* the meaning of a concept by associating it with a large range of other concepts with which it has vital statistical or cognitive connections.

I will assume, then, in what follows that the above architectural principle, the *Transparency of the syntax–semantics mapping*, is substantially correct and a fundamental insight into the structure of language: semantic interpretation takes its cues from syntactic form. Applied to atomic or derived words, Transparency means that word boundaries *matter* for semantic interpretation. Something that does not *seem* to have constituents, like *kill*, does not have them covertly, or at some 'semantic level of representation', either. In fact, the decompositional view leaves us puzzled why a 'word-component' (derivational morphology, viewed as a structural system independent of syntax) should exist in the first place. It seems a plausible explanation of its existence that it has significance at the semantic interface: as I will subsequently argue in this book, words *name* concepts in an irreducible and rigid fashion and no other syntactic object does so.

Beyond the lexical level, transparency in particular means that interpretation is strictly local: the interpretation of a higher projection is computed from that of its syntactic sister (complement). Overall, the principle has been empirically very fruitful, and is the strongest hypothesis.[5] It also makes formidably good sense from the viewpoint of acquisition, for there are good reasons to believe that the meanings of verbs and sentences cannot be bootstrapped from the phonetic form of speech and contextual parameters alone (see Gleitman *et al.* 2005 for a review of the problems). The child's problem of mapping complex meanings from complex expressions analysed phonetically is magnificent; adding a syntactic dimension to the analysis of the expressions in question strongly helps, and is perhaps necessary to get the task done, as Gleitman's line of research suggests. However, that dimension could only really help if something like the transparency of the syntax–semantics mapping is in fact assumed. Assuming an *arbitrary* relation between syntax and semantics, as in the philosophical tradition, seems hopeless from the point of view of the acquisition task.

2.2 The essence of an 'atom'

We will return to conceptual (D-) structures in Chapter 3, and to intentional structures with a significance for discourse (as opposed to thematic) interpretation in Chapters 4 and 5. For now, having described language as a particulate system that bottoms out with atomic concepts that make up the meanings of words, we have to ask, as a part of our general internalist exploration: What makes these atoms mean what they do? In particular, we have to raise the question of whether we can analyse concepts in terms of anything other than themselves. That is, is there another layer of description in the study of reality that would account for them? The answer to that question depends on what actually is the 'essence' of a concept. By this I simply mean that, as in the case of any other object, there presumably are aspects or properties of a concept that it could miss while remaining the concept it is—these would be *non*-essential properties. And then, there should be properties that it could not miss, while remaining the concept it is. It seems that any theorizing about objects in nature will depend on an essentialism of this modest sort: it depends on determining the nature of things, or having a criterion of identity, which in turn is a matter of separating out essential from non-essential properties.

So, what is the essence of an atom? Clearly, the *content* of any concept C is essential to it, whatever notion of content or meaning one has (e.g. a referential

[5] For recent defences of transparency, see Larson and Segal (1995), Borer (2005), Uriagereka (2005), Fodor and Lepore (2002), Roeper (2003).

or a use-theoretical one): concepts are *semantically individuated.* This is simply to say that without meaning *house,* the concept of a house, whatever it is, would not be the concept it is. I take it as undeniable that, again, whatever one's notion of meaning, one will concede that our concept of a house means *house* and not *horse,* say, *chair,* or *piccadilly.* However, if we say that what makes the concept HOUSE the concept it is, is that it means *house,* we are not talking informatively, or non-circularly, since the concept itself is made use of in specifying what is essential to it. Thus the question arises:

THE CIRCULARITY QUESTION:
Can we specify any atomic concept C in *other* than *circular* terms?

In particular, are there other properties essential to it than its content, as circularly specified? This question will occupy us for the rest of this chapter, and I will give a negative answer to it. This negative answer surprises many, I have found, but seems to me actually quite expected: if the explanation of the meaning of a *complex* concept involves an appeal to the meaning of its (ultimately) atomic parts and their structural relations, then for these very parts *another* kind of explanation must be found than for their complex hosts, an explanation *not* appealing to their parts and their structural relations, and necessarily *consistent* with their compositional behaviour when entering complex expressions. But it is thoroughly unclear—and certainly unknown—what that explanation is. I will argue we do not know how it might remotely look, showing a fundamental impasse in current human inquiry into the nature of mind. Suppose also that I am right that the structure of a complex concept (as expressed by a syntactically complex linguistic expression with a compositional semantics) is intrinsic or essential to it. Then the *lack* of such a structure of an *atomic* concept should be equally essential to *it,* too. Hence if conceptual atoms are analysable in terms of anything other than themselves, that must belong to their *relational* rather than their intrinsic aspects. And it is precisely here where the externalist intuitions that have structured the analytic philosophical discourse in the twentieth century come in. But we can also predict why they will not succeed: for arguably, it is the conceptual essence of the very notion of an 'atom' that a *relational* specification of it should not be possible.

So let me return now to the most paradigmatic attempt to explicate the content of a conceptual atom relationally: on this attempt, the meaning of a word or concept is specified by appeal to a mind-external object out there in the world that we use the word or concept in question to refer to: a *referent.* The relation supposedly connecting the word and the referent is called *reference*. It is reference that explicates meaning, and on many views exhausts it. Its formal analysis is the relation between an individual constant and an individual in the model of the semantics of a first-order regimentation of natural language.

The paradigmatic form of reference in the sense of the Fregean/Russellian tradition is *naming*: the meaning of *John*, a name, is John, an object in the world, and ideally, there is no more to its meaning than that. Most analytic philosophers appear to believe that reference is at least one tier on which meaning rests, and contemporary semantic theory as such is based on it. It is thus a remarkable point of disagreement indeed that we find Chomsky stating that

> there is no *reference*-like relation for human language, hence no semantics in the technical sense of Frege, Peirce, Tarski, Carnap, Quine, and others, or contemporary 'externalists'. (Chomsky 2006: 5)

I aim to explicate this statement in this chapter, adopting my own understanding of it, which may slightly differ from Chomsky's. I will then link this discussion to the paradigm of 'naturalizing meaning', which I argue is fundamentally opposed to what its name suggests, quite apart from its lack of empirical results. Proper naturalization, I will conclude, abandons an externalist line of explanation which is a behaviourist heritage, and assumes the irreducible existence of concepts, with metaphysical consequences.

Formal semantics formalizes the referentialist intuition in a paradigmatic way by positing (i) an ontology of *individuals* that act as the external referents of singular terms, (ii) a domain of *symbols*, and (iii) a relation of reference (technically, an interpretation function) that connects individual constants and variables with external individuals and properties (or sets of individuals). Note that the domain (ii) is standardly thought to be specified in non-semantic terms—this is 'syntax' in the formal-language sense, hence does not involve intentionality intrinsically. The domain (i) is also a non-semantic one: if a physical ontology is adopted, all the individuals in the model's domain will simply be physical objects. All the intentionality or semanticity that there is, therefore, lies in (iii), the reference or satisfaction relation. If the latter can be specified in non-intentional terms too (for example, causal ones), the project of 'naturalization of the intentional' or semantic is complete. For 'natural' in this project means 'physical', and physical is defined to exclude 'mental' ('intentional', 'semantic'). Crucially, this is different in Locke, where 'matter can think' (see Yolton 1983), and in much of the rest of eighteenth-century thinking on the matter, a point worth noticing. If the human mind is interpreted as a Turing machine implementing a formal semantics of this sort, moreover, the intentionality of thought will be naturalized in the same way—that is, again essentially without implicating the mental at all. A closely-related externalist intuition boosts up a causal notion of reference by a notion of *function*: meaning is then not analysed merely causally or by relations of co-variance between occurrences of symbols and occurrences of worldly entities, but by appeal to the way they function in a context. Often, that notion is understood in a biological adaptationist sense. In short, the origin of concepts and meaning are thought to lie in our dealings with and functional relations to the world, as physically and biologically analyzed.

Turning now to the claim quoted above, that the reference-relation does not exist, I begin by noting the claim's empirical nature. Obviously, defining a reference-relation in mathematical terms between individual constants in a formal language and posited entities in a 'model' is *not* to make an empirical claim. We cannot establish the existence of a reference-relation by stipulatively positing referents in a model. The referents in question have to be argued for on empirical grounds. This demand may sound somewhat bizarre: are we supposed to argue for the existence of London, say, the referent of *London*? Isn't it utterly ludicrous to ask for an argument for the existence of something that our very language use commits us to? I will argue that this entire notion of an ontological commitment, around which analytic philosophy of language and epistemology has been centring since Quine, is highly questionable: there are no ontological commitments from the way we talk to what the world is like. What we say can be true and false, but for that to be so the world does not have to consist of independently identifiable entities that exactly correspond to whatever cognitive categories we as a species use to make sense of the real. We may be conceptualizing things as objects, relations, substances, and events, but from a physical point of view, everything out there may as well be a wave.

An analogy with phonology that Chomsky (2000) often suggests may help. Understanding the phonological patterns of a language involves no commitment on there being external objects corresponding to phonemes and their internal features. Although the construction of PHONS in the language faculty has acoustic repercussions of a causal nature in production (although not necessarily), they are not themselves external objects. Nor does a PHON *represent* any such external entity, like a collection of air molecules, or can it be explained from them. So even though an internal representation can be functionally and causally effective with respect to physical events in the external world, this does not mean it represents or refers to the various external events with which it stands in causal relations. A PHON refers to nothing at all. Why couldn't the same be true of SEMS, or more true even, given that, since PHON is about sound, its causal relations to physical entities in the external world are so much clearer? In that case, even though humans engage with acts of reference to cities, cats, mountains, desires, or hopes, and these acts of reference are adaptive and carry a communicable content, there would be no external objects that explain how this can happen.

To see whether this is not only possible but true, consider how we refer to London. Suppose we find that *London is polluted, London is enjoyable, London is grey, London is corrupt, No city is noisier than London, London is a big city.* Here we are thinking six thoughts that in one clear sense are all *about* the same single object, London, and each predicate identifies a certain property of it. Yet, in each of these examples, we are referring, in an equally clear sense, to quite different things, viewing the same object under radically different perspectives: in the first we view London under the aspect of its air quality, a perspective that we ignore in the second (supposing the enjoyment lies elsewhere). In the third we refer to London's visual aspects, which are irrelevant in the fourth, where we focus on, say, business or governmental practices; in the fifth we are contemplating its acoustic aspects; in the sixth, population size. So, descriptively, in one sense the reference-relation remains entirely stable; in another it shifts as our perspectives and predications do. The relevant question now, once again, is this: Can we specify *what* remains stable—hence what alone can qualify as being *essential* to whatever meaning our concept of *London* has in the first place—without *appealing* to that meaning? Or, to formulate it differently: *Is there anything other than our concept of London that stabilizes and de-contextualizes our reference to London?*

For the externalist the answer is yes, and that thing is London itself. Yet he must hold that this cannot possibly be so. For what is meant to stabilize the very meaning of our concepts is what external referent they refer to, but whatever external object we take, none has properties that will make it serve our explanatory purposes. Naively, for example, we might have thought that the object in question, London, is a *place*, and that it is that place which is the stable referent of all of our acts of using the word *London* and fixes its meaning. So, if we are referring to a different place, it is definitely not London. But this is not true. As Chomsky (2000: 37) points out, a city is crucially not a place, as his following striking example reveals:

(8) London is so unhappy, ugly, and polluted that it should be destroyed and rebuilt 100 miles away.

On the recommendation of (8), a decision might be made to totally destroy London and rebuild *it*—the same city—on which we might then comment by saying:

(9) London has remained the same, although it is now located elsewhere.

Others would refuse to agree and insist that with the move in question, London is gone forever. But this very disagreement shows that the facts 'out there' leave our judgement in such cases *open*. And in this very sense, they do not determine our judgements, which are determined by something else. From a *physical* point of view, the city of London rebuilt elsewhere is not the same. For us, it may be. We judge according to our *concepts*, not 'the facts'. These judgements moreover are *individual* ones. Others who disagreed with the judgement in (9) could not claim its proponents are 'incoherent' or have made a conceptual mistake. They may disagree, but there is no conceptual incoherence in the view they oppose.

In short, our concepts *allow* cities to move places, and in this precise sense London is not a place, even though perhaps it is *at* a place, at least for now (we might fancy a situation of technological advance where London is not even *at* a place any more but is a 'virtual city', with no physical existence or location at all, again without conceptual contradiction). No matter whether London is at a place or at no place at all, it would be something inherently *abstract*: for no concrete object can be in two places which are 100 miles apart. Being the concept it is, LONDON allows us to take the perspectives mentioned above on regions of the physical world: depending on the perspectives taken, London will involve the air in and above it (although only up to a certain height); its colours and visual aspects; its smell and noise; its size, history and future; its morality or all of these perspectives at the same time, as (8) shows: there it is the same object—London—which has all of these properties. Chomsky's claim is that no mind-external physical object—and surely not simply a place—can possibly qualify as being this object of reference. Not only is its place not essential to London; none of its other aspects are, or are believed to be. If London were washed away by a tsunami and only an odd number of houses was left standing, it—London—would not even be a *city* any more, but, as we might then think, a village, or an island. If you fall deaf, or all traffic goes underground, we will not conceive London as noisy any more. Repainting its inner city completely will not make it necessarily a different city, in our judgement. If the ozone layer becomes too thin and a layer of dust and ashes covers most of London's surfaces and interiors, the city would be 'gone' to many. The layer of dust might thicken and the city become a solid, amorphous block, called the 'London hill'. Yet, with the recovery of the ozone layer, life might slowly come back after many centuries or even millennia, with London rising to *its* old beauty, as people then commenting might find.

The conclusion here should be that London, while having myriad physical and non-physical aspects, has *none* of them essentially: it remains stable and self-identical across changes in apparently *any* of the properties that we might predicate of it. Any of these predications is synthetic, none analytic. There simply is no external object that we could point to and claim: *this* object is London, and it is the referent of the word *London* no matter what predication it is a part of, and it determines its meaning and how we use it to refer. No such object qualifies as what gives our word *London* the referential powers it manifests in language use, which creates a world of referents more than it passively mirrors one. The attempt to spell out non-circularly—without reference to the very concept expressed by a word—what the word in question refers to, fails. The only thing that remains stable in perspectivally different acts of reference to the 'same thing' *is* the concept we have of that thing, and that concept, alone. It is the concept that stabilizes human reference, not reference (as non-intentionally specified) that stabilizes human concepts. (How it is even *conceivable* that concepts, which we see to behave in these ways, should be 'learnable' from causal encounters with physical objects or inductive generalizations from them alone, remains rather obscure.)

The case of cities reiterates in analogous ways with our concepts of houses, persons, substances, or artefacts. It is not the external physical world that determines when two persons are the same person, for example. Kripke (1980) argues that Gödel remains Gödel instead of becoming another person, if we discover that he did not discover the famous Incompleteness Theorems of 1931, which we identify with him. Just that is explained by the nature of our concept of a person: that concept is such that we consider mathematical genius not an essential feature of a personality, and that we can be *mistaken* in ascribing genius to a particular person. Deprived of our concept of a person, by contrast, and left with causal relations to the world, we might as well judge that after such a discovery there wasn't anything like Gödel any more. For the same reason, we might judge that he becomes a different person by combing his hair differently, or that the sorcerer I referred to in Chapter 1 becomes someone else by looking like a mouse. But these are not the judgements we make. We think these judgements are false. So the truth here does not track 'the facts', or an independent world. It tracks our concepts.

Topology is the science of how to fold, bend, and project, in short 'warp', a single object in dimensionally different spaces without ever tearing it apart. In the same way, a concept we have of a thing allows that thing to undergo the most various physical and geometrical transformations, while remaining the same thing all the way through. A person can be flattened physically to a two-dimensional surface (when pressed on both sides, as in a Tom & Jerry movie), and restore its three-dimensional body only upon recovery; it can become a mass of meat rather than an individual entity, losing much of its boundaries, as in some paintings of Francis Bacon. It is a fascinating (and empirical) question precisely which transformations concepts *dis*allow: perhaps a sorcerer's disappearance into thin air would terminate his fate; or a person's losing her ability to feel emotion might, in which case it might be rated a machine. These limits to the transformations that our concepts allow are subject to empirical inquiry, and have been so for millennia in philosophical reflection, but the externalist drive of the Kripkean argument has things backward. The stability ('rigidity') of the object of reference across possible worlds that he points to finds explanation, not in this object, but in the concept that our predications involving it include (see further Chapter 5).

The situation is not essentially different with substances or putative 'natural kinds' such as water or gold. Putnam (1975) famously concludes that the content of concepts expressed by such words as *water* is fixed by what substance the world factually contains. What kinds ordinary nouns denote is a question of what kinds there are in nature. But kinds are not like physical objects, to start with: the kind *gold* is nothing like a piece of gold, nor presumably the mereological union of all the pieces of gold that exist. So what sort of thing is this kind? It is, presumably, something abstract (a universal, in traditional terms), but would we posit its existence if we did not have the option to intentionally refer to kinds by means of general terms? And is there anything apart from the facts determining which concepts are the same concept that could determine when two posited external 'properties' are the 'same' properties?

As we shall see in Chapter 5, nouns take kind-denotations only in particular syntactic contexts, in fact. It is not obvious at all that there *needs* to be a device in human intentionality or language for referring to kinds. The existence of such a device may just be evolutionarily contingent. What we have got is such a device, and hence we can use certain nouns in certain of their uses to denote kinds rigidly across possible worlds (although we do not have to do so, as I point out below). We can then also think of some of these objects of reference as objects of the world—or 'project' them onto the world—namely those that we hope have some underlying constitution that can be the object of a scientific theory. Generally, though, science will give our ordinary concepts technical meanings, in which we do not recognize our ordinary intuitions. Science does not vindicate the conceptual intuitions of common sense, but largely ignores them. It employs whatever concepts and explanatory schemes make sense of the phenomena, and is uncommitted to finding underlying kinds in nouns that we use. We should not wait for a natural kind in the case of *sadness* or *jogging* any more than in the case of *water*: even whether the ordinary word *water* depicts a natural kind is entirely unclear: in scientific terms, there is 'light' and 'heavy' water, in particular, and only one of them is H_2O, which shows that being H_2O is not after all necessarily part of the essence of what we use the term water to refer to.

According to the predominant Putnamian view, that water happens to be H_2O is *not* an accidental feature of water that it could lose. Nothing that was not of this composition could *be* water. And yet, people do not necessarily follow this recommendation. So, suppose we were all beamed to Twin Earth yesterday unknowingly, and that this was where you, the reader, and I are now.[6] Look around yourself, everything seems normal to you. Take a sip of water—all normal. All, that is, until you check on the molecular structure of water, get stunned, do some inquiries, and slowly find out the truth of all that happened yesterday. Shocked, you state:

(10) Water on Twin Earth isn't H_2O!

No doubt this is all conceivable; nor would there be a sense of conceptual contradiction or a misuse of the word 'water' if a newspaper were to print the same sentence as a headline the next day. Hence there is no constraint to use the word 'water' to stand for H_2O. Nothing else we expect: for 'water' and 'H_2O' are, quite simply, different words; hence by the general principle of synonymy avoidance that appears to be operative in the human lexicon, they should have different meanings.[7] This is what we empirically find. There is no more conceptual incoherence here than in the case of a person that is reincarnated and remains the same person, in our judgement, or a city that changes its place, remaining the same city. Two substances, relevantly enough, may be 'similar' in a way that we let them bear the same name. When travelling frequently between Earth and Twin Earth we might come to call Twin-water something else, to avoid confusion. But, and this is important, we might also not. Just as I am me even with a different face or body,[8] our concept of water happens to be such that it allows our object of reference to differ in chemical constitution if it is otherwise the same. Its chemistry is a

[6] Twin Earth is a fictional planet introduced by Putnam on which there is a substance looking, feeling, tasting, etc. like water on Earth, the only difference being that it is chemically XYZ rather than H_2O.

[7] In this particular case, we should note that 'H_2O' is not even a term listed in a human lexicon: there is in this sense not even an issue of potential synonymy here.

[8] As I write this (summer 2006), news reaches me that the first person ever was given the face of a different person declared brain dead.

feature of it that is in fact completely irrelevant for many of the uses of *water*, given our conceptualization of the kind in question. As Chomsky (2000: 149) notes, tea has essentially the same molecular chemical constitution as what comes out of most normal taps; yet, what comes out of the tap is water for us, and decidedly not tea. This reveals one way in which our concept of water delimits its uses: water is decidedly *not* tea, we judge, even if looking the same (when the water is polluted, say), but it *can* be XYZ.

What the Twin Earth thought experiment tells us is that concepts in terms of which we think may come to refer to different entities out there, as historical circumstances change. Just that would have happened to us, had we indeed been beamed to Twin Earth yesterday (something that, if it had happened, we might have never found out). Linguistic reference is not necessarily sensitive to changes in the referents we happen to pick out by the words we use. We cannot take such accidents as whether we have been beamed away or not into account when laying down the semantics of a language. So, as *we* use the word *water* now, its actual referents could be *various* substances, in the chemical sense of this term: this is a matter of how the linguistic system happens to be embedded in a context. The system itself cannot determine that embedding, or what it is actually applied to, an aspect that is radically external to it. Externalism is right, then, in that the actual referent we pick out by a word is not determined by 'what's in the head'. But that insight is no deeper than the insight in biology that how an organism is embedded in an environment and survives in it depends on that environment. The internal organization of the organism does not decide what natural selection will select or not. Nor can our concepts determine what they will be factually applied to, even though they will be delimiting their uses. We cannot use the concept of a person to talk about a stone, for example (unless we personify the stone, a change of perspective).

It does not look like a promising idea, then, that *non-circularly specified* referential relations could possibly be rated *essential* to a concept as used in acts of intentional reference. How would one decide the question of whether one was referring to the same person, Jack, once he had lost an arm, *if not* by consulting the concept we have of Jack, which will mark him out as a person as opposed to a physical object? I submit that nothing else will tell. So our concepts are the measure of reality, and not the other way around. The way our referential perspectives are configured is not a matter of non-intentional relations to the world, be they biological-functional or causal, but of the internal organization of our minds and our species-specific modes of thought. An explanatory theory of human reference has to start *from* our concepts, not from the world, as anticipated in Chapter 1. The project of 'naturalizing semantics' as virtually universally conceived fails; it omits the prime causal factor involved. Naturalization should be sought by developing actual *theories* of the forms of thought, and why they are the ones they are, making no ontological assumptions on the kind of entities that the universe contains, and hence allowing for concepts as primitives.

Let me now contextualize the naturalization of meaning as here conceived with regard to some different and prominent attempts to accomplish such a naturalization. Dennett (1995: ch. 14) argues that if the meaning of natural kind terms such as *horse* or *water* is taken to be their reference, an appropriately 'naturalistic' or 'Darwinian' point of view would show the referents of these terms to be radically *indeterminate.* But there is a tension between the externalist stance of fixing meaning from without, on the one hand, and the intuition of the determinacy of meaning, on the other. The examples above make this clear: if the meaning of *water* depends on what external object it refers to, it means H_2O in one circumstance, XYZ in another, and who knows what it might mean in a third, or fourth. Precisely this indeterminacy, however, Dennett continues, is to be expected and appropriate when taking a 'Darwinian' stance. Thus consider the question of what the frog's eye tells the frog's brain when it sees (as we would put it) a fly. We know that the frog snaps out its tongue in exactly the same way when flies are removed from its environment and small digestable and similar-looking black pellets are placed there instead by a nasty-minded experimenter. More generally, flies are necessarily co-instantiated with a large number of other properties in the frog's environment, such as the property of being a small black moving item looking like food. Hence, what property *exactly* does the frog's mind represent prior to its snapping? What 'content' does its 'mental' state have, what 'truth-conditions' does it determine? It seems there is no determinate answer: if we take *our* conceptual scheme and the distinctions we make therein as basic, it seems quite radically indeterminate what the frog's brain is referring to. But it is simply a radically mistaken philosophical presumption, Dennett argues, that makes us *expect* a determinacy where Darwinian biology does not grant any. As he puts it succcintly:

> the idea that there must be *something determinate* that the frog's eye really means—some possibly unknowable proposition in froggish that expresses *exactly* what the frog's eye is telling the frog's brain—is just essentialism applied to meaning (or function). (Dennett 1995: 408)

In short, if reference, in a biological-functionalist sense, is all there is to meaning, the representational content of a mental state will precisely and only track that function, or co-vary arbitrarily with it. It will, in particular, not *constrain* the function, which I argued human concepts do. Dennett argues we mistakenly *presume* the human case to be different, and in the conflict between the determinacy of reference and 'Darwinism', we should sacrifice determinacy.

To support his case, he asks us to imagine that there are animals on Twin Earth looking exactly like horses and also called *horses*, while not being horses by some scientific criterion. Call them *schmorses*. One morning you are beamed from Earth to Twin Earth without realizing it. The first thing you see is a schmorse, by that criterion, and the first thing you say is 'Lo, a horse!'. A Twin Earth native who speaks Twin-English and overhears this utterance utters the same sounds. In this situation, the externalist insists: what the Twin Earthling says and thinks is *true*, as he has expressed and thought the proposition that a schmorse just ran by. But *you* said something *false*, for the proposition you expressed by your utterance is that a *horse* ran by, this being what your *English* (as opposed to Twin-English) word 'horse' refers to. Let us get this intuition clear: by being a speaker of English, the idea is, your words carry certain denotations around with them, even as you utter them on different planets, where the phonetically same words are used with a different denotation attached to them. Using the word *water* you'll be talking about a specific chemical constitution as hypothesized on Earth, and using the word *horse* about a particular entity as biological taxonomists on Earth view it. It is under that supposition (alone) that what you will be saying on Twin-Earth will be false, although you think it is true. Dennett comments:

> How long, though, would you have to live on Twin Earth, calling schmorses 'horses' (just like all the natives), before the state of your *mind* (or what the eye tells your brain) is a *truth about schmorses* rather than a falsehood about horses? (When does the aboutness or intentionality leap to the new position (...))? (Dennett 1995: 409)

The implied answer to this rhetorical question is that there is no fact of the matter: there is no more determinacy to be had here any more than in the case of the frog. As long as *horse* is *used* to denote both horses and schmorses, it can *mean* both. Depending on what environment we place you in, the meaning of your words shifts, and it can mean *as many* things as it can take up functional roles, which is *indefinitely* many (schmorses, lorses, whorses, Trojan ones, reincarnations, etc.). If there is really *nothing* in our concept of a horse itself to internally constrain the function of the word *horse*, there is nothing to prevent that word from meaning just about *anything*. So if it came to be used to refer to horse skins, riders of horses, or landscapes behind horses, there would be nothing to prevent us from saying it does not refer to that. It follows that Dennett cannot possibly mean anything other by 'the word *horse*' than what is effectively a *phonetic label*. For it is of course true of phonetic labels (and of them only) that they can be attached to any concept whatever: there can be no objection to lexicalizing our concept of a landscape with the same phonetic label that now lexicalizes the concept of a horse.

But any word of any natural language is more than just a phonetic label: it is, at any moment of its history, connected to a particular concept. For any such concept, say the concept horse, it is just plain untrue that it could come to mean what any other concept means, say landscape. So, although the *label* can of course be used to refer to just anything, the implication of this observation for what the concept that is attached to the label means, is nil. There is, factually speaking, *no* way for HORSE to mean LANDSCAPE. We could sincerely try and construe our concept of a horse so as to make it usable for talking about a landscape. This is marginally possible, if, for example, we imagine looking at a horse's flank from very closely, and use its surface structure as a metaphor for a landscape consisting of fields, hills, bushes, etc. But it is perspicuous that even in such a metaphorical extension, the concept HORSE comes nowhere closer to meaning what LANDSCAPE does. To the extent that we succeed in our re-conceptualization, what we are talking about *is* a landscape, not a horse, and the two concepts in question are as distinct as ever, even though they can be used to refer to what is physically the same thing.

Does this response answer Dennett's question of what determinate referent the concept horse is supposed to refer to, horses or schmorses? It doesn't. Again, the determinacy and rigidity that characterizes human intentionality does not lie in the *referent*, but the *concept*. You and the Twin Earthling share a concept, and that concept determines a notion of 'same thing' relative to which you are both referring to the creature in question under a certain perspective, not necessarily a biological one. The concept, although it constrains its possible application, cannot of its nature fix what external object it ends up being used to refer to in the course of history. They may be horses, schmorses, or something else, although within the range of applications that the concept permits. But there are simply no consequences following from this indeterminacy of *reference* for the determinacy of the *concept* in question.

Might Dennett reply that what I am calling concepts here and putting in small caps simply do not exist? That all that exists is the phonetic labels and the functions they contingently acquire as we add appropriate contexts? No, because not anything can have any function. An organism's neurological machinery will take up certain referential functions only if it is suitable and equipped for that. A frog would not refer to horses. We *cannot* intentionally refer to a landscape as a landscape (or under that perspective), without having the concept of a landscape. Without it present, the external world will not as such have to provide it. Biological function in general is necessarily conditioned by the presence of the appropriate internal structures, and these structures do not swing into existence the moment it would be useful to have them. Dennett's entire meaning-theoretic story, which claims to 'naturalize' meaning, does not do that, as it constrains meaning by adaptation alone; but while it is constrained by adaptation, adaptation itself is a process operating *within a range of possibilities* that internal capacities delimit. The origin of these capacities remains unaddressed; as does the fact that linguistic expressions do not reduce to their phonetic forms and have functions which their physical aspects alone could not support. If meaning was nothing over and above, (i) the structure of the physical world, (ii) the structure of the organism, as biology, physiology and neurology describe it, and (iii) natural selection as an explanation for the organism's adaptive complexity, then the concepts we grasp could not be anything other than reflections of the structure of the external environment in which we survive. Any concept would need to have a physical or biological meaning, and be more or less directly linked to an adaptive significance. The claim seems radically false for virtually all human concepts that a normal child acquires by the age of five, where virtually *no* concept's content is determined by the physical or biological determinants of the referents it is used to refer to, and we witness a radical *disparity* between our modes of thought (concepts) and the physical structures in the environment to which we apply them.

The origin of concepts remains *radically* unclear today, to the extent even that constructive suggestions are missing. Somehow, the problem does not seem to be on the scientific agenda. In the brain sciences, we can and do label certain brain sites or even single neurons with certain concepts or semantic significances: but we seem unable to even contemplate what it would be for the electrical activity of the brain to give rise to these concepts, or to them as opposed to other possible concepts. This seems true no matter whether we are talking about sensory concepts or others; it is unclear even how colour concepts are to be derived from causal encounters in the world and neurological computation (see Mausfeld 2002, for discussion). With more abstract problems, the whole issue becomes just mind-boggling. Take, as Juan Uriagereka notes in personal communication, the fact that human concepts have an intrinsic *topology* to them. Thus, our concept of water is that of a mass: an object with a substance to it, unlike abstract terms like friendship or sadness, but still no boundaries to it that would make it countable. So, a mass is just an object that extends indefinitely in time and space, and there can be more or less of it, but there is not one or two. How would the cells of the brain give rise to such a concept? The question appears to be so far beyond the scope of current scientific inquiry that evocations of Neo-Darwinism seem essentially meaningless. In that sense, the enterprise of 'naturalizing meaning' in the standard sense appears off the mark, no matter whether built around the externalist notion of reference or a Neo-Darwinian notion of adaptation.

The opposing stance is to accept concepts as a primitive layer in nature that is as real as anything else and that can be and has been studied empirically and naturalistically in its intrinsic structural features. Concepts are internal structures in the mind of an organism that lend themselves to certain uses, but, as generally from a Darwinian point of view, these uses or functions are not the cause of why they exist. Like other organismic traits, concepts open up an environmental niche that the organism can then exploit; they are like keys that, if we are lucky, will fit certain locks, although these are not the reason for why the keys come to exist. Whatever the *degree* is to which our concepts *are* usable to talk about the external world, it has an explanation in the workings of natural selection, which selects structures for a use.

As noted earlier, the indeterminacy of reference does not translate into an indeterminacy of meaning (or concepts). In fact, there does not appear to be any indeterminacy or uncertainty in our knowledge of lexical concepts at all, and it is not clear what mental operation we should perform to check whether one of our concepts *was* indeterminate. We *know* the concepts of a horse, a house, a person, or truth, and perhaps there is little more to say than they mean HOUSE, PERSON, and TRUTH. Although, when learning a language, we can be in doubt whether we have attached a particular phonetic label to the same concept to which others attach it, it is dubious how a similar uncertainty can possibly arise over a concept *itself*. We *can* be uncertain about whether a substance we call 'water' is H_2O or XYZ, for example; but can we be uncertain about what water means, the concept itself, or the concept PERSON? Is it imaginable that we should have to *correct* ourselves about its meaning? The only way for this to happen, it seems, is to realize that we have ascribed a wrong property to the concept. But this very idea presupposes that concepts are objects to which our thoughts can be directed somehow, so that properties can be ascribed to them and withdrawn. But we think about and refer to *things* (John, London, justice, the Last Supper, etc.) and predicate properties of *them*, where these properties are expressed by concepts. Do we ever refer to concepts? It seems that we do not stand in any *epistemic distance* to concepts, as it were. We do not face them, or think about them; they *are* our thinking. If so, there is no such thing as being wrong about a concept that one grasps. We are right or wrong in *predications*, which are inherently structured, not in (atomic) concepts, which are not. Something that is connected in thought, like a subject and a predicate, can be wrongly connected. A concept as such is not connected at all.

Even the sense in which experience may correct us in making a judgement involving a predication is not very clear. Even a plainly empty space under your table need not cause you to concede that there is no rhinoceros there. If you insisted on more evidence, there is nothing an opponent could do. Nonetheless, a sense of corrigibility remains: it is exceedingly difficult, for example, to construe your visual experience as you look at these lines right now as a sunset. Experience refutes this construal no matter how much effort is taken to imagine a possible world where this paper is a sunset. But this is not quite because it is 'wrong' that the paper you are looking at is a sunset. Rather there is a very practical, indeed physiological, sense in which our mind *fails* in the assigned task of construing its experience in the insane way envisaged. We can do a lot with our experiences and construe them according to quite different concepts, but not everything. To certain experiences our concepts will not stretch. None of this has anything to do with concepts being right or wrong. It is simply a matter of what they prove applicable to and to what not.

Do concepts *change*? That, it seems, could only be if they had parts, which could change. From this point of view, atomic concepts *ipso facto* could not change. Frege's intuition of their immutability would be vindicated (on quite different grounds). There are ever new houses we see and persons we meet, and perhaps some day we will ascribe personhood to a dolphin. None of this shows our *concept* of a person changes in the course of this, as opposed to that same concept's proving applicable to ever new instances, hence not being exhausted by any finite number of them. The compositionality of concepts demands the context-independence of the meanings of the concepts that make up complex structures, too: they must mean what they do irrespective of what complex judgements they figure in, in order for compositionality to hold. *Person* cannot mean what it does because we can plug this word into an argument slot of, say, the expression *Flipper is a person.* On the contrary, *Flipper is a person* means what it does because it contains the constituent *is a person*, which in turn contains *person*, which context-independently means PERSON.

Countless treatises elaborate on what a person is, and obviously we might learn from those and apply our person concept to instances we would not have applied it to before. Yet such treatises may be interpreted as doing no more than making a suggestion as to what our notion of a person is or comprises. They tell us what we know, or what our concept entails. We will find them convincing only insofar as its insights are sufficiently in tune with the intuitions we find ourselves having over what a person is. Studies of certain human concepts are in this way conditioned by our possession of them, and they will never exhaust their content. There is no end to what we can find out about persons, and no end to the forms that houses can take. We cannot fathom any such thing as having enumerated 'all the possible houses'. The indefinite combinatorics of walls, floors, windows, doors, colours, cupboards, beds, ceilings, functions, etc.—which we may think of as the 'lexicon' from which houses are built—forbids this: an enumeration of all the houses would be like an enumeration of all the thoughts we can possibly think. None of this combinatorics implies anything against the simplicity, atomicity, and unity of the concept HOUSE itself.

This is the time to more briefly address the other major tradition that claims to analyse atomic concepts in terms of something other than themselves, that is relationally and non-circularly. This is the *inferentialist* tradition, which proposes that the content of a conceptual atom is its inferential relations to other concepts. But conceptual atoms are *ipso facto* not individuated by relations to other atoms that they co-occur with: that is why they are atoms. To be an atom is to be (syntactically and semantically) structureless. If inferential relations to other concepts *were* essential to one such atom, they *would* be part of its structure, hence we cannot be dealing with an atom; the other concepts would *figure* in that very atom, just as, if the concept kill *was* essentially related to the concepts CAUSE and DIE, the concept KILL would literally *be* the concept CAUSE TO DIE, and thus the concept CAUSE would *figure* in it as a constituent. Independently of this argument from atomicity, there is no known case where such relations literally *constitute* a concept. Consider the concept BELIEF. There is no known way to relate this concept to other concepts in a way that possessing these other concepts and some means of combination of them would account for possessing or acquiring belief. As Leslie (2000) explains in painstaking detail by analysing a number of available proposals, either the other concepts in whatever combination are *weaker* than the concept of belief (in the sense of not entailing it), or they are *at least as* strong. Either way, they do not account for it. The concept of a belief is not known to follow from anything other than itself.[9]

[9] The same conclusion can be reached by looking carefully at available proposals on how concepts like (natural) NUMBER are acquired by the child (see e.g. Carey 2004). One would expect that the child does so on the basis of strictly *weaker* concepts; but then the *transition* to NUMBER would be unexplained. Or the concepts that it starts from are *equally* strong, in which case the account is circular again. Carey claims to solve this problem via the notion of *bootstrapping*, but bootstrapping is

None of this, again, is to deny the intuition that there are numerous and even countless necessary relations between conceptual atoms and other concepts. But it simply does not follow, as for the inferentialist it must, that the connections in question are *semantic* or *conceptual* in nature. Evidence that there is such a conceptual connection, say between the concept of killing and that of (causing) death, would be that one could not conceivably think the one concept without thinking the other (just as, indeed, one cannot think the concept KILL BILL without thinking BILL). But that one cannot do this is extremely implausible.[10] Similarly, it is plausibly the case that despite the *mathematical necessity* that the number 2 is the only even prime, there is no *conceptual* necessity to that (a claim that, if true, makes mathematical truth synthetic rather than analytic). It is quite untrue, it seems, that, by having a

a process of mapping between *given* (semantically individuated) representations. It does not make the representational resources of the mind *strictly stronger* than they (implicitly, prior to the explicit mapping) were. It is not clear at this point how our concept of number, with the infinitary property it has, could follow from anything other than itself. That bootstrapping in Carey's sense is strictly circular (it presupposes possession of the concept in question, and at best makes a comment on its maturation) has recently also been pointed out by Rips *et al.* (2006). For further discussion, see Section 3.1.

[10] Consider this dialogue:

You : Hi there, didn't you just kill somebody?
A : Yes.
You : Isn't there something you *did* to accomplish this?
A : Yes.
You : How would you describe this?
A : I killed him.
You : Yes, but *how* did this happen?
A : Well, I decided to kill him, I strangulated him, and then he was gone.
You : What do you mean? Wasn't he, in the end, ...
A : ...*gone*?...*killed*?
You : Hm. Never mind. And when you yesterday *boiled the beans*, don't you think there was something in *common* between what you did today and what you did yesterday? You did *some*thing, ...X..., and then something got to be the case as a result of that.
A : Huh...? Well, yesterday I boiled the beans, and they became boil*ed*, and today I killed someone, and then he became kill*ed*.
You : Hm, hm. But look, suppose your victim today had fallen over a stone instead and got... *killed*, as you put it, without *your* having done anything to *accomplish* this. What would be *different* in this case?
A : I wouldn't have killed him.
You : Right, right.... But the stone clearly didn't *kill* him, it rather merely *did* something, X, so as to make him *be* in a lifeless state, Y. How would you call what he did?
A : Made him lifeless, perhaps?
You : Rats. And when you killed this poor fellow, what would you say is the relation between *you*, and *him*, that had the *consequence* of his being killed?
A : I am his *killer*, of course!

I think this conservation could continue for a very long time, without A ever hitting upon or using either the concepts CAUSE or DEATH, despite A's best efforts to trigger these concepts, if, for some (perhaps neurophysiological) reason, he simply *lacked* these concepts. This is evidence that one can lack the concepts CAUSE and DEATH, and yet have KILL, and shows that the former are neither constituents of the latter, nor essential to it in our required sense.

thought about 2, we thereby have thoughts about primes (a belief ascription involving the concept TWO, for example, could be felicitous in circumstances where a belief ascription involving PRIME clearly would not be) (see Fodor 2004, for discussion). While there arguably *are* analytic inferences where we have a *structured* expression—thus, arguably, it follows from the grammatical structure of the linguistic expression *brown cow* and not our beliefs about the world that a *brown cow* is *brown*—there are no analytic inferences where we have a *structureless* lexical atom. Except for the property of being a cow (or for London's property of being *London*, etc.), there is no known property that we think a cow has, the lack of a possession of which would lead us to judge that we are *not* dealing with a cow, or the possession of which would necessarily make it a cow.[11]

Inferentialism does not seem to succeed in a non-circular specification of an atomic concept even in the special case of a type of concept for which an inferentialist analysis is *prima facie* most suitable: the logical concept CONJUNCTION. For this concept there at least *are* known inferential rules that with some plausibility exhaustively capture its logical or Boolean content, which is all the content there is to it: the Gentzen introduction and elimination rules. But, as Fodor (2004: 45) points out, understanding these rules of inference (recognizing their validity) *depends* on a grasp of the meaning of '&', which occurs in the statement of the rules. It does *not* merely depend on an appreciation of the intricate physical shape of this symbol, say. It is the very grasp of the meaning of '&' that must explain why this inference and no other inference is drawn and judged valid (it should not be drawn merely by means of some sort of physical reflex, or a drug, in particular, if the relevant agent is to be rational and to be credited with a possession of the concept conjunction). In short, the Gentzen-rules may well specify what conjunction means, for someone who already *has* that concept. They explain what it *is* to have it, not how we do, or why.[12]

[11] Clearly, e.g., we need not agree that a creature whose *genome* was not like that of standard cows, would therefore not be a cow (in fact we could comment: 'That cow is a rather nonstandard one!', in which case we think of it as a cow, although a non-standard one). Equally clearly, having a normal cow genome would not *ipso facto* (i.e. necessarily) *make* something a *cow* for us (note I am not denying that it factually *could* lead us to infer that we are dealing with a cow).

[12] An inferentialist account of the content of a conceptual atom has affinities with the behaviourist view that the meaning of a word or utterance has an intrinsic connection with the behaviour that ensues from it in the hearer, or his dispositions to such behaviour. If rational as opposed to conditioned, this response will have to depend on an independently given understanding of the meaning of the utterance. Even distinguishing between types of speech acts in these action-related ways appears futile. As Chomsky (1959) noted against such proposals, one 'cannot distinguish between request, commands, advice, etc., on the basis of the behaviour or disposition of the particular listener': something is an advice or request even if not followed; a question does not become a command if a speaker answers it merely because he suspects punishment otherwise; ignoring a warning as opposed to heeding it may be positively reinforcing, and so on.

A final problem for an inferentialist view is that we know on formal-logical grounds, as Hadley (2004) points out against connectionist and neural network-based reductions of concepts, that *no* manipulations of representations in neuronal activation spaces can possibly implicitly define any specific semantic content: no finitely specifiable axiomatization of such symbol manipulation, for example through Peano's axioms of arithmetic, will determine the content of our ordinary number concept uniquely.[13] As Hadley argues, even today the moral may have to be the one that Fodor and Pylyshyn (1988) inaugurated: if meaning is compositional, and inferential roles are not, then inferential roles cannot be meanings. Compositionality entails that the meaning of BROWN COW is determined by that of BROWN, of COW, and the syntax of this representation. But the inferential role of BROWN COW in your thought might license an inference to DANGER, and that aspect of the meaning of BROWN COW is not necessarily derived from that of its constituents plus syntax, hence is not compositionally determined and is non-intrinsic to this complex representation (see Fodor and Lepore 2002: ch. 1).

My overall conclusion is that neither the referentialist nor the inferentialist tradition has much purchase on conceptual atoms. We seem to be stuck with them, as primitive entities in nature, with nothing to analyse them further, let alone to analyse them in non-semantic terms. Put differently, *only* its content is essential to an atomic concept. Ultimately, the only way to spell out what is essential to a concept like HOUSE is to say that it means *house*: this is the disquotational way, which goes no way towards explaining concepts, and doesn't even try, because it recognizes that there is no *non-circular way of spelling out a particular concept*, if it is an atom. Again, all this is quite expected: for such a way to exist, the atom would have to essentially relate to something other than itself. This *is* so for complex concepts, but it is *not* so for atomic concepts, whose very atomicity precludes it. The meaning of BROWN COW *can* be derived without appealing to that very concept and its content, and it can be reduced (although to other concepts, not the non-semantic); the meaning of BROWN cannot.

That a concept that is an atom has no relational specification also has the consequence that it is not *functionalizable*. Its being functionalizable would mean we could define it by appeal to a particular causal role that it intrinsically plays; but if the above is right, the *right* causal role, if there were one with which the concept could be identified, is not identifiable other than circularly,

[13] This is due to non-standard (non-isomorphic) models of axiomatized languages that will necessarily exist (at least for first-order languages), and in which such an axiomatization would still be true.

that is by reference to the concept. In an explanation of the form: 'A physical symbol S plays such and such a causal role iff it means...' would have to evoke a reference to the intended meaning on the right hand side. Functionalizable, indeed, is only what is *computable*; but computable is only what has structure; and atoms have no structure, by definition. Functionalism as an account of semantic content fails for *atoms*, even if nowhere else.[14]

2.3 Spencerism then and now

In discussing Dennett above I have been contrasting a Darwinian 'selective' view of concepts from an 'instructional' view according to which cognitive structure is a mirror of or moulded by environmental complexity. Historically, I associate the classical formulation of the latter view with Herbert Spencer, but as I shall point out in this section, its general intellectual mode remains as alive today as in his time. Dennett (1995), to be concrete, develops a 'naturalistic' view of meaning that he calls 'Darwinian', but it is not a selective one in my sense, and much closer to a Spencerian instructive one. Indeed, Dennett (1995: 393) calls Spencer 'an important clarifier of some of Darwin's best ideas'. 'Spencer was a Darwinian—or you could say that Charles Darwin was a Spencerian', we read, and also: 'the modern synthesis is Spencerian to its core'. As a self-confessed 'good Spencerian adaptationist', Dennett adopts Godfrey-Smith's 'Environmental Complexity Thesis' (ECT), according to which 'there is complexity in the organism in virtue of complexity in the environment' (1995: 395; see Godfrey-Smith 1996). Spencer presumably defended a strong version of this paradigmatically externalist claim, to the effect that environmental complexity is both necessary and sufficient for organic complexity. Godfrey-Smith opts for its mere necessity—a claim I will here also claim to be too strong—and proposes, more succinctly, to understand the ECT as a thesis about the *function* of cognition and its

[14] It is interesting that Fodor—known also as a functionalist—reaches what essentially amounts to the above conclusion in Fodor (2004). There are not, Fodor argues, '*any epistemic clauses in the analysis of concept possession*' (2004: 32), where any such epistemic clause would constrain possession of a concept C by the having of certain epistemic capacities, say to be able to sort C from non-Cs, or to draw inferences in which C figures. But, as Fodor plausibly argues, the question which *kind* of sorting would substitute for possession of a concept C can ultimately only be answered by letting C *enter into* the description of the sorting, which means the sorting cannot be essential to C or explain it. e.g., if the concept TWO is the concept whose possession we wish to specify, then not even a sorting according to a necessarily equivalent concept like THE ONLY EVEN PRIME will do, for a person can sort according to the one, but not the other. Yet, the person's sorting will overtly or physically look the same in both cases. What sorting, then, *will* do to specify possession of the concept TWO uniquely? Only a sorting according to the concept TWO, Fodor argues (2004: 39), which is precisely the circularity I argued for above.

evolutionary *rationale*, in the teleonomic sense of function: cognition evolved for the sake of enabling the agent to deal with environmental complexity. While that appears as an answer to a deeper 'why'-question—it aims to explain why cognition exists in the first place, by appeal to a notion of what it is 'for'—the thesis can also be read as an empirical/explanatory claim (which it was in Spencer's version of it): structural complexity *outside* causes/explains structural complexity *inside*.

Understood in the latter way, human language would seem a particularly unpromising start for the ECT. If the ECT had its way, externalist structures in the environment should predict or at least stand in some systematic relation to the core structural properties that we can empirically attest in the workings of the computational system underlying human language. To my knowledge, little evidence suggests this, as long as one accepts standard textbook accounts of that system (e.g. Haegeman 1994).[15] The very operation Merge, as noted, appears unmotivatable in these terms, and this operation has claims to be what is minimally needed to get a system like language that exhibits discrete infinity into place. At the same time, the case of language shows that more than the mere *necessity* of environmental complexity for the origin of the internal structures would have to be invoked in defending an externalism as underlying the ECT, since otherwise even a strong internalist such as Chomsky (2000) need not disagree: in particular, there surely *are* various physical and environmental preconditions that are necessary for the language faculty to evolve phylogenetically and mature ontogenetically. Godfrey-Smith agrees that the

> critical feature of a Darwinian mechanism is that the variants produced do *not* bear a systematic relation to the environmental factors that exert selective pressure on the organism (Godfrey-Smith 1996: 87, my emphasis).

For Darwin but not Spencer, the environment is silent on matters of 'design'. It does not act on the organism so as to mould it and confer structural complexity to it, or so as to create adaptations. Darwinian environmental selection is like a spectator sport: choosing among forms that present

[15] As rehearsed in MMD, language is created by children even in the absence of a 'language model', that is, severely impoverished linguistic structure in the environment. See Goldin-Meadow (2003). Neander (1997: 567–8) considers one version of the ECT as 'obviously true', or as 'trivial' as the claim that 'circulation is for transporting blood around the body'. But even such 'trivialities' regarding the externalist's notion of what something is 'for'—even if they make empirical sense in other cases—may be unavailable for human language. In particular, all species *communicate*, but the specific way in which we do does not seem to explain specific linguistic structures, but precisely depends on them. Quite plausibly, mechanisms allowing language processing evolved irrespective of their later use in the human communication system (Hauser *et al.* 2002; Chomsky 2006). It remains unclear today what theoretical and practical purpose some identification of the 'function of language' serves (see further Chomsky 2003: 312–13).

themselves, as a consequence of which these forms get redistributed in following generations, and evolution becomes progressive. But this process works with forms that are already there, which arise with no preferred orientation in an adaptive direction. At least in this sense, there is, for the Darwinian, no direct transfer or induction of structure, a direct causal or explanatory path from environmental complexity to internal systemic structure.[16] By crediting the environment with a more 'active' role in structuring the organism, Spencer falls on the Lamarckian side in the Darwin–Lamarck divide, with direct repercussions for his paradigmatically associationist psychology. He took it for law that 'all psychical relations whatever, from the absolutely indissoluble to the fortuitous, are produced by experiences of the corresponding external relations; and are so brought into harmony with them' (Spencer 1855: 530). As Godfrey-Smith puts this view: 'the environment brings about an organic change exactly in its own image' (1996: 86), a mechanism meant to account both for within-generation and across-generations change. Since variation is acquired for Spencer, by the direct causal flow of environment to organism, for the sake of an increasing optimization in the latter, there is a diminished importance for the process of selection, as what is there to be selected is *already* brought in harmony with environmental pressures. Spencer remained essentially uncompromising in his 'Lamarckian' psychology based on learning by classical conditioning (Godfrey-Smith 1996: 88–92). Only the former form of learning can be termed 'Darwinian', in that new variants are produced randomly or spontaneously. Spencer's hyper-externalism radicalizes Lamarckism, in fact, in that the Lamarckian organism's 'creative response to felt needs'—as when the giraffe stretches for

[16] There is an ongoing debate on whether natural selection has a creative role to play on the evolutionary scene. Thus, Neander (1995) argues that 'natural selection has a creative and not merely distributive role to play' (1995: 586). The 'statistical' as opposed to the 'dynamic' interpretation of evolutionary theory (see Walsh *et al.* 2002), supports the present view. Neander crucially appeals to the *cumulativity* of the adaptive process, in which some earlier preservations and proliferations of some co-adapted sequence of genes change the probability of what subsequent variations will arise. Still, natural selection cannot but influence what subsequent variations will '*randomly* arise' (Neander 1995: 586; my emphasis), no matter whether they occur with other probabilities on the population level, given a changed gene pool in which previous mutations took place. Neander's argument, one might say, depends on mixing two 'cycles of causation'. In a single-step selection process, as she points out, there is a 'causal isolation' between each random/select sequence. Here the causal processes invoked are the organism-internal ones giving rise to a random mutation. In cumulative selection, she further argues, one random/select sequence is *not* causally isolated from the next. But, now, the notion of 'causality' has widened and invokes the gene pool in which certain distributional shifts have taken place. That said, the whole issue about cumulativity is possibly orthogonal to the concerns of this paper. What explanatory role, if any, natural selection needs to play for the origins of human language is a widely open question (cf. Hauser *et al.* 2002); and as regards human concepts, if these are *atoms* in the sense of Fodor (1998), hence primitives, it is not clear how they should have arisen gradually by cumulative selection.

a longer and longer neck to reach up to the treetops—is now *itself* thought to be moulded by the environment. Lamarck by contrast crucially appealed, internalistically, to *drives* towards adaptive complexity ('inherent tendencies', 'innate proclivities') as well. But these must come from somewhere, Spencer (and Dennett 1995) would object here, and the environment is meant to turn that trick, too.

There is a severely distortional caricature of Lamarck, according to which, as Gould puts it, 'a giraffe felt a need for a long neck, stretched ever so hard, and then passed the results of these successful efforts directly to its offspring' (Gould 2002: 179). An analogy to this caricature in psychology would be: a human, feeling the need to name a certain—given, yet nameless—kind by a concept, thought ever so hard, came up with a suitable concept, and passed it on. The Darwinian response to that caricature would be that no need for a new concept will as such bring it into existence: functional need does not account for genesis. While Lamarckism in biology is nowadays regarded as *factually* wrong, if not *necessarily* (Dawkins 1983), its analogy in psychology, I here argue, is much alive, an indication for a methodological dualism as regards 'body' and 'mind' which MMD, following Chomsky (2000), centrally rejects. Specifically, if ontogenetic *learning* is conceived as an 'instructive' rather than a 'selective' process, it *is* the sort of direct flow of structure or information from the environment to the organism that Darwin denied. The classical case would be Skinner's (1969) theory of learning as an accumulation of learned habits or operants, a view not strikingly different from even some current accounts on how language is learned as a system of 'social conventions'. But it is part of Dawkins' argument that the Darwinian theory of evolution of the non-random selection of randomly varying replicating entities is universally and necessarily true, not just contingently and empirically, hence that all learning, if understood as adaptive improvement, must in principle be governed by a Darwinian selective mechanism (Dawkins, 1983: 20–3). Structure in the organism may be induced from the outside, but none of these changes are intrinsically adaptive. Hence, as long as explaining *progressive* evolution is our goal, Dawkins' argument shows it is not coherent to merely *add* a Darwinian mechanism of evolution to an independently operative Lamarckian one.[17]

[17] Dawkins (1983) argument for the universality of Darwinism nevertheless has a limitation as well, however: it confuses the question of the law of *change* for the form of life with that *form* itself. Dawkins would be right if life reduced to its adaptive history. But the history of a thing, and the various functional relations in which it enters in it, is conceptually or logically distinct from that thing itself and its intrinsic form. The history of life needs no more to account for its form than the history of the universe needs to account for planetary motion. There is no question that laws and formal principles *interact* with historical circumstances, certainly also in physics. But to say that, in physics, laws of form

Lamarckian instructive views applied to learning create a basic and unresolved paradox: it seems inconceivable that a human could 'stretch for a concept it lacks'. The problem in its Ancient Socratean formulation is that if you do not know what you are looking for, lacking the relevant concept, you can neither look for it nor find it. To look for it, you have to know what you are looking for, which by hypothesis you do not. You also cannot find it, for lacking the relevant concept you would not recognize that it was the solution to your problem. In the reformulation of this classical problem by Fodor, it runs as follows. Suppose you wish to acquire a concept you lack, say the concept expressed by the word 'red', presumably a primitive concept. Suppose, too, that learning it would require an inductive process of hypothesis-formation and testing. If that is the case, you have, at some stage, to form the hypothesis that some object falls under the concept expressed by 'red' by virtue of being *red*. But that is not possible, because, by assumption, you lack the concept involved in this hypothesis (Fodor 1998: 124). You can *only learn what you can represent* with given conceptual resources.

The internalist response to the paradox is that 'learning concepts', if these are primitive, must be a different process than hypothesis-testing. A child's learning certain concepts at certain times in ontogenetic development will be no more than mapping given phonetic labels to given representational resources that are in place at those developmental stages, resources that themselves originate on independent and internal grounds (see e.g. Gleitman *et al.* 2005; Spelke 1994, 2003; Hespos and Spelke 2004; Mehler and Dupoux 1994). The externalist and Spencerian response is also that the concepts are already there, but now they are supposed to be *there in the environment*: learning is the transfer of this structure to the organism. In line with this, Spencer, discarding the need for any internalist creative and non-functionally driven element in mental development such as Lamarck's innate proclivities, committed himself to show that the 'mind, supposed passive, is moulded by its experiences of "outer relations"', as James (1880: 188) put it:

> The cohesion between psychical states is proportionate to the frequency with which the relation between the answering external phenomena has been repeated in experience. (cited in James 1880: 184)

and history collapse (are one) would not be sensible. That *life* and its history do essentially fall together in this way is perhaps the received philosophy of biology. If I am right, and that view is no more than an empiricist and externalist presumption reflecting our ignorance of the principles structuring the forms of life, Dawkins' argument is question-begging. It presupposes a functionalist vision of life. Relative to the latter, Darwinism may well be universal. Hence, even though it does argue against the conceptual coherence of the externalism of Lamarck or Spencer, it does so on the basis of an important premise concerning what the prime explanandum in biology is: progressing in an adaptive direction. If by contrast we appeal to logical distinctness of form and function, the need for the external inducement of form is questioned on more fundamental grounds.

That is, what we know is a function of what happened to us (or our ancestors). James objected to what he argued was 'an obsolete anachronism, reverting to a pre-darwinian type of thought'. Instead,

> new conceptions, emotions, and active tendencies which evolve are originally produced in the shape of random images, fancies, accidental out-births of spontaneous variation in the functional activity of the excessively instable human brain, which the outer environment simply confirms or refutes, adopts or rejects, preserves or destroys,—selects, in short.... (James 1880:184)

That picture is true, James sensibly concedes, for the 'higher mental departments' only, as the lower ones are clearly not creative (or stimulus-insensitive, or non-input driven) in the sense James emphasizes: while there is (some) sense in which I am under the direct influence of the environment when I feel pain, say, there is no external or internal physical fact or configuration that, as far as we can tell, will force me to say or think anything in particular. On James' 'Darwinian' alternative to Spencer, an environment selects a concept for a use, but it does not create it, or shapes the organism so as to let it have a concept where it lacked one before.

Dretske (1988) develops the Spencerian conflation of function and genesis into a whole explanatory framework. He centrally defends the claim that what our words or mental representations mean is a function of how they came to be, namely through 'learning'. His explicit theoretical goal is 'to install the informational processes underlying concept learning as the source of meaning and content' (Dretske 1994: 260), a goal that in turn subserves another, to show the intentional contents of the mind to be causally relevant in the explanation of behaviour. Concepts, according to Dretske, flow naturally (without the mediation of intentional propositional attitudes) from our encounters with external environments. Behaviour is strictly conditioned. It is not even a Lamarckian 'creative' response to recurring situations, and even more clearly not a Darwinian 'selection' of an independently originating internal structure. Dretske argues it is inconceivable that the acquisition of a concept could depend on anything other than learning, hence have an *internal* cause, since only its having an external cause in the sense of being appropriately conditioned makes it *acquire* causal relevance in the explanation of behaviour:

> the content of beliefs and desires, of fears and intentions, the representational content that is featured in every explanation of behaviour by reasons, *must* derive from the development in learning of those circuits that constrain and structure voluntary action. (Dretske 1994: 262; my emphasis)

To get intentional contents with causal relevance, one must 'look to systems whose control structures are actually *shaped* by the kind of dependency relations that exist between internal and external conditions' (Dretske 1988: 95, my emphasis). Meaning is causally relevant to behaviour *only* in situations in which it is 'associatively learned' (1988: 96), by way of a 'mechanical' response (1988: 85):

> By the timely reinforcement of certain output—by rewarding this output *when*, and generally *only when*, it occurs in certain conditions—internal indicators of these conditions are recruited as causes of this output. (1988: 98)

But in a Darwinian frame of mind, Dretske's insistence that internal structures sub-serving intentional behaviour *must* derive from learning is just the fallacy of conflating genesis and function. Darwin showed us how even the seemingly most perfect adaptedness of an organism to a given environment does not require us to invoke Lamarckian 'shaping' or environmental 'instruction'. There is *no* inherent relation between adaptation and genesis, function and causal history, how something works and how it came to be. And there are standard empirical objections to Dretske's need for learning, too: in the course of normal ontogenetic maturation children come to know a lot more for example about language than they can have learned from their experience alone, as well as associationist processes of an empiricist provenience. The notion of 'development in learning' as such, informally understood, may involve any amount of creativity on the side of the organism, based on its native systems of core knowledge, each of which involve learning mechanisms of different kinds, in which case there is no such thing as 'learning in general' (Gallistel 1990; Gallistel and Gibbon 2001). For Dretske, by contrast, the internal control structures of behaviour that are acquired are supposed to crucially *not* depend on the organism's active contribution and the internal resources it brings to bear on its understanding. They depend on what they factually *do* mean or indicate about the external circumstances to which the organism's behaviour is appropriated during learning, hence an appropriately conditioned causal–functional relationship (Dretske 1988: 88). As Dretske (1994: 260) points out: '[w]hat converts a physical state—some condition of the brain—into a belief is outside the head'. This latter assertion has a reading on which it is trivially true, for the embedding of an organism and its concomitant functioning in the environment in which it is placed is nothing that the organism strictly speaking causes. But this is not the reading Dretske intends, where the conceptual structures subserving intentionality are *mechanically induced*, as in empiricist learning theories more generally. But it is an *empirical* question, when we look at particular processes that we intuitively describe as 'learning', whether the process we look at is more than the selection of a given neural structure, whatever its origin. Wherever this would be arguably true, we could still, if we wanted, say that:

instances of a mental representation, R, carry information about instances of an external property, P, if 'Ps and only Ps cause Rs' is a law,

which is how Fodor (1990: 57) summarizes Dretske's view. But, on the present view, these co-variance relations would indicate a *consequence* of the evolutionary process for given forms of cognition. The forms of cognition in question may as well have a different cause. The question cannot be decided by philosophical or conceptual means, in the way Dretske appears to envisage.

Behaviourist and neo-behaviourist views of meaning as deriving from associative learning or conditioning are as clear an expression of Spencerism as one gets. Dennett (1995), for one, endorses this heritage unabashed, as we saw. Even Fodor (1990) is explicit that he regards Dretske's as well as his own causal co-variance-approach to meaning as continuous with that of Skinner's. Skinner's account of language acquisition reduces language learning to social reinforcements mediating alterations in the strength of verbal operants: an operant response comes under the *control* of a type of discriminative stimulus as a function of the frequency with which the response elicits reinforcement when produced in the presence of stimuli of that type. Although Chomsky's critique of this view, Fodor (1990) argues, has effectively demolished his learning theory, it has done nothing against the *semantics* that went with it. This seems immediately problematic for a view such as Dretske's, where learning precisely is what grounds semantics, and the difference between a learning theory and a theory of meaning becomes moot. Fodor, by contrast, gives up on the learning theory, and focuses on what he calls a 'Skinnerian semantics' alone, which he regards as independent of a learning theory.

But Chomsky's critique affected Skinner's semantics as much as his learning theory. There is no non-circular way to specify what utterances like *What a fine way of making a compliment*, *Remember the quarrel we had last Christmas?*, *Slightly darker than the one on the left*, or *Calming*, uttered when standing in front of a painting in a museum, refer to. Skinner (1957) explains their utterances and meanings by 'subtle properties of the controlling stimuli'. But positing an external 'controlling stimulus' (or a meaning-determining 'referent' or 'property', for that matter), is a scientifically vacuous proposal, as the stimulus is identified in the light of the 'response'. As Chomsky (1959) argued, the notion of 'stimulus', whatever well-defined meaning it may have had in a laboratory setting in relation to bar-pressing experiments with rats (where behaviour *is* 'conditioned' in a meaningful sense), loses this objectivity when metaphorically extended to cases of verbal behaviour that only vacuously fall under such externalist explanatory schemes.

Chomsky (1959, section VIII) explicitly extends this line of criticism to an externalist Skinnerian semantics for words. Regarding descriptive terms such as *vertebrate* or *creature with a spine*, he points to the familiar problem that 'there is no good way to decide whether two descriptive terms designate the same property'—independently of invoking the meanings of the descriptive terms in question. If which properties we posit is a trivial consequence of which meanings we understand and which ones are synonymous for us, the postulation of such properties as the 'meanings' of such terms is explanatorily vacuous. Saying that the reference or denotation of descriptive terms is under the causal control of physical or abstract features of the external environment thus again involves an arbitrary shift in meaning, with 'causal control' having no objective status. Thus, for example, the meaning of the word *fox* as uttered by a speaker, A, for a hearer, B, is said by Skinner to consist in B's response to it (looking around, running away, etc.). That response is explained by appeal to a history of causal control reinforcing these behaviours given a sequence of earlier such activities of looking around, running away, etc. that were followed by occurrences of a fox. Moreover, B is said to 'have an interest' in seeing a fox on the occasion of A's utterance. Chomsky points out that B may have never seen a fox, nor have a current interest in seeing one. Current 'causal' theories of meaning and reference are different from this behaviourist analysis and its obvious failures, but the idea that meaning is causally controlled and referents can be non-circularly identified, appears not too far removed from the earlier story.

Let us consider Fodor's (1990) view more carefully. On this view, again, instances of the mental representation underlying the word *dog* denote dogs because the former are under the causal control of instances of dogs in the environment. Fodor renounces behaviourism, of course, but for a wrong reason, from the present point of view. The Fodorian reason is that his Skinnerian theory of how meaning comes about is reformulated as a theory of the semantics of *thoughts* ('propositional attitudes'), the existence of which Skinner denied (Fodor 1990: 55). The advantage that Fodor claims for this reformulation is that while speech acts are *actions*, and it is plain that what we *say* is not a function of the situation we are placed in, what we *think* is no action in this sense. However, what I *think* in a situation seems no more a function of what is true in it than what I *say*, not least because what can happen in it from my point of view is a function of what thoughts I, as opposed to a monkey, can think. For a concern with Spencerism, not the view we take on the 'metaphysics of propositional attitudes' matters, but the view we take on *semantics*. What the Darwinian is opposed to is the idea that concepts—rather than functional relations to an environment as *based* on such concepts—are causally or mechanically generated by an environment.

Explicating externalist content by appeal to causal relations between expressions and things in the world would a priori seem to be most promising as a theory about *unstructured* (atomic) concepts or expressions (that is, expressions that are not the result of operations of the computational system). For take an arbitrary structured expression, like *a nice cow with brown spots that I can eat for dinner*. In what causal relations does this concept, having the sound and the meaning that it does, stand with the environment? Consider my mind when it represents this expression, which has the form of a complex DP containing a quantified and modified NP, a TP, and CP, and so on, put together by Merge operating on the mental lexicon. Does this structure, when it occurs in my mind, stand in causal relations with anything in the environment, so that these causal relations are responsible or explanatory for its occurring in my mind? Has a particular cow, perhaps, or a situation, part of which was a cow, caused the assembly of the above expression in my mind? Was there something that caused the NP to assemble, and projected it, together with a TP, into a CP, and so on, yielding a new sound and a new meaning at each phase of the derivation?

I will trade this rather extraordinary hypothesis for the more modest one that our minds have certain operational resources intrinsic to them, which are not a passive reflection of physical conditions in the environments, and can be freely generated without any need for an external stimulus or referent. If a causal theory of meaning is upheld, we would do well to restrict it to strictly *unstructured* concepts, concepts that do not depend in some obvious way on the mind's intrinsic combinatorial resources. A close reading of Fodor's (1990) presentation of the informational/causal approach to meaning, however, suggests that he does not pursue this course. Consider the following quote:

> It will do if contents are assigned only to the *atomic* expressions, the semantics for molecular symbols being built up recursively by the sorts of techniques that are familiar from the structure of truth definitions. (Fodor 1990: 58)

Note first that contents are said to be 'assigned', which is inconsistent with the view taken here, that contents are *intrinsic* to the linguistic expressions that express them. Only in formal languages are contents 'assigned'; in natural languages the view presupposes the independent givenness of the contents in question. Note secondly that Fodor suggests that the contents of all structured expressions are fixed when those of the contents of the atomic ones are. This is true by my lights, given that if we add a combinatorial apparatus to a given lexicon, the full language, with its infinite sound–meaning pairs, is in principle thereby determined, without any involvement of the external world. A Tarskian truth definition, however, plays no explanatory role in how the computational system of language is described in standard current accounts; and the clauses with which it specifies relations of satisfaction between symbols of arbitrary formal complexity and infinite sequences of posited individuals in the external world simply bypasses the problem of how meaning is assigned. It has nothing to say about the problem of reference. So, I contend that the genesis of structural complexity and ensuing complex meanings in the language faculty is an internalist affair entirely.

Why does Fodor think otherwise? The answer may be that grounding the combinatorics of language in a definition of truth for language or thought is a way of keeping the close tie of linguistic meaning and the external world. Once that link is secured at the level of atomic expressions through the relation of object-reference, the idea seems to be, we can secure the same link at the level of complex expressions, given that truth is standardly viewed as a paradigmatically external relation as well. In short, making complex expressions intrinsically bearers of truth, and viewing truth as a relation between structured symbols and things in the world, we go some way towards completing an externalist vision on linguistic meaning. The following assertion confirms this interpretation:

> When we use 'it's raining' to specify the intentional object of the thought that it's raining, we are picking the thought out by reference to the state of affairs that would, in certain circumstances, cause it to be entertained. (Fodor 1990: 61)

We rephrase the bare bones of this proposal as follows:

> When we use 'it's raining' to assert that it's raining, we are doing this by reference to situations that would, under certain conditions, cause us to think that it's raining.

The problem with this assertion is that it seems quite false: the situations in question do not seem to exist. They are presumably those in which it is true that it is raining. But why would such a situation cause us to think that it is raining? We may think in such situations that it is raining, but we may also not. What if it rains all the time? If we do think that thought, this may patently be true in the way that a historical fact is (hence not be a lawful matter), and in the light of an infinite range of alternative thoughts in the same situation, it seems we simply cannot sensibly talk of 'causation' here at all, except by arbitrarily changing the meaning of the word. Looking out of the window, I realize the day makes it paradigmatically true that the sun is shining (Fodor's hedge clause 'under certain circumstances' will surely be satisfied). Yet, I have not entertained this thought once today. Fodor will thus have to code into his notion of 'certain conditions' whatever rules out such an infinity of counterexamples. At a trivial extreme, one might stipulate that nothing short of a situation will do in which I actually have a *concern* with whether it rains. But this would be to say that the circumstances that would cause me to entertain a thought of a specific type cannot be specified without making reference to the thought in question and its intrinsic content. Without a creature that can think such thoughts, has the concepts in question, and the right sort of concern, no causal relation will turn any trick or make anything mean anything. Since the point of the project is to specify the relevant content in non-intentional terms, it would in this sense be self-refuting.

As far as I can see, there simply *is* no lawful correlation between occurrences of syntactically structured expressions like 'It's raining' and environmental conditions. We *can* specify conditions under which this sentence would be true: these are conditions in which it is raining. But these are not different from conditions in which the sentence is true, and the specification is circular.

So let us turn to the application of the proposal to unstructured or atomic symbols and ask whether they stand in causal relations to the environment that explain their meaning. The following statement is Fodor's (1990) way of capturing the spirit of so-called causal-informational approaches to meaning as inaugurated by Fred Dretske in the late 1980s (Fodor's own causal-theoretic proposal in the same book is a variant of it):

(Dret) Symbol S expresses the property P if instantiations of P are nomically sufficient for instantiations of S *in situations where only things in the extension of S cause occurrences of S.*

The idea, then, is that symbols have 'extensions' (a notion to which I turn momentarily), and that, supposing that the symbol *cow* has all and only cows in its extension,

cow means cow just in case only cows cause tokenings of *cow.*

To assess this claim, let us first consider the three theoretical entities involved: (i) physical symbols, (ii) concepts, and (iii) extensions of symbols. To begin with the notion of the *extension of a symbol*, this notion is rather perplexing, as symbols properly speaking are no more than physical patterns: either they are phonological words or, if we consider some 'language of thought', they are neurological equivalents of words. But neither words nor neurological equivalents in a language of thought in the sense of Fodor are intrinsically meaningful: words are phonetic labels connected to a meaning, but no more intrinsically so than John is named 'John'. A phonetic label, simply being the physical object it is, does not seem to have an 'extension' either. It seems that what has an extension, at best, is the *concept* cow: it is the concept that means something, and which in virtue of this meaning determines a set of objects falling under that concept, that is an extension. But the Fodorian proposal above really has no use for concepts, which are what on his externalist view *reduce* to non-conceptual and non-intentional *interrelations* between symbols and extensions. So, it is not concepts that should be said to have extensions on this view, but only symbols, which is impossible if I am right that symbols have extensions only because of the concepts they express.

An extension of a symbol is thought to be either an abstract property expressed by a predicate or else simply a number (or set) of things to which that same predicate objectively 'applies'. On the former of these views, a symbol picks out an abstract object thought to exist 'out there'. But it is not clear what 'out there' means. Outside our bodies is a physical world, but no abstract properties: scientists study phenomena, usually unspecified for ontological category, and hypothesize them to have certain abstract properties that explain their behaviour. Positing these properties is based on explanatory constructs that scientists creatively come up with in their heads. For these explanations to work we need no ontology of external objects called 'properties' that one-to-one correspond to these explanatory constructs. No scientist studies 'properties', in the sense of natural objects; they could not, I suppose, if these are abstract objects.[18] Neither does a scientific realism depend on such specific *ontological* assumptions. If we replace talk about properties with talk about explanatory constructs in a scientist's head with which some sense is made of the phenomena out there, we will be talking about mental objects (aspects of the human mind) that are different from the symbols (or their neurological equivalents) that were assumed to have extensions: there is

[18] Moreover, if the Neo-Darwinians are right, there simply is no such thing as an objective property of being a cow that natural objects such as cows have: species do not form 'natural kinds'. Accordingly, no symbol could pick one such property out, in this particular case; whether there are natural kinds in the metaphysical sense in the non-biological case is an entirely open question. Its answer should likely not depend on semantic analysis.

nothing mental or semantic about a symbol as such, or as a physical object. So we could not make do with an ontology that discards concepts. If the meaning-theoretic problem of how symbols get to mean what they do is not resolved by positing external properties they pick out, we need to appeal to mental concepts that make their meaning happen and allow their referential uses.

Let us then discuss instead whether symbols refer to extensions in the sense of *sets* of entities *falling* under a particular mental concept. The idea is to make relations between a symbol and things in the world explanatory for our account of what concept it expresses. If that is the purpose, however, things in the world individuated by appeal to a concept under which they fall are definitely not what we look for, for reference to an ontology of concepts was precisely what was to be avoided in the physicalist proposal above. So to understand what it is for a cow to fall under the concept of a cow we cannot conceive it *as a cow*, that is as instantiating the concept in question. A set of cows (an extension, or a number of occurrences of them) cannot explicate what the concept COW is, because such a set is simply a set of things falling under that concept. Human languages make this very vivid: the extension of the concept COW consists of, as we say in English: *cows*, but what the externalist approach aims to explicate is the concept (as we put it in English) *cow*. A grammarian will rightfully object to any such attempt to explicate *cow* by appeal to *cows*: for the latter word is linguistically *more* complex than the former. Grammatically, the concept COW-S contains the concept COW as a proper part; it *presupposes* it. The concept COW also cannot be used to talk about one individual (countable) cow, for in this case we have to speak of A COW or THE COW, using the intrinsically complex concepts that these expressions respectively express.

These considerations suggest that the word *cow* as such does not refer to a set of individual cows as its extension. Interestingly, where it occurs without any syntactic or morphological complexity, it seems to denote a mass of a cow (cow-stuff), as in (11) or (12):

(11) a bucket of cow
(12) I ate cow [rather than pork].

Example (11) cannot mean that there is a full and individual cow stored in your bucket, and (12) means that you ate an indefinite amount of cow-stuff. However, as Chapter 5 will point out, and as Longobardi (1994) has argued, the appearance of a bare noun in these instances is misleading: the nominals in question are in fact syntactically complex, having an empty determiner position that accounts for their quantificational reading. By consequence, a truly bare noun *cow* will neither denote a set of individual cows nor a cow-mass. It denotes—irreducibly names—as I will conclude in Chapter 5, a pure concept, which we need to think of as something distinct from both individuals and masses.

If, on the other hand, the extension in question is not meant to be explicated in intentional terms (it does not matter how we think or conceive of the entities in question), then the stipulation of the extension will not explain anything about conceptual understanding at all. That extension as such will then neither cause any concept of cow, if none exists, nor necessarily trigger it, if it does exist. And if there *was* anything in the world out there that the word *cow* as used in English co-varied with, it would have to be cow-stuff, or a pure concept, but not individual cows. But whether something is cow-stuff or an individual cow is not something that reality fixes: it is in the mind of the beholder, in how we look at things given what concepts and ways to combine them we have. To see this, suppose I slaughtered Mathilda, a cow, cut her into pieces, and put them all in one bucket. In this circumstance, I can say

(13) I have a cow in a bucket, namely Mathilda

making individual-specific reference to a particular cow. But if I say instead, forgetting about the history of the meat-stuff in my bucket,

(14) Here I have a bucket of cow,

the scene in question will not have changed one jot. *Apprehension* varies, not causation: by making a simple syntactic change—dropping the determiner in front of *cow*—we cognitively configure an entirely different scene, although it physically does not change. In this sense, the world does not co-vary with our apprehension of it.

There is also a logical argument that concepts never are sets of entities falling under them. Take the set of natural numbers, N, and our *concept* of a natural number, C. Now, C is not N: our *concept* of a natural number is not the natural numbers *themselves* (of which there are many, for example, whereas our concept of a natural number is only one). An extension like N is not a concept because it is simply a number of things. In general, no such number of things or ordered series of them can determine any concept, or be itself the cause of its underlying unity. Enumerating N *explicates* C, but no *n* natural numbers in an ordered sequence will as such tell us anything about the law of generation that underlies them. Any such law of generation or concept can be *illustrated* by a finite number of samples, but it is logically impossible for it to *determine* it. This is true of sets of cows as much as of sets of numbers. Talk about sets evades talk about concepts as primitive elements of our mind.

Talk about symbols and their extensions is another such evasion. Words as phonetic labels are connected to concepts but do not tell us anything about what these are. Stipulating a relation of 'reference' or 'representation' between phonetic or neurological labels explains nothing. Looking at the Dretskian proposal above, the supposition seems to be that certain occurrences of symbols will lawfully co-vary with occurrences of external objects that exert causal power on us. Concepts will essentially *consist* in such co-variance relations, as I understand the proposal. But that there is a cow in the visual scene is neither sufficient nor necessary for my entertaining either the concept or the sound associated with the actual English word *cow.*

Talk of 'dispositions' to use a word in a certain way is another example for an evasion from crediting concepts with an explanatory role. Fodor (2001) considers a theory according to which the relational properties of 'proto-concepts' (innate concepts, considered prior to being externally triggered), relations he supposes to be constitutive for them, supervene on the proto-concepts' (possibly unactualized) *dispositions* to enter into causal world-to-mind relations: 'Maybe what makes a mental representation a token of the proto-concept type cat is its disposition to be triggered by cats' (Fodor 2001: 137). Hence what makes the concept in question *that* concept as opposed to another one is not that it means CAT or has that content, but a disposition to enter into certain causal-referentially specified external relations. But talk of such dispositions explains nothing, and seems like a misleading paraphrase of the idiom of concepts and what they mean. It is having the relevant concept that accounts for the behavioural disposition to react to cats by saying or thinking a proposition involving the concept.[19]

We face a similar tension between a biological nativism and an externalist individuation of content in Fodor's discussion of the Platonic learning paradox described earlier in this section. Fodor's (1998) response to the paradox is interestingly rather more in line with Spencer's than Plato's. Fodor starts by considering giving up on *cognitivism*, the view that concept acquisition involves a process of hypothesis-formation and testing, and stipulating instead that acquiring a concept is *nomologically locking* onto the *property expressed* by the concept (so an external ontology of 'properties' is assumed). Internal operations of the mind—forming beliefs, testing of hypotheses,

[19] It seems similarly unclear how, if part of what is innate about a concept is a specification of its 'proprietary trigger' (Fodor 2001: 138), we would know *what* trigger is 'proprietary' if we do not know the concept it is proprietary for.

concepts—drop out of the process, and since these internal operations caused the problem in the first place, the learning paradox disappears. This moves us into an externalist direction of explanation, and a predictable internalist response: If, indeed, having a concept is 'resonating to' the property that the concept expresses, we do not seem to know what, if not having the concept itself, *explains* our resonating to *the particular* property expressed by it, rather than some other property; and why this dualism of 'concept', on the one hand, and a 'property' directly corresponding to it, on the other, should obtain (see above).

While finding the above externalist and anti-cognitivist move attractive, however, Fodor himself raises the problem that even locking on to a property does ultimately not seem to be a process that is unconditioned internally. It clearly seems to depend on exposures to the *right kind* of things given in one's experience: things *falling under* the concept to be learned. The concept of a doorknob is learned from exposures to (typical instances of) *doorknobs*, not giraffes or oysters, say. For Fodor this means that hypothesis-testing must be a part of the picture after all, for the learner has to use experiences with *doorknobs* to test and confirm hypotheses about what property the word *doorknob* denotes. If, instead, the process of concept acquisition was *not* cognitively mediated in this way, or 'brutely causal', we would not predict that the concept of a doorknob is typically acquired from exposure to doorknobs and doorknobs only. But it is. Therefore the process is not brutely causal, and the relation between a concept and the experience from which it is learned or which it is 'true of' *is* a special case of the evidential relation between a generalization and its confirming instances (Fodor 1998: 127, 132).

But then again, ask just *when* an experience of some thing would be a confirming instance of a generalization formed over what the word *doorknob* expresses. Clearly, only if it was a doorknob. But this thought the learner cannot think, lacking the concept that figures in it. Thus hypothesis-testing is not involved, the internalist would again conclude. The process in which a concept that originated on independent grounds is triggered *must* be 'brutely causal', and the doorknob/DOORKNOB problem raised is a *reductio* of the hypothesis-testing model. But why then *is* doorknob acquired from doorknobs and not giraffes? The appearance may be as unsurprising as the one that organic structures not fitted to particular uses are not selected for or selectively retained. The relation between the concept of doorknobs and doorknobs is the relation of selection among pre-given variants. It is non-cognitive (and in this sense: brutely causal, though still not arbitrary), and it is selective as opposed to instructive.

2.4 Conclusions

Meaning begins, not from relations of reference between words and things, but atomic concepts. This is an empirical claim, although it can be read metaphysically as well. Metaphysically, it should be as acceptable as any conclusions arising from scientific theorizing unpremised by *a priori* metaphysical assumptions. That there are meanings in this universe, or that these make up a layer of reality, seems way less troublesome than more popular assumptions such as that the universe contains objects and structures 'corresponding' to our concepts and 'mirroring' them structurally. The empirical plausibility of the claim in turn resides in the adequacy of the model of language as a naturally occurring particulate and self-diversifying system in nature, and the lack of success or even coherence of externalist attempts to bootstrap meaning from what depends on it, like reference to the world as creatures like us undertake it. As a particulate system, language has a bottom layer in its hierarchy of complexity, and there is good evidence that the word boundary no less than the phrasal boundary is semantically significant and distinctive: whatever internal structure a lexical item will have, it will not have a compositional semantics itself. In short, standard quotidian, 'middle-level' concepts do not have complex representations 'at the semantic level'.

Behaviourists in the early twentieth century inaugurated the project of a 'functional analysis' of verbal behaviour: such behaviour consists in input–output relationships that get into place through conditioning, learning, or causally specified relations of reference. None of these, I have argued, likely provide even a basis for understanding the origin of human conceptual thought and reference—not for where conceptual thought begins, at the level of conceptual atoms, nor in the structured thoughts that are built up from there. Philosophical 'functionalists' have crucially followed the behaviourists in assuming that the meanings of the internal representations mediating between relevant input–output mappings could somehow be functionally or computationally explained. This externalist project remains with us to this day. Most certainly, though, the *primitives* of the combinatorial system of human language cannot be so explained, if indeed they are atoms. When current approaches to the neural correlates of consciousness (NCC, Koch 2004) aim to integrate a theory of semantics into their account of consciousness by connecting it to Churchland's associationist 'neurosemantics' (Churchland 1998), this enterprise similarly depends on assuming the falsehood of what is asserted here, the non-functionalizability of lexical atoms, the particulate nature of human language, and the failure of meeting systematicity and compositionality constraints by the kind of neural network modelling underlying the neuro-semantic enterprise (Hadley 2004; Fodor and Lepore 2002).

Hinzen (2006b) constructs an argument not only for the primitive status of lexical atoms but for their logical independence from their physical representations and their neurological or external correlates. This would mean that even though there can and should be a programme of finding the neural correlates of single concepts, the problem of why these correlations exist and how the correlates can be explanatory for the concepts will not be resolved by more empirical inquiry. Given these contentions, it is unclear why we should wed the NCC programme to the connectionist commitments of the neuro-semantic programme that only seem to revive a behaviourist and empiricist heritage, in the absence of explanatory breakthroughs at least in the case of the cognition of creatures that have found access to the particulate system in nature that this chapter has been about.[20]

[20] For comments on how the neurosemantic programme depends on philosophical assumptions of an empiricist nature for its workability, see chs 8–9 in Fodor and Lepore (2002), and in particular pp. 171–2.

3

Structures for Concepts

3.1 Stage-setting: The analytic content of a concept

An interesting implication of the previous chapter is that the notion of an 'analytic inference' appears to be an essentially unproblematic notion when appropriately restricted in its application. It has been rated as a highly problematic one in the entire twentieth century—indeed, it has been rated as obsolete—on the grounds that no principled distinction between analytic and synthetic knowledge can be drawn. The foregoing account of language as a particulate system however makes this distinction virtually trivial: analytic knowledge is knowledge that follows from the laws and combinatorial principles of language, which are, if I am right, equally laws of meaning. So, as noted in Section 2.3, *brown* is an analytic implication of *brown cow.* Similarly, (1) has the analytic entailment in (2), (3) the one in (4):

(1) [portraits of himself], Bill thinks Hill would never purchase
(2) What's purchased are portraits, which are portraits of either Hill or Bill
(3) [portrait himself], Bill thinks Hill never would
(4) a. Hill is the one whose doing a portrait is in question here, not Bill
(4) b. the person Bill thinks Hill would never portrait is Hill, not Bill

The entailments are analytic because they have structural explanations in terms of the binding theory and other modules of Universal Grammar (UG), which depicts the architecture of the language faculty, an intrinsic aspect of the human mind. An entailment is analytic where there is an algebraic (syntactic) structure that explains it, the structure being what our best account of the language faculty posits for explanatory reasons. Claims about analyticity are thus relative to a particular theoretical scheme, but this does not mean that the analytic is relative. Different explanations compete for correctness on what the analytic entailments are.

Rejecting the entire idea of the systematicity of language and its particulate character, one could as well argue, of course, that (2) and (3) are simply firmly enshrined 'beliefs' in a speech community enforced by social conventions, with no relation to anything like a biologically grounded 'language faculty'. But this option seems unlikely to be as explanatory as a current linguistic account. The entailments surely do seem to depend on the actual structures of the expressions involved; and speakers do not hold beliefs about abstract phrase structures, co-indexed traces, locality, c-command, and other such notions that characterize the expressions in question and explain their properties. A child needs no beliefs about laws of UG, nor does it need to 'represent' them. They just have to be there, and be operative. Similarly, in arithmetic we may indeed *believe* that after 74, the next natural number is 75. But the fact in question is a structural fact, and whether or not we have any such beliefs is no more relevant here than in the case of recognizing harmonic principles in music or relations between spatial dimensions in geometry. A child not recognizing the arithmetic fact in question would eventually adjust its proclaimed beliefs to the structural realities: we can be confused about the contents of our own mind, or be 'out of tune' with our own systems of cognitive competence. But only up to a point.

In short, Quine's deepest problem, how to distinguish putative analytic entailments from merely firmly enshrined conventions or beliefs, only arises on a conception of language as a system of conventions subject to communicative constraints alone. It does not arise from a naturalistic, biolinguistic stance. So analyticity is not a problem, nor is the analytic/synthetic distinction, as long as the biolinguistic stance is adopted (which in turn is just a question of the fruits it yields): in that case, our best theory will simply delineate a number of explanatory principles for linguistic structures and their properties, and separate others from them which are not part of narrow syntax, but a consequence of convention, beliefs, or context. The distinction will not be an absolute or conceptual one, but this does not seem to matter very much. Nor is it now a surprise that the analytic/synthetic distinction breaks down for lexical items. Atomism predicts this very fact: if there is no structure, there can be no analytic entailments either. So one should not in fact speak of the impossibility of delineating the analytic content of a lexical concept (whether PRIME is part of TWO, for example, or DEATH is part of KILL), or the breakdown of the analytic/synthetic distinction: it does not break down, but is firmly in place. The distinction precisely *predicts* and *explains* why lexical items do not seem to have analytic entailments (I return to another sense in which they do).

Analytic knowledge is also *a priori*. The structure of the initial state of the language faculty, described by UG, whatever it is, is *a priori* by definition. Therefore, whatever principles structure our knowledge of language that the child brings to bear on its acquisition task, as opposed to reading them off the data, are *a priori* too. Such principles determine what a (human-biologically) possible human language is. They do not determine *which* such language will be spoken in the environment. The child's eventual knowledge of *English*, therefore, that is the fact that it is English that is spoken in its environment as opposed to Japanese, is entirely *a posteriori*. No amount of study of the language faculty, at least in its initial state, would predict any such thing. This particular knowledge is therefore also *synthetic*: it is a piece of knowledge *about the world*, which does not follow from the internal organization of the organism in question. Analytic knowledge, by contrast, would be (implicit) knowledge of a competent speaker of an infinity of meanings and sounds. For, if that speaker knows the items of a mental lexicon and the combinatorial principles of language (that is, she has the computational system of language), she will know an infinity of sound–meaning combinations including those never generated before. This knowledge is entirely independent of what is contingently true in the world, and in this sense, again, analytic.

From the above it finally follows that there will be knowledge which is *synthetic a priori* too, as Kant proposed. This is for the simple reason that the child's concept of a 'possible language' has a real-world content too: it is about *contingent* features of any possible human language that may be spoken in an environment. The child's concept of a possible language will acquire such a real-world content the moment that it becomes *restrictive* and our theory of the initial state gives rise to an insight into what an '*impossible* language' would be: a language not learnable natively, by being just 'puzzling' for a mind structured like ours. Typological studies of linguistic universals and universal restrictions on distributions (Greenberg 2005), psycholinguistic inquiry into language learning (Smith and Tsimpli 1995), and theoretical inquiry into the language faculty all substantiate such a notion of what is possible *and apparently impossible* in human language. The child's knowledge of these restrictions insofar as it is attested is not therefore purely *formal* knowledge (in the way that knowledge of logic would be), but truly content-involving, in the sense that it concerns substantive features that human languages *contingently exhibit*, such as recursivity, the necessary headedness of phrases, the categorial hierarchy of the clause, or the structure-sensitivity and locality of linguistic dependencies. A communication system used in an environment *need* not exhibit any of these features. If it does, this is contingent information about features of an environment that follow from nothing in the organism. The knowledge is therefore synthetic. But it is also *a priori*, to whatever extent this knowledge is part of what is specified in the initial state. In sum, I neither see a problem with the existence of *analytic* and *a priori* knowledge, nor with the existence of *synthetic* knowledge *a priori*.[1]

It could be that word meanings (concepts) are an inherent part of the language faculty, or at least are *a priori*, as well. This is what would follow from the general Socratean/Fodorian puzzle on how we could ever acquire a concept that we cannot (yet) represent, which I mentioned before. For certain specific concepts this conclusion seems virtually forced by their infinitary aspects, as in the case of the natural number concept. Take the numeral 'seven'. Understanding this simple term hides a whole system of knowledge that takes many years to mature. Full understanding of this term does not mean, for example, that it denotes a set with seven objects, or that it comes after 'six' and before 'eight'. It requires a grasp of the fact that the number seven is part of an *infinite series* in which every member is generated by the same generative principle.[2] As one number is given, all numbers are. No experience seems capable of determining that insight, supporting its *a priori* nature.

Indeed, it is *unknown* how children acquire the number concept, typically by the age of four. Extensive current developmental and comparative studies suggest that the maturation of arithmetical knowledge is guided by two systems of core knowledge, both present in humans as well as non-humans: a system of representation for *continuous magnitudes* ordered by relations of more and less, which falls short of precise numerical knowledge; and a system of discrete and precise numerical cognition that is however limited to sets with a cardinality of one, two, or three (Carey 2004; Gallistel and Gelman 1992; Spelke 2000, 2003). On Carey's specific proposal there is, moreover, a *counting routine* by which children recite the number series without, at early stages, fully grasping the meaning of the number terms involved. What they gradually learn according to Carey is a *mapping* between the position of a particular numeral in an ordered (count) list, on the one hand, and the position of a set in a series of sets ordered by a step-wise addition of a single element. In her own words, the child makes the following 'wild analogy':

If number word X refers to a set with cardinal value *n*, the next number word in the list refers to a set with cardinal value *n*+1. (Carey 2004: 67)

[1] That knowledge guided by *a priori* components takes many years to mature and be usable by the organism is of course no reason to reject the *a priority* of those components. Instantaneous presence and usability at birth is not, on my reading, a feature implied by the notions of *a priori* knowledge that either Plato or Kant defended.

[2] Knowledge of that series can be captured by various axioms, for example by the Dedekind axioms that 'zero' or 'one' (depending on where one begins) is not the successor of any number, that if the successor of k is equal to the successor of j, k must be equal to j, and that nothing else is a natural number.

The term 'wild analogy' captures nicely why this process of acquiring the number concept must be mysterious for a creature that does not possess it already. The system that recognizes continuous magnitudes is too limited to represent the recursive process '+1'; and so is the process of discrete numerical cognition aided by the counting routine. As Rips *et al.* (2006: 7) point out, unless the stipulated notion of the 'next element in the counting sequence' is actually *equivalent* to the notion of the successor of a natural number, so that the counting sequence is effectively equivalent to the natural number sequence and understanding of the latter is presupposed, the notion of 'next element' will leave undetermined what comes next. To state the point more generally, one does not get from two systems which singly and in conjunction are strictly weaker than the number concept, to a system that captures it.

An exactly parallel argument can be construed for the child's acquisition of its notion of any recursive unit of language, be it the possessor phrase, as in *John's father's sister's friend's shirt*, the clause, as in *John said Mary said her brother wanted Fred to get Bill to understand Rothko*, the adjective or adverbial phrase, as in *this sad, honest, beloved, deep smile of yours* and *beautifully, slowly, leisurely, passionately paint the car*, or in iterative structures like *very very very very tired.*

There is no such recursion at the bottom layer of the human conceptual edifice, where primitive concepts live. Using our concept of a person, we can construct an indefinitely extensible number of possible persons in our imagination. But that will not give rise to any person recursively containing another person as a part, in the way a sentence or clause can contain another. Some of my father may be in me, just as there may be much Wagner in Strauss. But this is more like one grape being part of another when wines are mixed. Nor should there be analytic entailments at this bottom layer, where there is no structure, as noted above. But now we face a massive problem, which is what the rest of this chapter is about. For there seem to *be* intrinsic lexical connections between *words*, seemingly driven by their intrinsic meaning. If these lack an internal syntactically and semantically compositional structure, we have no resources to *explain* these connections. I am calling them 'intrinsic' because they have a *necessary* character and because they seem to depend on nothing *other* than the lexical items (specifically, their conceptual contents) in question.

For example, consider that a given man is not only an animate individual being but also—by implication—a lexical 'space' that is quantifiable and countable (e.g. *few/three men*), a mass or substance (as in *man-eater*), and even an abstract kind: something that's *manly*, or is *more man than woman.*

The last, purely abstract denotation of man, where 'man' basically is the same as 'manhood', is neither a mass nor countable/individual nor animate. Any given concrete man, by contrast, *is* all of animate, individual/countable, and mass. There is thus an entailment hierarchy, and it is asymmetric. The higher in the hierarchy we are, the richer the entailments. A merely abstract space entails nothing: it has no structure. To arrive from an abstract denotational space—manhood—at an animate entity, we have to gradually add topological complexity: first, we have to subdivide the space into parts, that is introduce a partition in it that allows us to have 'more' or 'less' of it and to apply mass-quantifiers like 'much' or 'a lot'; then we have to present the space in more articulated fashions so as to present it under an individual guise, allowing us to count the individuals in question (men), and quantify the man-space in all kinds of ways: *two/some/all/few* men. Finally, we have to add a change potential and make our space dynamic, so as to capture an animate entity. These ways of mentally 'warping' a given space, to use a term coined by Uriagereka (1995, 2002), are not of course specific to the item *man*: having this specific conceptual architecture in place in its language faculty, the child would grasp relevant entailments for *any* nominal concept it acquires, simply by knowing where in the hierarchy it is lexicalized. Thus, *man* is lexicalized at the highest animacy level; *justice* or *beauty* are merely abstract spaces; *car* and *house* are count nouns; *coffee* and *beer* are masses.

Lexical hierarchies in fact are not restricted to the nominal domain but extend to the verbal one, with concomitant structural similarities cutting across both domains, which hardly seem accidental. To illustrate, a verb depicting a *state* like *lives* (in the sense of being alive) is intuitively simpler semantically than an *activity* like *run*, which in turn is simpler than an *achievement* like *reach*, which in turn is simpler than an *accomplishment* like *construct*. The latter two imply telicity and boundedness in a way that the former two do not. The second implies a dynamic character, which the first again does not. Again we get asymmetric entailments: accomplishing entails achieving entails being active entails being. I take it these are conceptual necessities: we could not think about a world in which they fail, hence could not empirically discover that they do.[3]

As Uriagereka (2007: ch. 2) notes, it is interesting that these nominal and verbal hierarchies may in some abstract sense be *the same hierarchy*, which attests to their formal reality. Abstract nouns and mass nouns intuitively lack intrinsic bounds in a similar sense in which states and activities lack intrinsic ends; and the way countable and animate nouns are bounded does not seem

[3] At least we could not express these thoughts in a *natural language*.

unrelated to the way in which there is an inherent telicity to achievements and accomplishments. Moreover, quantifiers like *a lot* modify both mass nouns and activities (*[a lot] of beer, Saddam runs [a lot]*), and numercial quantifiers like *two* modify both countable objects and achievements (*[two] mugs of beer, Saddam reached his hideout [twice]*). It is as if an initially least specific mental space is stepwise 'folded' onto itself, so as to give rise to gradual enrichment in formal specification, whether 'verbal' or 'nominal': beginning at the least specific (abstract) level, it first gets extended indefinitely (mass/activity), then boundaries are added (concrete/achievement), and finally we have a fully entangled space (Uriagereka 2007: ch. 7; Hinzen and Uriagereka 2006).

Note that the formal-topological analogies between the nominal and verbal spaces in question are not denotational, or do not hold at the level of reference: there is nothing out there which would make us discover, independently of the conceptual spaces in question that can configure acts of reference, the intrinsic topological boundaries characterizing both telic verbs and individuals. At the level of reference, the boundaries imposed by a glass of beer do not compare with the temporal boundaries of an action of drinking it.

Let us now discuss what would *explain* the hierarchies in question. Could not, for example, lexical entailment simply be a species of world knowledge plus rational inference, construed normatively? This would seem the right option, if, say, we are learning some logical system, such as first-order logic. But entailments between types of nouns and verbs, I daresay, are of a rather different kind. It seems odd to say that we hold 'beliefs' about these things; and, clearly, the entailments in question are not merely externally imposed, but find a reflection in syntactic complexity that we see appear in countless languages. For example, a speaker who was told that he was *trinzing*, for example, having no clue what trinzing was, would know that trinzing is at least an activity, not a state, in the verbal hierarchy; and if told that it is impossible in principle that he might be trinzing John a house, he would thereby know it is not an accomplishment but only an activity. These inferences seem structure-driven, or structurally analytic in the sense above. So it is rather crucial for the present view that analytic entailment is not construed normatively, in the sense of externally imposed and ultimately arbitrary norms. An analogy with the phonetic side of things helps here as well. Alliteration and rhyme are naturalistically explained by the internal phonological structure of sounds. Here the explanation has nothing to do with beliefs or norms of reasoning either. If rhyme is naturalizable, by virtue of what phonology tells us about the internal structure of sounds, the question is why lexical entailment could not be naturalizable in a similar way, by appeal to the internal architecture of concepts.

As for the option that the rationale behind the lexical entailments in question is broadly 'semantic', as I have depicted them the entailments *are* prima facie purely semantic ones, and 'entailment' is a semantic notion to start with: so why *is* their explanation not simply a semantic one as well? Well, one methodological difficulty here is that 'semantics' is what we are trying to explain. It *is* what we want to have following from something else. That aside, for a semantic explanation to be an option, we would have to be talking about a semantics that is not systematically and perhaps trivially mapped from syntax or takes its essential cues from it. Semantics would have to be a separate component in the mind that worked by independent principles and was *linked* to syntax somehow, at worst by some essentially arbitrary 'correspondence rules'. Jackendoff's system (Jackendoff 2002), mentioned earlier, is one version of this. There the relevant component is called 'Conceptual Structure' (CS), and its semanticity is internalistically construed. Explanations for lexical entailments would have to come from right there. But a rationale for the above entailments could be semantic in an externalist and relational sense as well: then they would hold because of the very structure of the real, the topology of the world out there. I will discuss the latter proposal first.

To start with, it is weird to say that abstract spaces denoted by nominals like *beauty* or *justice* are something 'out there' at all. Nor do physicists find anything semantically wrong in asserting that most of matter consists of 'mass without mass' (John Wheeler's phrase); or that solid objects are actually mostly empty space (Newton), or even unextended in space (Boscovich, a post-Newtonian). All of these are essentially conceptual impossibilities. So, what we see is that as science progresses, constraints imposed by the human conceptual system may be simply dismissed; the world out there imposes no constraints of the sort we found operative in human concepts. Nothing is more irrelevant to modern physics as the notion of 'body' and other such naïve terms of native 'folk-physics'. Nor do any predictions for an ontology of animacy, objects, masses, and abstract spaces *follow* from the posits of modern physics, where we think of matter as travelling in waves through space, and objects are events or turn out to be 'actions' (cf. Stapp 2005). In short, if 'semantics' means 'relations to objects in the external world', then the ontology I have sketched is not semantic in character, not grounded in such relations. To put this in different terms, the entailments in question do not formulate any *truths about the world*, but truths about the organization of our concepts, and these kinds of truths can come fairly radically apart. Nothing we will be dealing with in this whole chapter involves truth (or reference) as yet.

Returning to the alternative proposal which appeals to an internalist semantics (Jackendoff 2002), the suggestion now is that CS is independent of syntax, exhibiting a productivity and systematicity that is entirely its own, as needs to be the case, given that, as noted in Section 2.1 against generative semantics, the combinatoriality which is taken to account for conceptual structure is not standard syntagmatic syntax. Only if that independence really held, that structure's ontology of objects, events, etc. could then potentially also provide an *explanation* for why the syntax of language exhibits the features it does: that is, syntax can potentially be rationalized as a system that evolved to *code* or *express* independently given semantic contents for the purpose of communicating them. Jackendoff (2002: ch. 8) is just such an evolutionary 'story'.[4]

Ideally, for such a story to be coherent, the independent generative systems of syntax and semantics should be somehow *optimized* with respect to one another: if the principles of the former seemed totally unrelated to the latter, it would not be plausible that syntax evolved in the service of semantics. Sadly for this project, Jackendoff argues at length, a *close* match does not exist, which then drives him to adopt his *parallel* architecture with multiple independent generative systems. For example, there are significant problems in rationalizing specifically the syntactic categories by appeal to their associated semantic or conceptual content. The category N, in particular, he notes, is surely not consistently linked with our conceptual category of an 'object' or 'thing' (*contra* e.g. Langacker 1998): nouns can denote objects of any ontological category or imaginable kind: compare earthquakes, concerts, wars, values, weights, costs, famines, redness, fairness, millennia, functions, perfection, enjoyment, or finesse (see Jackendoff 2002: 124). On the other hand, mismatches of the kind Jackendoff points us to—which make language look less perfect than we would like and harder to rationalize—may reflect how we look at the object more than the structure of the natural object itself. Linguistic facts are always also of our own making. Employing another idealization, language design may look differently and more elegant.

In the case of the category noun, for example, it is perfectly true that things like fairness, weight, justice, and war do not ontologically seem particularly 'thing'-like. But maybe ontological category at the level of reference is not

[4] Two problems with this is that the rationalization of aspects of syntax by constraints on communication seems circular and teleological: one cannot rationalize the evolution of a structural pattern from its later use. Secondly, language and communication are two distinct issues and evolutionary problems. A syntactic language may evolve for purposes of expressing thought independently of whether or not these syntactic structures will find their way into the open through a phonetic or visual channel. Put differently, a rationalization of syntax by appeal to the nature and structure of thoughts that can be encoded in it makes no predictions on the evolution of communication and need not depend on it.

what we should look at. Consider that all the above entities which the relevant nouns denote are *objects of reference* nonetheless, at least if reference is a use-theoretic notion relating to the intentional acts of a speaker: for we *refer* to these things in some direct fashion using the terms in question (when embedded in appropriate functional projections, irrelevant for now). But we do not use *verbs* for the purpose of referring to an object; we could not do so, as much as we tried. In this sense there is a neat semantic distinction between nouns and verbs. Verb denotations are not concrete objects to which we can point. Not all noun denotations are concrete and pointable, to be sure, but verb denotations are not in a more drastic sense, and the idea that a child can bootstrap verb meanings on the basis of non-linguistic factors such as 'saliency', independently of help from syntax, is naïve (e.g. Gleitman *et al.* 2005). If we were to *refer* to the event depicted by a verb, we would likely use a nominalization of the latter for the purpose, like *the kissing, the act of smiling*, etc. Consider how (5a) and (5b) or (6a) and (6b, 6c) differ conceptually:

(5) a. kisses
(5) b. the kissing
(6) a. John runs
(6) b. John's running
(6) c. the running of John

Intuitively (5a) and (6a) depict something dynamic and ongoing, whereas this dynamics is, as it were, frozen in (5b, 6b, 6c), where an 'object' is created out of something inherently dynamic. Importantly, these remarks again do not hold at the level of denotation, or the physical objects out there: an event of John's running has whatever physical correlates it has, which are independent of whether we intentionally refer to it through an objectifying nominalization like (6b) or a sentence like (6a). Similarly, if we refer to a friend as *John*—that is, by simply naming him—there is, when considering the denotatum in question, a whole dynamic life history and future behind the object we name, plus all sorts of paraphernalia like his style of clothes, family, job, home, and so on: but all that is not the object of reference in that act of naming, which as an act of reference is maximally economical in comparison to more elaborate forms of descriptive reference that would invoke one or more of these properties (*the man with the blue pants who lost his job*...). In naming, then, it is again as if the object of reference is frozen, moved out of space, time, and context, being much more abstract, as if we had a condensation of an enormous (in fact, in principle limitless) complexity into a single point with no internal complexity at all: just *John*.

In short, it is not implausible that a verb is something like the 'dynamification' of an object, and an object is the freezing of such a dynamic event, and that these two categories are fairly closely linked to a distinction at the level of the syntactic categories. Possibly, this insight is even a path to a still missing definition of 'verb', as Juan Uriagereka suggests in personal communication: perhaps a verb *is* nothing other than its Theme or internal argument viewed dynamically. Thus, an event of *drinking a beer* is a *beer* viewed dynamically as a gradual reduction of its volume, until it disappears. Once more, we are not talking at the level of reference here. The world might be such that a man drinking a beer does not finish it, say; or that there is an instantaneous mechanism that makes beer glasses full again the very moment they are emptied, so that an event felicitously described as *drinking a beer* would actually involve the drinking of several; or none, for, because of a hole in the glass connected to a hole in the table and an appropriate cable, in conjunction with the refill mechanism, a person occasionally sipping from his beer would always sit in front of a full one, never even finishing a single glass. All these are the vagaries of the world; they do not affect the intrinsic meaning of expressions.

On mismatches between syntactic form and semantic content at the level of argument structure and atomic concepts I will comment in the following two sections. What is interesting here is that because of the supposed mismatches in question, Jackendoff obtains a worst-possible result in relation to grammatical architecture: he is compelled to assume a radical *autonomy* of syntax with respect to semantics, captured perspicuously in his maxim that we should 'evacuate all semantic content from syntactic structure' (Jackendoff 2002: 124) and regard it as an independent system that has no semantic effects (although it has been adaptive in other ways). In other words, the entire idea of 'Transparency' I have defended in Chapter 2 becomes moot. The generative semantics programme comes out as essentially right, except in the most disastrous way: the programme set out to discard a syntax–semantics separation, striving for a system in which syntax is trivially mapped from whatever generative principles underlie semantics, a generative system of 'thought' independent of language. That project has failed by Jackendoff's own assessment: although semantics *is* antonomous, that is now *along with* an autonomous syntax totally separate from it.

In contrast to this, I have argued in Section 1.4 that language—in conjunction with other abilities partially unique to humans, such as operational memory—is very likely to have been semantically innovative at least to some *extent*, hence does not merely *answer* to independently given semantic conditions. In this chapter, I will more specifically argue that a part of the explanation for fundamental aspects of argument structure in human language—a crucial element of conceptual structure—is syntactic in origin. Correspondences between the two systems are too systematic to warrant Jackendoff's parallel architecture, which assumes independent generative systems wired together loosely by arbitrary correspondence rules. This makes the explanation of conceptual structure as well as lexical entailment an internalist–syntactic one, in the general spirit of this book.

An initial motivation for this conclusion is that the lexical entailment hierarchies above, although pretheoretically semantic in character, seem directly linked to specific facts of syntactic structure. Hinzen and Uriagereka (2006) point out that as we go up the ladder of entailment and semantic complexity increases, syntactic complexity increases stepwise too, in both the nominal and the verbal domain. Thus, consider that an abstract nominal like *serenity* is a prototypical 'bare' noun, with little or no syntactic complexity. For example, in standard, non-metaphorical uses it does not take articles such as *the* or demonstratives such as *this*, in the way that *beer* does; it is not measurable or countable, and does not take a plural (**we saw different serenities in Spain* involves a metaphorical shift in reference or else in ungrammatical). In turn, *beer* is only classifiable or quantifiable by the rough estimates *much* or *little*, whereas, if it comes to *mugs*, we see languages applying more classificatory (e.g. number and gender markers, where these exist) and precise quantificational resources (e.g. *four mugs*), with still further such resources showing up in the case of animate nouns like *man* (e.g. 'personal' markers in many languages). In short, grammatical complexity tracks lexical-semantic complexity, an important insight from the functionalist tradition, as Uriagereka (forthcoming: ch. 2) notes.

A similar such correlation can be observed in verbal spaces, as Uriagereka notes too. Thus states cannot be progressive (*Saddam lives* but not **Saddam is living*), and they do not tolerate bounding modifiers (**Saddam lives [in two months]*). Activities, by contrast, can progress (*Saddam is running*), but they can still not be bounded (**Saddam runs [in two months]*). Achievements can both progress (*Saddam reached his hideout*) and be bounded (*Saddam reached his hideout [in two months]*). Yet, they can still not appear in so-called 'affecting' circumstances (**the hideout's reaching (by Saddam)*). Finally, accomplishments can appear in all contexts: they can progress (*Saddam is constructing a hut*), be bounded (*Saddam constructed his hut [in two days]*), and occur in 'affecting' circumstances (*the hut's construction by Saddam*). It seems to be the most immediate explanation of these empirical correlations, and a conceptually highly natural one, that semantic complexity is not supported without a 'matching' syntactic complexity. That is, we cannot *think* (construct representations of) certain thought contents, before the structures expressing them have reached a certain matching complexity. We cannot, say, refer to an individual without giving the noun in question a determiner; or make a generic statement without supplying the noun with a plural morpheme. (The case of proper names *seems* to contradict the former claim, which is precisely what makes it interesting; see Chapter 5.)

The rest of this chapter explores this idea and argues for an internalist and syntactic origin for conceptual structures containing lexical concepts, as well as such structures internal to lexical concepts, and an explanation for analytic and lexical entailments that follows from this.

3.2 Conceptual structures

The term conceptual structure is ambiguously used: sometimes, to depict a recursive phrase-structural encoding of the lexical requirements of a head, built by external Merge in the absence of (that is, prior to) any movements transforming the structure in question; at other times, to depict a putative structure internal to a lexical item, which then is said not to be atomic at a semantic level of representation, but the coding for a complex 'thought' or conceptual structure at that level. These two kinds of conceptual structures—phrasal and sub-lexical syntax—obviously need not be the same. In GB models of UG, conceptual structure is inherently phrasal or hierarchical, hence of the first sort: this is what was called 'D-structure', a level of representation where all lexical items figuring in a derivation are inserted (a 'locus of lexical insertion'), semantics is strictly compositional, and recursion takes place (D-structures can be infinitely long). I will argue in what follows that *both* of these kinds of conceptual structures exist.

Crucial to a GB architecture is that the derivation passes a D-structure level prior to transforming the phrase marker by dislocating constituents, leading up to LF (or S-structure, before that), with D-structure providing the lexico-conceptual material on which (or on whose projections) the transformations operate. D-structure is the proprietary domain of one module of UG, Theta Theory (in conjunction with X′-Theory). For an expression to pass the filter that this level represents, syntactic structure has to match the 'logical' structure of an expression with its syntactic one. For example, the 'logical' subject of the expression has to be in the position where its surface-syntactic subject is, too. This is not the case, for example, in passives, whose syntactic subject is their logical object, which is one of the reasons for thinking that passives are actually 'derived' rather than 'base'-structures. Nonetheless, the term 'logical' is misleading, since there is nothing 'illogical' in a derived structure that is obtained through transformations. Indeed, it is a basic insight of generative grammar dating back to the early 1970s that semantic interpretation is read off S-structure (later LF), hence that derived structures as well feed semantics and logic in systematic and distinctive ways.

D-structures capture one aspect of the logico-semantic structure of an expression, but *only one*: there are other dimensions of meaning which are structurally more complex, and particularly affect the embedding of a thematically complete expression into an ongoing *discourse*. Note that this *semantic* significance, or (in more recent terms) *interface* dimension of D-structures, transpired after empirical arguments for them were developed that are of an essentially *syntactic* sort (such as the distinction between raising and control, see e.g. Hornstein *et al.* 2005: ch. 2): that is quite interesting, for it suggests that we can discover essential cuts in the system on formal grounds while finding later they have a specific interpretive dimension to them as well. If this differentiation of semantic information into (at least) thematic (argument) structure and discourse semantics were transposed into a more contemporary minimalist framework, it would naturally lead at least to the view that SEM representations cannot be unitary: there must be an *internally differentiated* interface (Chomsky p.c., 2005), or a 'distributed' one (Uriagereka, forthcoming). According to the second of these ideas, a derivation interfaces twice with the semantic component, first with conceptually structured material, then with intentionally structured material.

The two kinds of meaning coded at the levels of D-structure and LF, respectively, are not merely different and supported by structures differing in nature and complexity. They are also asymmetrically related, with the latter uni-directionally mapped from the former. As for their difference, consider that information of the sort that an argument of a verb plays the role of a patient or a theme, or that the verb is interpreted as telic or non-telic, is very different from information such as that one operator takes scope over another in a given conceptual structure, that a variable is in a referential position, that some item is focalized, or some given proposition is presented as true. Put in different terms, there are purely lexico-conceptual relations between words, which our mind can configure without yet making any particular sort of *judgement* about how things are in the world, and which are the material conceptual basis for these judgements. For example, we may have the lexical items *rotten* and *potato* and put them together to get the conceptual structure *rotten potato*, without yet judging that some particular object *is* a rotten potato (or that it *is* a potato, or that it *is* rotten). Having *concepts* of something, and having them arranged in a conceptual structure involving thematic and predicational relations is in this sense not the same as (using these concepts in) making judgements, talking *about* something, creating truth-functional and referential *commitments*, embedding a proposition in discourse—all things that I associate with the term 'intentional'. Analytic entailments, on the present view, are purely conceptual. They do not depend on how the world is or how one judges it to be. Hence their existence indirectly support the existence of this distinctive layer of information. You know from meaning (or linguistic structure) *alone*, and in fact could not know it from anything else, the claim is, that *The soup boiled* is necessarily entailed by *Sue boiled the soup.*

As for the *asymmetry* in the relation of the two kinds of information, LF is clearly mapped from D-structure and not vice versa, and the former cannot overwrite information coded in the latter. Typical LF-processes such as scope fixation are blind to conceptual information, and do not mesh with it: processes which fix, say, whether *a man* has wide or narrow scope in *Sue loves a man*, would not care what sort of thematic role Sue takes in this event (agent, experiencer, etc.), or whether its *referent* can have such a role, say if Sue is a computer. In this way it makes no sense to map concepts from judgements. Similarly, recall from Chapter 1 that if you think about people loving other people, you may arrive at the judgements in (7). But we cannot introduce two lexical items corresponding to these two judgements, as in (8):

(7) a. There is someone, x, that loves every y.
(7) b. For everyone, y, there is an x that loves y.
(8) a. x ping y
(8) b. y ping x.

Of course we can, but not if we do natural language analysis. This conclusion suggests that the old notion of D-structure did capture something real and needs to find a place in a Minimalist syntactic architecture with no levels of representations as well, a point we will revisit once more below.

If there were to be linguistic constraints on the structuring of conceptual information, are they syntactic ones? Could conceptual structure be non-linguistic altogether? Could it be, for example, that the only representational condition imposed on syntactic argument structure by external systems of thought would be that a verb like *love* requires a lover and a beloved, hence that its syntactic structuralization provides two argument positions? On this minimal view, Theta Theory would be denied a role in the grammar: the verb *love* need not have anything in common with the verb *stab*, for instance—except for having to have two arguments. Beyond that, no generalizations between what connects stabbers and lovers, on the one hand, or stabbees and beloveds, on the other, are asked for, wanted, or necessary. Syntax is a pure reflection of semantics, and the latter carries the explanatory burden. This view is attractive from a standard Minimalist point of view in one sense, for now we need not think hard about what linguistic constraint makes **Sue felt* ungrammatical; or what differentiates the role that *Sue* plays in sentences such as *John adored Sue, John kicked Sue, John hit Bill with Sue, John threw a kiss to Sue, John stood on top of Sue, John came from Sue,* or *Sue felt John on her skin.* Whatever conceptual differences there are between the thematic roles that Sue plays in these sentences (differences that cannot be denied), will, from the point of view under discussion, merely have to do with what we know about the world, but not syntax. We *know*, say, that adoring something is not the same as standing on top of it, or that kicking something is different from using it as a weapon, or feeling it. Similarly, it would not be a *grammatical* property of a word like *destroy* that the event it denotes has a natural end point (when the thing being destroyed is destroyed), or of a verb like *work* that the event it denotes *lacks* this sort of 'telicity'. All this is simply a matter of what we know about the world: we are not talking about facts here that we have to code somewhere in the linguistic system. Call this the 'austere view', which diminishes syntax or argument structure as an explanatory factor for verb denotation.

Despite the *a priori* attractiveness of the view, constraints of an apparently linguistic nature remain: constraints like the organization of linguistic expressions into head-complement relations that do not seem to follow from anything in the external world, or lexico-conceptual entailments that intimately correlate with syntactic complexity, hence do not seem independent of the latter's derivational build-up. As far as I know, visual aspects of the physical world in particular do not engender these constraints; nor do the necessary adaptivity of functional discriminations. Even if it were evolutionarily particularly adaptive to distinguish between actions (events) and their participants, or between behaviours and entities, and the relevant mental structures were available, this would not have to give us more than a distinction between predicates and arguments, for the coding of which we do not need even verbs.

The austere view will equally have to incorporate or deduce the *Thematic Criterion* as a condition on representations at LF (since there isn't D-structure, on the austere view): that, at this level, all syntactic arguments will have to have thematic roles, and all heads must have distributed all their thematic roles. Dispensing with such a representational constraint would mean that the Thematic Criterion is something that would be checked in *performance* (it would be a brute matter of meaning, not of grammar, to fix the thematic properties of a verb's arguments). For example, in the case of expressions like (9) or (10), nothing will be wrong grammatically:

(9) *Bill loves
(10) *John stinks the room

It will be *performance* only that balks at such objects, not our system of linguistic *knowledge*. Put differently, *Bill loves* should be as grammatical as *Bill loves Jim*, although it might cause some more difficulties of intelligibility (rather than grammaticality). But this seems to be the wrong prediction. If *Bill loves* receives an interpretation at all, it is the interpretation that *Bill loves someone or other*. It is not merely *hard to understand*, that is, but *outright impossible* for someone to love, although not to love something or someone. In (10), in turn, it seems like an intrinsic property of *stink* that if stinking is what you do, you do not do it to something or someone else.[5]

We are stuck, then, with something like the Thematic Criterion, no matter how austere a minimalist framework we would prefer. Minimally, we would have to assume that verbs are idiosyncratically endowed with thematic features that the grammar must respect; and thematic structure will now have to be checked, not at the level of D-structure (phrasal configurations prior to movements), but at LF, since D-structure, on the austere model and minimalism generally, is thought not to exist. But then, deprived of a syntactic level of D-structure, there essentially is no *rationale* for the Thematic Criterion any more. It becomes a gruesome, because brutely empirical, constraint with no principled explanation. As just pointed out, LF, which is the realm of chains rather than arguments, seems to have no concern with purely conceptual matters such as thematic relations, and the latter should thus not *be* constraints on LF-representations. A more specific problem is that it would be surprising that (9), repeated here as (11) should be ungrammatical, and not have the meaning of (12):

(11) *Bill loves
(12) Bill loves himself.

For on the austere view, we would precisely predict from the *semantics* of *love* that there is a second thematic feature that needs to be checked: something or someone has to be loved. But then, if *Bill* was lexically inserted as a complement to *loves* (or in object position), and there is a second role to be checked, that of the lover, why does *Bill* not move up the tree into the specifier of the verb and then T? The same argument would check

[5] Of course there is a meaning that hearers might assign to this expression for non-linguistic reasons (such as conversational charity, etc.), such as *John causes the room to get stinky*. But arguably, this is not a possible meaning of the verb *stink*.

two thematic roles, but if thematic roles are a matter of LF, why should this not be so?

In short, if the thematic structure of an expression that used to be coded at a level of D-structure becomes an LF-matter, we lack an explanation of why *Bill loves* is ungrammatical, or rather, marginally grammatical only with a different meaning, that Bill loves someone or other. Similar worries apply to the pair (13)–(14):

(13) Bill loves Bill
(14) Bill loves him.

These would seem to be the immediate ways, on the austere view, to express the thought that Bill loves himself. There are two arguments to be licensed, and the immediate way to license them in the way that you get co-reference is that you insert the same item. But the two arguments in both cases above crucially are not co-referential, and in fact we are facing what seems to be a cross-linguistically well-established fact: co-reference of two nominals is obviated under c-command within the local bounds of a clause.[6] There seems to be no semantic reason at all why the grammar should impose such an interpretive condition. The Thematic Criterion should better not be a constraint on LF-representations, then. As Chomsky himself remarks, theta-relatedness

> is a 'base property,' *complementary to feature checking*, which is a property of movement. (Chomsky 1995: 313; my emphasis)

But then, again, why is this not to admit that there is a purely configurational stage of the derivation, prior to movements and the creation of chains, with a correlating kind of semantics? Theta-relatedness, Chomsky says, is a 'property of the position of merger and its (very local) configuration'. Hence, by implication, it is not a property of movement. Chomsky since (1995) also discusses favourably a version of Hale and Keyser's (1993) theory of argument structure, in which theta-roles *are* in fact nothing other than configurations, attesting to the formal reality of D-structures, which capture these relations. Base properties of expressions, surely, projected monotonously into the rest of the derivation, are as real as ever. I therefore think that Uriagereka (forthcoming: ch. 2) is right in questioning the rhetoric behind proposals to 'abandon D-structure'. Chomsky (2006) argues that the idea of D-structure has become obsolete and in fact 'unformulable' in a system based on Merge. One early bad reason for this

[6] If there is to be co-reference within a clause, the grammar demands an explicit grammatical formative—*self*, which correlates with (or forces) an interpretation of obligatory co-reference.

minimalist conclusion is that D-structure as a level of representation in the grammar should not exist because it is not an interface level. This reasoning is circular, however, since it assumes an answer to what is the very question at issue: whether there might be two interfaces rather than one, one relating to thematic and conceptual information, one to intentional properties of the expression and its embedding in discourse. A more interesting reason is that levels of representations in the early technical sense had several properties that in the case of D-structures are neither empirically supported nor conceptually sound. To start with, any D-structure is a *unified* object that as such acts as a filter on derivations, but in current Merge-based accounts of the computational system, a derivation is built in separate chunks, which may be separately assembled and are then merged as units by a generalized transformation. Hence for a full derivation, there simply is no single locus of 'lexical insertion', although in some models there is a 'locus of lexical assembly', the Numeration (but this is intended to be a non-structured object).

However, this objection to D-structures, based on the existence of generalized transformations, can be countered by simply splitting a derivation into several phases or 'cascades', and thinking of each of these chunks of structure as having their own D-structure and LF-properties. This will be reasonable as long as other conditions on a structure's being a 'level of representation' are satisfied, such as having its own kind of assembly operations and relations established by them. In the case of D-structure, such distinctive features do seem to exist. As for operations, these are external Merge in the case of D-structure, and internal Merge in the case of LF; as for relations, these are configurational and theta-theoretic relations in the case of D-structure, and chains in the case of LF. Given that both kinds of structures have distinctive semantic correlates, we can sell them as 'interface representations' and thus save D-structures from the minimalist instinct of eliminating them, without thereby having compromised in any way the general methodology of the Minimalist Programme.

Another piece of support against the austere view and in favour of syntactic constraints is the extent to which conceptual relations are coupled with cross-linguistic *syntactic* generalizations and principles, with a possibility even to *deflate* theta-theoretic notions into syntactic (configurational) ones, as in the Hale–Keyser programme. In particular, it is peculiar that the thematic roles of the arguments that a given verb selects should be ordered into what is called the *thematic hierarchy*. There is some disagreement on what exactly the hierarchy of thematic roles is, but the following (the 'Larson–Baker' hierarchy: Baker 1996, 1997; Larson 1988) captures a wide agreement (the most deeply embedded argument being the lowest in the hierarchy):

[Agent [Theme [Goal/Source/Location]]].[7]

Cross-linguistically, the phrase containing the Agent argument is always higher in the underlying syntactic structure than the patient or 'Theme' argument. An Agent always becomes the *external* argument of a verb (the Spec of VP), while a theme is an *internal* argument, a complement of V. An instantiation of this hierarchy would be the transitive verb construction *Mary passed the ring to John*, where Mary is the Agent, the ring is the Theme, and John is the Goal. The picture is complicated through an alternation of the previous example with *Mary passed John the ring*, in which the Goal acquires prominence over the Theme. Indeed, if there is disagreement on the relative positions of thematic roles, Goal is placed typically above Theme (as assumed, for example, by Hale and Keyser (1993: 65), who also assume a slightly richer hierarchy by having the role of *Experiencer* just below that of Agent). The case of unaccusative verbs such as *come*, on the other hand, universally seems to allow for no ambiguity in the respective Goal/Theme positions and supports the Baker–Larson hierarchy (Baker 1996). If that hierarchy is adopted, one will have to adopt a movement analysis for the cases where the Goal appears higher than the Theme. This would be to say, not that the other hierarchy is not real, but that it is derived. It mediates and restricts the mapping of lexical items into their respective syntactic positions in a universal and systematic fashion.

According to the hypothesis of 'universal Thematic Alignment', if the theta-role of an argument X is higher than the theta-role of a second argument Y, then X c-commands Y at the level of D-structure.[8] To the extent that this is true, we can systematically predict, from the grammatical position of an argument in a syntactic tree, what role the filler of this argument will play at the event picked out by the verb. This is very surprising and unexpected, at least on the austere view we started out with: intuitively, if the conceptual structure of a mental representation is nothing that intrinsically connects with the syntactic structure of language, and syntax is just a reflection of it, there should not be any universal restrictions on the ordering of argument roles. Thematic roles like Agent or Patient, *prima facie*, are *conceptual* notions, not grammatical ones, and they should have no direct correlation with grammatical notions such as subject and object.[9]

[7] This is a basic hierarchy: there are other thematic roles one might differentiate, but they can be accommodated on the above scheme. I will assume this applies, in particular, to *Instrument* (see Baker 1996: fn. 18).

[8] See Webelhuth (1995: 31), Baker (1996, 1997).

[9] The thematic hierarchy in particular correlates grammatically with the fixation of subject function: if a verb has a single Theme argument, it becomes its subject, as in *The man came*; in the context

The correlation between argument role asymmetries and structural relations is expressed in Baker's very general *Uniformity of Theta Assignment Hypothesis* (UTAH), according to which for any two languages (or any two items in a single language) (Baker 1988: 46) the following holds:

UTAH:
Identical thematic relationships between items are represented by identical structural relationships between those items at the level of D-structure.

UTAH hypothesizes a homomorphic relationship between conceptual and syntactic structure, on a universal scale. Indeed, if I told you that *Gors barkled the gloob*, you would immediately understand that *the gloob* was the Theme, and *Gors* the Agent: syntax tells you this. In fact we know not only that syntax plays that role, but also that it takes *dominance* over other sources of information that help to determine the conceptual structure of an expression, such as semantic or morphological information (like the English suffix *-ize*): thematic information determined by the latter sources may be overruled by the former (Lidz and Gleitman 2004).

Again, such findings are unwanted from the perspective of the austere view. Non-linguistically conceived event conceptualizations should be translatable on this view into syntactic forms without encountering such constraints, which thus again raise their heads, just as they did above in the case of *Bill loves*. As Massimo Piattelli-Palmarini points out in personal conversation:

by means of adjunctions we can optionally specify any 'thematic' information we want (source, composition, common/exceptional, effortless/effortful etc.) but the *kind* of mandatory information given by theta roles is fixed and universal, even when more of the same kind can be recursively inserted. It's not too far fetched (though evidence is hard to be found) to imagine that some animal species can have some concepts of source, composition, effort etc. but the emergence of the machinery of language constrained this in us quite severely, making some conceptualizations mandatory and structurally fixed while others are optional and expressible only by means of adjunction. (Piattelli-Palmarini, p.c.)

One way of rephrasing this is: something appears to have happened in evolution that restrained the recursive generation of ever more thematic roles added adjunctively to an event description, and as long as we see linguistic/syntactic constraints operative in the kind of thematic structures that we universally find in human language, there will have to be something about language that is

of a Goal, the Theme always outranks the Goal in the sense that the latter can never become the subject—unless there is an Agent, in which case the Theme can never be subject (and remains higher than Goal, one may assume, if it was higher in the absence of the Agent).

responsible for them. The UTAH above is explicitly defined to apply at D-structure, moreover, which, as we have argued, a Minimalist grammar should and can accommodate. By contrast, defenders of the austere view will tend to assume architectures of grammars that are 'monostratal' in the sense of assuming one single level of syntactic representation. Baker remarks on these:

> Since the syntax proper is so tightly constrained, these [monostratal] approaches tend to take on a rather asyntactic flavor, with much of the explanatory burden being carried by the lexicon and/or the semantics rather than syntax. As such, they shade into functionalist approaches, which downplay the existence of syntax as something distinct from semantics, discourse, pragmatics, and diachrony. (Baker 1997: 74)

Minimalism *is* monostratal in intention too; moreover, the connection between functionalist approaches and Minimalism seems to become stronger the more we see it sneaking in purely representational conditions such as the Thematic Criterion, motivated as demands imposed by assumed external interpretive systems. Functionalist approaches play down the role of syntax as worthy of separate study and focus on the way it subserves and interfaces with cognition, lexical semantics, and discourse. But Minimalism is an attempt to reduce the syntactic apparatus too, to eliminate what is not a reflection of a (preferably optimal) way of satisfying the assumed bare output conditions. Referring to the Principles and Parameters framework, Baker continues:

> This approach allows nontrivial syntactic derivations internal to the language faculty, and... attempts to constrain the interface between conceptual representations and syntactic representations in a particularly tight way. (Baker 1997: 74)

The more tightly constrained syntax becomes, the more feasible the project of explanatory adequacy for conceptual structures becomes. Maybe unsurprisingly, however,

> in practice the result of this approach [P&P] was often not deeper analyses of interesting phenomena, but rather a banishing of those phenomena from the domain of syntax—typically into the realm of the lexicon. Within the terms of the theory, this seemed regrettable: if one is going to have a nontrivial syntax at all, then that syntax should be required to pull its own weight. (ibid.)

But then, something like the UTAH precisely makes us hope that lexical-conceptual matters *need* not be evaded in syntax, and syntax can account for at least some aspects of conceptual structure. UTAH is intended to *show* that syntax can pull its own weight, since it allows us to systematically predict, on a universal scale, thematic relationships between lexical items from *structural* relationships between them on a syntactic level of D-structure. The fruitfulness of Baker's UTAH in language analysis would in this way seem to be a strong empirical argument *against* the austere view of thematic structure, which makes it basically a reflection of non-linguistic constraints, and a fortiori *for* a D-structure component.

Again, if one is committed to giving up on D-structure, one might code the relevant syntax of event conceptualization at LF. Then the UTAH will become another representational condition on possible LFs. This representational condition, one will stipulate, is met through derivational history: the *order* in which arguments are merged with the verbal head. To be at a different position in the thematic hierarchy, one will say, *is* to be merged with a given syntactic object at different stages of the derivation. Whatever is 'first-merged' becomes the internal argument of the verb; whatever is higher must be merged later. We in particular make the prediction that if there is a Theme *and* a Goal, the *Theme* will have to be later-merged. If there is, in addition, an *Agent* argument, it will have to be *last*-merged, outside the maximal projection of the verb. One will moreover have to ensure that UTAH is a constraint, not on the syntactic organization of verbal arguments, simpliciter, but on that of the *foots* (the lower parts) of the relevant LF-chains (given that the UTAH does not hold of structures derived by transformations). This indeed is what Baker (1997, section V) suggests, when considering the possible implementation of the UTAH in the Minimalist Program. Yet, recall that the moment one admits that all that matters to the UTAH are the foots of chains and the grammar is structured so as to have to keep track of them, one would once more seem to concede that the grammar makes a crucial difference between what is base-generated and what is not, or between what I call conceptual structures and intentional ones.

This argument affects conceptual structure in the sense of a D-structure component only, however, as opposed to a sub-lexical syntactic structure *internal* to a lexical atom. And as we saw in Section 3.1, it is the apparent necessary semantic entailments at the level of the lexical *atom* that we need to explain—and yet, paradoxically, that it seems we *must not* explain by appeal to internal semantic complexity in these atoms. Even if conceptual structure is essentially subject to syntactic constraints, as I have suggested in this section, this is not to say anything about whether sublexical conceptual structure is syntactic, too. Let us, however, rewind the tape of generative grammar and try replaying the generative semantics theme of splitting the lexical atom, hopefully without falling into the mistake of equating conceptual structure internal to lexical atoms with normal syntagmatic syntax, on the one hand, and avoiding the Jackendoffian option of entirely separating conceptual structure from the structures inherent to language, on the other.

3.3 Play it again, Sam

Hale and Keyser's (1993, 2002) theory of argument structure suggests we can go beyond Baker's conclusions, discussed above, to a stronger one. Hale and Keyser (HK) make a particularly important contribution to the question whether, and in what sense, conceptual structure *is* (a part of) syntax, after all, hence nothing non-linguistic or 'thought'-like that is then somehow 'mapped' to syntax or 'coded' by it. The basic idea is that theta-roles can be *identified* with certain phrase-structural configurations:

Argument structure is syntactic, necessarily, since it is to be identified with the syntactic structures projected by lexical heads. (HK, 1993: 55)

Moreover, on their view the configurational position of an argument may be the result of processes of head-movement that are subject to standard syntactic constraints—lending again support to the inherently syntactic character of conceptual structures of the basic thematic kind. Strictly speaking, in this framework, theta-roles are theoretically *redundant*—it is not that they are not for real, but that they fall out from properties of the grammar. This view would also explain a fact noted by Pietroski and Uriagereka (in Uriagereka 2002), that theta-roles are never a part of any natural object-language (they are not formatives in it). Why is it that no language seems to have lexical synonyms for the (metalanguage) expressions 'Theme', 'Agent', and so on? If HK are right, we could envisage this simple explanation: they are *formal* notions, following trivially from the architecture of the system itself. It is not that non-linguistic event conceptualization directs the forming of linguistic event representations, but that syntax as given on independent grounds directs the organization of the thematic relations needed to configure mental representations of events, and interpret ongoings out there in the light of them—an internalist conclusion again.

Assuming heads *can*, though *need* not, take complements and specifiers, we should, HK predict, first find argument structures that consist of a head *alone*: this is an argument-structural configuration which in English is paradigmatically realized by Nouns (see 15a below): possibly, complement and specifier—true heads is what Nouns *are*. Secondly we should find simple transitive patterns corresponding to a head taking a complement (alone), a pattern of the form H-XP, with H=Head, paradigmatically realized in English by the category, V (15b). Thirdly, we should find heads projecting *both* complements and specifiers resulting in a structure YP-[H-XP] (15c), canonically realized in English by prepositions. These we may view, more generally, as being organized around a 'relational' head, *R*, whose complement can also be an adjective A. This case realizes the fourth *a priori* possibility, that we have a head and a specifier alone, for this is precisely what adjectives in HK are: heads requiring a specifier. Fifth, HK argue that there should be a 'free' option of *combining* the previous lexical representation structures. In particular, if we plug the third configuration (15c) into the complement position of the second (15b), we obtain the configuration H_1-[Y-[H_2-X/A]], in which the specifier of the lower head (H_2) has now become the object of the higher one (H_1) (see 15d). Moreover, (15c) itself at least in its verbal version may be seen as composite, since it contains, on the one hand, a simple transitive structure as in (15b) (the relational head needs a complement), and satisfies the specifier/subject requirement of the adjective (the verb as such makes no such demands), on the other:[10]

(15) a. H — e.g.: *trouble*

(15) b.

```
   H
  / \
 H   XP
```

e.g.: *[$_V$ make trouble]*

(15) c.

```
   H
  / \
 Y   H
    / \
   H   X/H
```

e.g.: (pound) *[$_R$ [the nails] [$_R$ into[$_{NP}$ the wall]]];*
(make) *[$_R$[the leaves] [$_R$ turn[$_A$red]]]*

(15) d.

```
     H1
    / \
  H1   H2
      / \
     Y   H2
        / \
      H2   X/H
```

e.g.: *[$_V$ pound [$_R$ [the nails] [$_R$ into[the wall]]]]*
[$_{V2}$ make[$_V$ [the leaves] [$_{V1}$ turn[red]]]]

These four configurations are, according to HK, the only ones in natural languages ever projected by a lexical head—and these lexical projections are all their theory is concerned with. Thus we see that their lexical conceptual structures in particular exclude the external argument (EA), which HK, with Koopman and Sportiche (1991), in their sentence-syntactic subject position, take to be an adjunct to the full verbal projection: it occupies no complement

[10] As HK (2002: ch.7) note, Navajo for example does not distinguish the two versions of (15c), with the adjectival version consistently realized by V.

or specifier position *within* that lexical projection. More specifically, EA and *v*P are adjoined in a *Small Clause* relation, which conceptually expresses a *predication* (see Moro 2000). That the EA ends up as a sentence-syntactic subject may still be said to be enforced by principles of lexical projection, though: the argument HK offer is that a fully specified VP with internal arguments specified is intrinsically a *predicate*, which as such, if Full Interpretation holds, requires a *subject*. HK argue on the same grounds for the fact that lexical syntactic structures of type (15c) must include a specifier: the P/R-N/AP configuration is a predicate too, its specifier being a 'subject' of sorts. So a fully transitive structure like *My age made my hair (turn) grey* basically contains two predications, with one a proper part of the other. It is interesting that this embedding of predications only works if what is the *subject* of the lower predication in (16a) in lexical syntax, is turned into a sentential-syntactic *object* in (16b). (16c) is the 'synthetic' form of (16b), in which the lower verbal head V_2 of the lexical-syntactic configuration (15d) has head-adjoined to the higher verbal head, V_1:

(16) a. *my hair* [turn grey]
(16) b. my age (made) [*my hair* [(turn) grey]]
(16) c. my age turned$_{V1 + V2}$ [*my hair* [t grey]]

For this account to work, predication needs to be carefully distinguished from the argument-taking of heads, as it is structurally different and has different semantic effects: it is only the interaction of these two syntactic relations that yields the universal structuralizations of theta-roles found in human languages.

To elaborate on this issue, if the argument structure configuration underlying (16a) is not inserted in a monadic configuration of type (15b), then of course the lexical-syntactic subject of (16a) eventually becomes a sentence-syntactic subject. Like all other arguments that require Case-licensing for their full realization, it has to vacate its initial place in its lexical syntactic configuration and associate to the higher functional projections of the clause. In short, it is only in a *bi-clausal* syntactic structure that the lower subject has to become an object (perhaps this is the very origin of objects). As for the external argument EA, we see that it does not receive its theta-role from a position within the verbal projection, ever: not in the unergative case of *John laughed*, where all the verbal head projects is an internal Theme-argument ([$_N$ laugh]); not in the case of unaccusatives such as *The leaves turned red*, because *The leaves* is an inner subject in lexical syntax first, and becomes an EA only in sentence-syntax; not in the case of transitives, where the EA is never even an internal subject to start with. In all three cases, then, the theta-role of the sentence-subject is licensed not by V but its full projection (*v*P), which as such (as a full projection, not a head) is predicated of the subject, in a process different from argument-taking in lexical syntax. In the unergative or unaccusative case, this moment of predication happens earlier in the derivation; in the transitive and bi-clausal case (where two verbal heads are involved), the process is delayed until after the second clausal unit is constructed. In that case, no predication takes place internal to the lexical projection: a sentence can only include one main predication, just as and probably for the same reason that it can only bear one truth-value, even though it may include multiple *clauses*, each of which is propositional (or has a subject-predicate structure).

It is interesting, as Noam Chomsky points out in personal conversation, that this very proposal makes it *harder* to draw a connection between human argument structure and agent–action–patient schemas that perhaps do exist in non-human animals (see in particular Arbib 2005 on this). For now we see that the agent-argument is not even *part* of lexical syntactic structures. In other words, human conceptual structure and event conceptualization in non-humans[11] may obey different structural principles. More generally, the process we have described is structurally very specific, and contains linguistically-specific terms, such as complement and specifier, predication, verb, and argument. It is hard to see how the same conceptual structure might be fabricated in the complete absence of these linguistic structural elements. It is also interesting that if we did wish to ascribe conceptual structures to non-human animals, it would seem most plausible to ascribe *mono*-clausal VPs to them, hence not bi-clausal *v*P constructions requiring a subject. But VP as such (the lower V projection in bi-clausal lexical representation structures) by hypothesis is not a predicate; it first becomes the complement of another V. In short, the VP is an encapsulated unit that might have evolved separately, without predication, in a way that a *v*P might not, which requires predication (and more complex processes of verbal head-movement, on which see below). Note also that the entire HK theory follows on the basis of a small set of basic elements of argument structure, and in particular the four (and further reducible) basic argument structure types. It is not clear what it should be in the non-linguistic (semantic, visual, sensorimotor, etc.) domain that would account for similar such severe limitations on which thoughts we can think in the initial D-structural phase of a syntactic derivation.

Example (16c) anticipates the most crucial element of HK argument-structure theory, the process of head-adjunction called *conflation*, to which

[11] This is to say: *if* there are indeed event-representations in, say, the monkey: although the difference is vague, I suppose there may be a crucial difference between having action schemata and having *thoughts about* actions that have a combinatorial syntax. Why in particular would the mental action schema 'I grasp banana' involve an act of predication, in the technical linguistic sense we have been analysing here?

we now turn. It is conflation that results in a version of lexical decomposition, and a replaying of the theme of generative semantics, although in quite another tune. HK's assumption is that in cases of conflation, the upper verbal head of (16c) is phonologically empty at the level of lexical syntax. Empty phonological matrices of this kind are not possible at the level of sentences, so they trigger the putative process of conflation, which *supplies* the phonological matrix needed by taking it from the lower lexical head. All this leads to the 'surface form', for example of (16c). In a bare phrase structure framework (Chomsky 1995) of the sort HK assume, this process will go from the direct complement of the selecting higher head V_1 to this very head (see (15d)), and hence be strictly local. Specifically, on the theory of labelling of Chomsky (1995), at the point in the derivation where V_1 merges with the configuration projected by V_2, the lower head V_2 is strictly all that the computational system (i.e. Merge) 'sees': it represents all the information that is syntactically relevant about the lower event. If V_2 is then conflated, we obtain forms like (16d, 16e):

(16) d. My age greyed my hair
(16) e. The cook thickened the broth.

Both of these HK would interpret as a sequence of conflations in strictly local head–complement relations, first of the A (grey/thick) into the V_2 (yielding the verbs *grey* and *thicken*, as in *my hair greyed* or *the broth thickened*), then of the conflated V_2 into the empty upper verbal head. NPs may conflate too, as in intuitively denominal verbs such as (17a) or (17b):[12]

(17) a. *bag, bank, bottle, can, shelve*, etc.
(17) b. *bandage, bar, butter, saddle, spice*, etc.

Here the NP, for example *shelf*, conflates with the head P, which projects, and in turn conflates with the V, to yield the surface structure *shelve the books*:

(18)
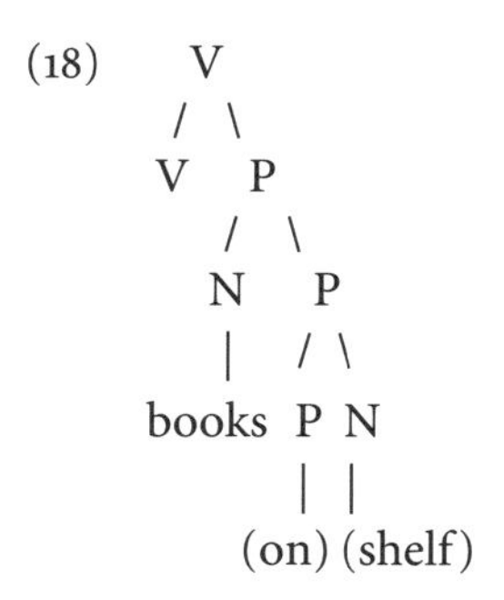

[12] I assume, following Uriagereka (forthcoming, ch. 2) that contrary to what HK propose the lexical representation structures for (17a) and (17b) are identical, on the lines of (18).

Semantically, the default relational head P on Hale and Keyser's view corresponds to a relation of 'coincidence': the books undergo a path of motion which ends with books being *on* the shelf (the saddle on the horse, the butter on the bread, etc.), which is their terminal location. Interestingly, Hale and Keyser categorize the relevant relation that is established as one of *possession*, in a broad sense of the term: 'the complement of P corresponds to the entity "possessed", while the specifier, or inner subject, corresponds to the "possessor" ' (HK 1997: 36). That is, the horse comes to 'have' the saddle, or the shelf the books (we return to possession in Chapter 5). What interests us in the rest of this chapter will be the idea of such syntax–semantics correspondences and what role the process of conflation plays in them.

One immediate answer might be: none, for the synthetic forms of these derived verbs are assumed to be neither syntactically nor semantically different from their 'analytic' counterparts, as in (19):

(19) a. put the books on the shelf
(19) b. put the saddle on the horse.

The same possessive relation is established in both instances. That is, conflation is a process that is semantically inert. Indeed, HK are as explicit as one would like that conflation on their view is a purely *morpho-phonological* process. The shift of the phonetic signature of the conflated items is invisible to the syntax, to which phonetic signatures are 'irrelevant':

> conflation leaves the entire structure in tact, unchanged, in respect to syntactic and semantic structure (HK 2002: 70).

But this, if we wish to avoid the pitfalls of generative semantics, is precisely the conclusion we have to *avoid*: sublexical syntactic structure is precisely *not*, at least in the general case, *transparent* to the syntax and subject to a compositional interpretation. If, say, the underlying structure of *We rolled the ball down the hill* was literally like that of *We made the ball roll down the hill*, or, even better, *We made-roll the ball down the hill*, we would run into entirely familiar problems rehearsed in Section 2.1 relating to ambiguities of modification in the analytic (decomposed) case that do not seem to exist in the synthetic one (with just the verbal form *roll*): a modifier attached to the synthetic form cannot distinctively target two verbal heads (although see below for qualifications of this claim).

I take this as evidence that conflation in fact *has* a crucial semantic consequence: specifically, it may create what is in effect a novel *name* for a more complex event than we had before. Being merely named (rather than described) by the conflated phonological matrix, its internal structure now cannot be 'seen'. This would in turn fundamentally cohere with the fact that denominal verbs are strictly *lexical* ones for HK: they are *words* listed in the lexicon which as such have to be *learned*, and are inserted as such in the D-structure component of the grammar.[13] For it is a crucial aspect of lexical items *that they are names*: their semantic function cannot be more complex than that (see Chapter 5). More complex forms of reference, as I will argue towards the end of the book, start *later* than the lexicon, at the level of *sentential syntax* with appropriate functional projections. As HK put it themselves:

> In reality, all verbs are to some extent phrasal idioms, that is, syntactic structures that must be learned as the conventional 'names' for various dynamic events. (HK 1993: 96)

In other words, once we have formed a complex word, its internal structure becomes largely opaque to semantic interpretation, as in an idiom (largely, because there is a limited extent to which syntax can 'penetrate' or is sensitive to the internal decompositional structure of a verb, again as in the case of idioms; see Section 3.4 for this extent). That this intermediate conclusion and the name-solution to the problem of lexical decomposition are nonetheless not *enough*, we shall see. The moral to be drawn for now is that *semantic atomicity and syntactic complexity (or being derived) are not mutually exclusive.* This is the crucial point to realize when we turn to assess the attack on HK argument-structure theory which Fodor and Lepore (1999) have launched under the heading *Don't play that again, Sam.* Before we turn to that in the next section, let us turn to the explanatory benefits of HK's account.

HK can explain, for example, why (20) is impossible:

(20) *He shelved the books on

It is impossible because the complement of the relational head in the lower transitive construction cannot, because of the locality of conflation, skip the prepositional head on its way up the tree. Moreover, it cannot conflate into

[13] The latter fact shows up in the case of *saddle* as with other synthetic words, also with respect to canonicity effects. Saddling a horse is not simply to put a saddle on a horse—just anywhere. There is a canonical place for the saddle to be. Which one is simply not a piece of systematic knowledge, but something that has to be brutely learned. *Saddle* is a typical lexical item (or idiom) in this regard, and characteristically *not* a syntactic structure.

the P-head because that head is not phonologically empty. We also understand why (21) is impossible:

(21) *The clown laughed the children.

For the argument-structure of *laugh* is the transitive (22):

```
(22)      V
         / \
        V   laugh
```

This is a fully evaluated argument structure which is not a predicate. If it comes to be part of a sentence, as in (23):

(23) The children laughed

then *The children* is an argument *external* to the lexical projection of the verb. For (21) to be possible, *the children* would have to be an internal subject of the verbal projection, and the latter's head would have to conflate with the higher causative head. The absence of an internal subject in (22) explains the necessary absence of a sentence-syntactic object in (21). A similar line of reasoning predicts the possibility of (24) along with the impossibility of (25):

(24) The pigs got mud on the wall
(25) *we got the pigs mud on the wall
(with the putative meaning: *We brought it about that the pigs got mud on the wall*)

Sentence (24) is possible because *mud* is the inner subject of the argument-structure projected by the lower relational head (there is no conflation in this instance). *The pigs* is an external (not a lexical) argument which becomes a subject of a predication. Only if it was an internal argument could the causative construction in (24) again be 'causativized', as in (25) (see HK, 1993: 87). But argument structure is too impoverished for that, and the predication of the subject *The pigs* cannot occur embedded as a further argument. Apparent restrictions on argument stucture explain why there is, conceptually, no such thing as causing a causing. As a final illustration, the theory of conflation makes us understand why we cannot, in any language (HK claim), say either (26) or (27):

(26) *He booked on the shelf
(meaning: *he put books on the shelf*)

(27) *It cowed a calf
(meaning: *a cow had a calf*)

In (26), the putative conflation of the internal subject into the higher *v* violates the locality restriction on conflation, which has to be from the complement. This makes sense if conflation is concomitant to Merge. In the lexical representation structure underlying (26), *books* is never complement of the higher V. As for (27), we can have *A cow calved*, with the noun *calf* being the complement of a lexical V-head. But for (27) to be possible, not the complement but the subject has to conflate (downwards), and this is impossible.

Note there is nothing *conceptually* impossible about (26)–(27). Language-independent semantics does not predict these facts. *Grammar* forbids assigning them the interpretations indicated.

3.4 Exploding the lexical atom

Let us turn now to Fodor and Lepore's critique of the idea of structure internal to words, for which all we have been rehearsing is just a bad revival of generative semantics—playing Sam's theme again, and not even in another tune. It is, in short, a failure to pay a dutiful respect to the reality of the word-boundary. But this is not true. First, they suggest (e.g. Fodor and Lepore 1999: 449) that on HK's view *do a song* is a derivational source for *sing*. But HK make no such claim. Thus there is a determiner projection in the structure underlying *do a song*, but there is no determiner in the complement lexical-syntactic argument-configuration projected by V. Nor is there an item *do* in their lexical representation structure of *sing*. If there was, conflation would not be possible in the first place. The configuration [V-[$_N$ song]] moreover is said by HK not to be 'derived' in any standard sense: it is a 'virtual' structure for them, to be conceived as a mere representation of the lexical-projective properties of the head in question. Conflation itself is not a movement rule, but an immediate accompaniment of Merge, which is the only engine of derivational processes that there is: once Merge discovers an empty phonological matrix in a local configuration, conflation happens. Hence there is no such thing going on in HK's argument as 'derivations' from an underlying paraphrase or 'semantic structure' with a compositional interpretation. If syntactically complex event representations are effectively names, this conclusion follows immediately, in fact.

Secondly, Fodor and Lepore misunderstand HK's argument of why (20), say, is impossible. The source of the confusion appears to be Fodor and Lepore's mixing up of a derivational approach to human syntax with a theory determining a set of 'well-formed formulas' of a formal language (a term irrelevant to the natural language that Fodor and Lepore address, cf. 1999: 451).

I interpret their distinction between 'impossible *rules*' (like subject lowering) and 'impossible *structures*' in this light. The latter, for them, are configurations that are forbidden by the grammar. They are impossible because of their phrasal 'geometry', their ill-formedness being 'intrinsic and hence independent of any assumption about how [the relevant configuration] was derived' (Fodor and Lepore 1999: 452). But the point of a derivational approach to syntax (which I take HK to endorse) is the *intensional* characterization of possible grammatical structures. Put differently, these *have* no existence irrespective of how they are generated. The very notion of a 'structure' that HK use should be regarded as a mere abstraction from derivational dynamics and their uses at interfaces. The structure underlying the impossible (20) is not impossible as a configurational structure that has some kind of Platonic existence, but it is impossible because it cannot arise through a sequence of permissible derivational steps and conflations accompanying them.

Thirdly, and relatedly, Fodor and Lepore charge HK with a confusion between an assertion to the effect that a certain *expression* is impossible and an assertion to the effect that a certain *meaning* is impossible. The charge is that HK do no more than show that a certain *expression* could not mean a certain thing (as in **It cowed a calf*), since its derivational history is an impossible one, but that this is not in the least an argument against the fact that there is that relevant *meaning*. At the very most, according to Fodor and Lepore, it shows that *no word of any natural language could have* that meaning. But there is a hidden assumption in this argument: that a word is a mere 'sign', and is as such more or less irrelevant, as meaning is something necessarily independent of it. Form is irrelevant, what matters is meaning (denotation). On this assumption, we could indeed ask: if generative grammarians come up with the idea that a certain word is impossible because of the violation of a certain syntactic constraint, so what? This shows only that a *word* is impossible, not a meaning. If a word is a mere sign, what, indeed, prevents us from inventing a *primitive* sign to denote it, if no natural languages—all the worse for them—succeed in denoting it, due to the disturbing idiosyncrasies of human syntax? From this point of view there is simply no sense we can give to the notion of a 'possible' (or 'impossible') meaning. In virtue of *what* should it *be* impossible?

But then, this is not how HK talk, or should talk. They make no claims about 'possible' (or 'impossible') meanings. This is because their notion of meaning (and word) is narrower than that of Fodor and Lepore. For Fodor and Lepore, if a Martian word corresponded to the English verb *cow* in **It cowed a calf*, this would show that HK are wrong in saying that a word with that meaning is impossible. But HK do not extend their claims to words and meanings in a Martian dialect. The topic is features of human language. If there is a structure that is not generatable in the latter, this says nothing about creatures with another nature; nor does it say anything about humans when they use other properties of their minds than language (and, for example, intentionally violate syntactic constraints). In our general cognition there is, to be sure, the thought to be found that *A cow had a calf*: that thought, if I am right, is the intrinsic linguistic meaning of an expression with a particular syntactic structure. But English could not express it in the form of a word *to cow.* What decides over possibility and impossibility in syntax is not that we can think certain thoughts, or wish to express them. To sum this line of counter-criticism up, HK deal with human linguistic meaning only—meaning *as depending* on linguistic form. At that level, the impossibility of a certain form is what explains the impossibility of a certain linguistic meaning.[14]

Let us now return to the question of the language-independence and possible semantic basis of the basic conceptual structures we are discussing in this chapter. We have made earlier remarks in the previous section suggesting that the language-independence of conceptual structures we express in the argument-structure system probably does not hold. Yet let us now consider another such proposal. Sometimes HK themselves—much as Baker (1997), who heavily builds on HK—give their theory a certain *semantic drift.* In Baker's paper, a semantic motivation for verbal decomposition is explicit in the strong sense that the structure is said to be supported by a (non-syntactic) 'conceptual structure' as provided in a 'lexical semantics' for words like *kill* (in the tradition of Jackendoff, cf. Jackendoff 2002: 337–9). Baker argues, in particular, that the conceptual structure (in this non-linguistic sense), (28), rationalizes the fact that in the Larsonian (1988) double object construction, which underlies the HK theory as well, the agent NP is the argument of the higher verb, while the Theme is the argument of the embedded one:

(28) [X CAUSE [Y BE/BECOME PREDICATE]]

This of course is reminiscent of the generative semantics analysis of *kill* in terms of

[14] None of this is to say that meaning in Fodor and Lepore's very general sense is not a topic of inquiry, but while there is a study of linguistic representations, visual representations, mental representations of limb motions, etc., it is not at all obvious how there could be, over and above these sorts of studies, a study of 'meaning'.

(29) CAUSES Y TO BECOME NOT ALIVE.

Taking this conceptual structure to be independently given on semantic grounds—an assumption that of course meets the full critique of Fodor and Lepore, and strikes me as circular, over and above arguments in the previous section—Baker specifically proposes that:

> it is very attractive to identify the causative part of the lexical semantic representation [28] with the higher verb of the Larsonian shell, and the be/become+predicate part with the lower verb position. (Baker 1997: 123, a view that is said to be shared by Hale and Keyser as well as by Chomsky 1995: 315–16)

Baker explicitly considers, if not defends, the option that 'syntactic structure is a projection of gross lexical semantic structure'. One remark of Baker's makes very clear what he takes that to mean:

> On the semantic version of the Larsonian structure, the agent NP is not generated in the higher VP shell because there is no room for it in the lower VP; rather, it is generated there because it is the argument of a cause verb (or configuration), and hence is an agent by definition. (Baker 1997: 124; see also Baker 2003: 79–81)

In short, the Agent argument appears where it appears because *v* (or V_1 in our presentation above) means CAUSE—the meaning, that is, of the English lexical word *cause*. Agents, by definition, are things that do such causing. But now, questions familiar from the history of generative semantics raise their heads. Uriagereka (forthcoming: ch. 2), in particular asks how we know what *v* means. We cannot rely on intuitions as to what the sublexical constituents of verbs like *cut*, *roll*, or *laugh* are. Moreover, the empirical syntactic evidence on the strength of which the existence of *v* can be made plausible is not what supports this 'semantic version' of the Larsonian shell analysis. What, in fact, does it show that other languages have *v* overt? On the face of it, *v* is not a word expressing CAUSE. Where it appears overtly, it might be a mere syntactic formative that marks the transitivity of a causative verb, but does not as such carry a particular semantic interpretation—or not that of the English word *cause*.

Baker's proposal in this way shares some of the problems of the earlier generative semantics attempts. It is an improvement over the latter to find syntactic arguments for lexical decomposition, if the alternative is the usual kind of 'conceptual' decomposition, as when it is said that *food* means *substance+edible, + something else*. The latter kind of decomposition is purely intuitive or introspective, and is obviously not a success story, since we seem to be unable to specify the 'something else' without essentially presupposing an understanding of *food*. But the improvement derived from replacing intuited conceptual structures by semantically relevant syntactic ones disappears once this kind of syntactic decomposition is again being grounded in controversial lexical semantic decompositions. Looking at some concrete claims, Baker argues that *laughed* really is a monadic predicate of events, meaning that laughter happened. *John laughed* specifically means that *John was the immediate cause of an instance of this kind of event.* I take this suggestion not to be entailed in anything that HK say, and it raises the old questions. Is John *causing*, in some literal sense, his laughter at all? It would seem the laughter just happens. When, in general, is one an Agent, and when, in general, is causation really 'immediate'? These are questions to be addressed if it is supposed to matter that *v* means CAUSE and its argument is a causer, in some determinate and conceptually defined sense.

It seems we might more usefully make a weaker claim (although this will not be my final proposal): that the external argument indicates an event participant that relates *externally* to given events of *rolling*, *shelving*, or whatever—events which as such have some completeness and semantic independence, by virtue of their two VP-internal arguments. That would imply that 'agentiveness' is a way of *relating* externally to a given event, but not, in a sentence where the verb *cause* does not appear overtly, that there are *two events*, one of causing, and one of rolling, shelving, boiling, or whatever. 'Relating externally to a given event' surely is an important *aspect* of causing it, in fact a logical precondition for it. But, on my suggestion, it is not a *new* event. Indeed, it does not seem plausible to say that once it comes to the question of the origin or efficient cause of a given fully configured event, *the causing of it* is another event (as e.g. Pietroski 2002: 100, argues, who calls Anton's action of initiating the event of boiling, an event). Intuitively, there is *one* event we talk about when we claim that *Anton boiled the soup*, not two, and the question to ask is how we derive this result. Matters are entirely different in the case of *Anton caused the soup to boil*, where we may crucially have two separate events in mind that need not even be very tightly connected. Thus the causing event may be of a very distinctive sort, for example in a context where we observe Anton to manipulate very infelicitously various buttons and wires on his stove, for a stretch of time that exceeds by far the usual time it takes to initiate a soup's boiling. Commenting on this scene, we might say *Look at this, Anton is causing the soup to boil.* It is clear here that the causing and the boiling are events that may be implied to be crucially distinct. These observations are exactly what Baker's 'semantic version' of the Larsonian construction does not suggest, where it is argued that the concept CAUSE figures as an interpretively relevant primitive in the underlying structure.

The concept–judgement distinction made earlier serves my purposes here well. The internal structuring of overtly mono-morphemic causative verbs indicates that a single complex event expressed by a doubly headed verb phrase is *presented* by the speaker/thinker in a certain way. *Anton boiled the soup*, as a whole and as a sentence-syntactic expression, encodes a *judgement* that contains a single event as its conceptual basis, an event that moreover contains a part, the result state of Anton's boiling the soup. The judgement is not a new event: it does not add any verbal head, nor any other substantive conceptual material from the lexicon. A judgement, of a given event, that event takes place, or that it is done by somebody, is not to change anything conceptually in the event. No analogue of such judgements exists *within* lexical argument structures. HK's argument structure theory is precisely not a theory of *judgement*, which in its full form in particular requires *tensing* a given, fully configured event, and A-movement to relevant sentential-subject positions. The HK argument structure is a theory of Themes and Goals, not Agents, which do not fit into the impoverished scheme that can be lexically projected. Judgements are transformationally *derived* entities, not lexical configurations: the lexicon does not know about them and cannot project them.

None of this is to say that HK have the last word on the matter, or that changing their view of conflation as a morpho-phonological process as suggested in Section 3.3 does all that is needed. For let us now go back to how this whole discussion started, with observations about particular *lexical* entailments: for example, an event of Jack's *boiling* the soup entails an event of the soup's boiling, an event of *shelving* books entails a state of the books being 'on' the shelf. We wanted to *explain* these entailments, which are *necessary* ones and should follow from the internal structure of these lexical atoms. So it seemed atoms *had* to be internally complex. In the meantime we have been offered one theory of conflation that tells us in what specific way they can be. We made a case for the conclusion that positing syntactic structural complexity internal to lexical items is not the same as positing semantic structure or a compositional interpretation, and in fact we excluded that option, saying that we should think even of lexically complex verbs as semantically atomic, like names. But that causes an obvious problem for lexical entailment. There are no semantic entailments between names. So it now transpires that the earlier solution to how HK escape the generative semantics trap is not sufficient. If we say that creating a name hides an underlying semantic structure or makes it opaque, we cannot appeal to that underlying structure to explain a name's lexical entailments. As we saw, for HK lexical representation structures exist at no stage during a derivation in narrow syntax; yet they are intrinsically complex, and in fact their intrinsic complexity is untouched by the process of conflation, which leaves their syntactic and semantic structure 'in tact'. Somehow, if we stick to their premises, either atomity or complexity has to go. These cannot both hold, and yet the problem is: they must.

This is not only because lexical entailment seems to be for real as a linguistic fact, but also because of the phenomenon of sub-event modification (this is the qualification regarding the atomist claim announced to come later in the previous section). Sub-event modification shows in examples such as (30), mentioned in passing before and adapted from Radford (1997: 371–2). Somehow it does seem as if the adverbial manages to attach to different layers of a complex event structure, with distinctive semantic effects, lending support to the reality of their internal event complexity:

(30) a. We gently rolled the ball down the hill.
(30) b. We rolled the ball gently down the hill.

The semantic difference is subtle, however, and maybe this is as it should be: clearly, the intended interpretation of (30b) is much better expressed by (31):

(31) We made the ball roll gently down the hill.

Here there is not even a question of 'gently' modifying 'made'. This lends support to lexical atomism: sub-event modification only comes into its own in the fully analytic form (31). Yet, the fact that (30b) can subtly mean what (31) means does suggest that there is a complexity there, internal to 'roll', which does not meet the eye. In conflict with this, Fodor and Lepore's lexical atomist position predicts that there really should not be *any* such thing as sub-event modification. If meaning is just denotation, and there is no internal structure in a lexical concept expressed by a verb, there is nothing in a lexical item as represented at D-structure that could account for an event's internal structure. But the example seems to show that there is sub-event modification and needs to be accounted for.

Note another example. Sentence (32) is again standardly taken to forbid the interpretation where 'on Monday' only modifies the soup's boiling but not Pat's causing of the boiling; this interpretation is unproblematic for a version of (32) with two overt heads, hence two events rather than one (33):

(32) Pat boiled the soup on Monday.
(33) Pat made the soup boil on Monday.

But consider a contest between various people competing for who is faster in soup-boiling on very slow stoves. They each have their separate kitchen, and get down to 'work' on Sunday. The following week, the external referees look at the result, and note truthfully the following:

(34) Pat boiled the soup on *Monday.*
(35) Chris boiled the soup on *Tuesday.*
(36) Only Anton boiled the soup already on *Sunday* night.

And indeed, in each case that's exactly what they did. Atomists cannot possibly propose that (34)–(36) are ungrammatical and the referees should have written down:

(37) Pat caused the soup to boil on *Monday*
(38) Chris caused the soup to boil on *Tuesday.* Etc.

On the other hand, if I drive a car listening to Mozart, inadvertently crashing into a café on the pavement killing four people including two children, why couldn't I call my wife later the same day and cry out: 'I killed four people today!' Why wouldn't this be felicitous and truthful, despite the philosophers who claim that the case in question instantiates an important difference between killing, on the one hand, and causing to die, on the other? In that state, the distinction in question would seem academic to me. Basically, I identify the two activities, and ignore their semantic differences. Yet, as the boiling case above shows, in a less agitated state of mind (as when dutifully recording who won a competition) I may well allow sub-event modification, in which case identification is too strong. *On Monday* then modifies an integral *part* of the whole event talked about (although not a separate event), a part that is the final effect of Pat's efforts (34).

What we have to find out is precisely what makes it happen that a separate verbal head that by itself expresses an event—the soup's boiling—comes to specify an inherent part of another event, instead of remaining a separate one. In both this and the identificational case, there must be a mechanism ensuring that, ultimately, it is and remains a *single* event that we are talking about and judging when we utter *Pat boiled the soup.* We cannot evoke conflation as that mechanism, as long as we stick to HK's conception of it: being morpho-phonological only it cannot have the needed consequences. Yet, conflation somehow seems to *be* the solution: the head-fusion it involves seems to somehow result in the identification of the two events, resulting in one event only of which the lower one becomes an inherent part. Still, the needed solution must go far beyond the mere assertion that a conflation creates a name that makes an underlying complex event structure opaque. Again, names entail nothing—unless *they are located at different layers of a conceptual edifice.* If syntactic processes could create lexical concepts at different such layers, and the layers are recursively built so as to asymmetrically entail one another, sub-event entailment will become conceptually possible, on purely formal grounds.

The paradigm for such an organization is that of the system of arithmetical competence, which, when we look at it in algebraic terms, has several dimensions to it; geometrically, we may think of these as spaces. In a standard vector space, the *algebraic dimension* of a particular space is the number of independent variables needed to specify the inhabitants of that space (more precisely, this is the number of vectors in the space's *basis*). Thus, for example, the number line is a mathematical object that has dimension one, as a single vector suffices to generate all objects along the line by scalar multiplication. Sometimes, when talking about dimensions, as in 'two dimensions of a problem', we mean two different sides of a problem where variables can change independently: they do not speak to one another. This meaning is not intended here. In the case of geometric objects algebraically described, we see that higher-dimensional objects may be *built* on the basis of lower-dimensional ones, and contain them. Thus while the space of the naturals is linearly generated from a single vector, the whole numbers are generated *from* the naturals by applying an inverse operation (subtraction). The rationals, in turn, are generated by applying inverse functions to the whole numbers (divisions), the real numbers are generated by applying inverse functions to the rationals, and so on for the complex and hyper-complex numbers. In a geometric interpretation of these hierarchical entailments, higher-dimensional spaces *entail* lower-dimensional ones as *parts*, in a purely formal way, much as the earth (qua planet) contains a two-dimensional surface, and a surface contains one-dimensional lines.

Put differently, infinite generativity as we find it in the natural numbers does not merely lead to a *linear* progression of a sequence of objects; it involves *jumps* in representational complexity, with asymmetric entailments following from operations recursively applied to lower-dimensional objects: each higher-order space is built from lower-order ones. On the other hand, it is also noteworthy that this recursive process eventually *stops* as we go too high in the hierarchy of spaces: in the region of the hyper-complex numbers, algebraic operations which characterize the lower-order spaces cease to be well-defined. It is as if our mind loses a grip on the structure of these spaces. So let us call the *limitlessly* recursive aspect of the generation of the objects of a single space, like the natural numbers, the '*linear*' one, and the only *limitedly* recursive aspect a '*hierarchical*' one. Using these terms, we can say that our problem above, how a lexical item (head) newly created in the course of a conflation process *can* engender a necessary asymmetric entailment, would be solved if language had, in addition to its linear aspect (which is captured by Merge), a hierarchical one as well. Two lexical 'names' that entail each other can do so (and necessarily) if they are generated in different algebraic dimensions that are recursively construed. If the transitive *boil*, say, is recursively generated from the intransitive *boil*, it will entail it with the same necessity that requires, say, the real numbers to be part of the complex ones, as the latter are construed from the former and presuppose them.

That human syntax has this multi-dimensional architecture would be unsurprising if indeed language as a faculty relates to arithmetic both formally and in evolution, as Chomsky has often argued. Chomsky (2005) specifically argues that Merge in language, on the one hand, and Merge in arithmetic, on the other, is essentially the same process: in the latter case, it is one-place and generates the successor function, in the former case it is two-place and generates an endless linear progression of phrases, brackets within brackets, each a set:

(39) {...{...{...{...} } } }

But (39), being linear, has nothing to say about hierarchy in the above sense, or in any sense that would illuminate the existence of semantic entailments within the hierarchical structure of the human clause. Neither does it tell us anything about the existence of points in the derivation where particular kinds of interpretations become possible (for example, evaluations of the generated structure for truth). Building up a full clause necessarily involves going through the main layers: VP, the middle layer (Agr), and TP/CP, and none of these may be left out in building a truth-evaluable proposition. Transgressing the boundary of each layer, we enter conceptually or semantically new territory. None of this is linear: it is the hierarchical aspect of language, which intrinsically involves the formation of specific syntactic categories that are hierarchically ordered with respect to one another and distinctive in their semantic functions. There are severe limitations and constraints at each step: this is true for HK argument structures, as we have seen; verb phrase composition in particular is limited to one layer of embedding, as when a lower verbal head conflates with a higher verbal head. In sentential syntax, structure-building stops at the CP-boundary, and no further hierarchical operations are defined there: there is no syntactic category on top of CP, except for ones that will already have been used in the construction of a CP (so one could build a VP or PP on top of a CP). Once having reached the CP-layer, we could also go on building more structure by adding adjuncts. But it is the very essence of adjuncts that they do not change the category or projection status of whatever they apply to. If we do not build adjunctions but stay in argument structure, we necessarily begin from the bottom again, until the next clause boundary is reached and so on, giving rise to a recursive sequence punctuated by CP-boundaries:

(40) [[V-T-C-[V-T-C-[V-T-C- . . .]

In other words, what makes the unboundedness of language so specific is the interweaving of merely additive or linear processes like adjunction, on the one hand, and hierarchical ones, which fall outside the scope of the adjunct system and give us new categories, on the other (see further Hinzen 2007). What is missing in Chomsky's (2005) arithmetic-language analogy is a theory of *categorization*, something that Merge (let alone the interfaces) does not yield.

Since this solution requires a quite radical rethinking of the architecture of the language faculty, let us compare it to a solution that HK themselves propose, and that faces serious shortcomings. This attempt is most prominent in HK's first large-scale account of argument structure (HK 1993), where it is tied to the notion of D-structure, which does not figure in their more recent work. HK (1993) claim that semantic relations between events as encoded in D-structure 'mirror' fundamental lexical relations as projected in accordance with their principle of 'unambiguous projection'. In particular, they note that the higher verbal head asymmetrically c-commands the lower verbal head, and propose:

> Corresponding to this syntactic relation, there is a similarly asymmetric (semantic) relation between the two events, a relation we will take to be that of *implication*. (HK 1993: 68)

This is very much in the spirit of the internalist program as understood here, as semantic relations are trivially mapped from syntactic ones. Yet, note that the correspondence is a mere stipulation, or axiom, and as such is not explained, natural as the correspondence may be. Moreover, a mere correspondence would seem to make no sense of the *necessity* of lexical entailment. Note also that in this quote HK explicitly talk about *two* events, which is not what is needed, as I argued earlier. On the other hand, this may simply be loose talk, since elsewhere they are fully explicit that they regard a word like *saddle* as a lexical item with a 'single event position'. HK also continue the passage above as follows:

> Accordingly, the matrix event 'implicates' the subordinate event [in a Larsonian double object structure], a relation that makes perfect sense if the syntactic embedding corresponds to a 'semantic' composite in which the subordinate event is a proper

part of the event denoted by the structure projected by the main [the light] verb. (HK 1993: 68–9)

But they denote this semantic relation '$e_1 \rightarrow e_2$', a notation that not only involves two events, but does not reflect what they effectively argue in the quote, where what accounts for implicational relations is said to be a *part–whole* relation, which is exactly right by my own reasoning above: an event representation arising from a head-fusion does not involve new conceptual material, but the *presentation* of a given event as a part of another one.

Neo-Davidsonian conjunctive event representations are another attempt to explain lexical entailment, and they run into the same difficulties. In particular it is said that *Anton boiled the soup* means (41) (see Pietroski and Uriagereka 2002, in Uriagereka 2002: ch. 12):

(41) There was an event e of causing, for an event e′ of boiling, such that Anton is the agent at e, e′ is the object of e, and the soup is the theme at e′.

Then if (41) is true, it will also be true that the soup boiled, or that

(42) There was an event e′ of boiling, such that the soup was the theme of e′.

But then again, from nothing in these representations could we explain why the relevant part–whole relations are obtained. Conjunction is the wrong notion from which to obtain such a relation, as a conjunction merely *conjoins*, and therefore is inherently inept to capture 'hierarchical' relations in the sense above. In short, by decomposing the verb into different phrases, one for each thematic role, and translating each phrase into a conjunct, we get the implications right. But the relevant part–whole relations will not follow from the structure. Moreover, what grounds do we have, *other* than that of getting the implicational relations right, that the phrasal structure underlying *Anton boiled the soup* maps into conjuncts (rather than disjuncts, say)? We should have a motivation *independent* from our desired result itself that conjunction rather than disjunction is the right notion. (Note that the case with postulating the *v*-element or the higher verbal head is quite different: there we *do* have evidence independent of a given semantic explanatory concern.) It may seem that no justification for introducing conjuncts into a semantic representation is needed, because it is the *simplest* notion, but this argument does not perhaps carry much explanatory force. Mathematically, at least, nothing really makes a mapping to 'or' rather than 'and' less transparent. Moreover, conjunction is a semantic notion paradigmatically suited to adjunctive modification. The problem is the integration of Neo-Davidsonian conjuncts into a single event—an event, moreover, with the right part–whole structure, and whose parts (sub-events) have the same themes as the main events of which they are the parts (the soup, in the example above).

Ideally, in short, we must show on the basis of our object language and its structure *alone*, why the implication holds, and not on the basis of largely arbitrary 'correspondence rules'. There should be something about the part–whole structure of our *representation* that justifies mapping it into a part–whole relation in the semantic representation without arbitrariness. The 'dimensional' solution, and as far as I can see only it, achieves this. Starting from a mere state such as *open*, lowest in the hierarchy, we arrive at the more complex event *The door opens*, with one argument (a subject), and at accomplishments such as *John opened the door*, with two arguments, a subject, and a previous subject now demoted to an object/complement of the matrix verbal head. More precisely, we begin with a mere property:

(43) PROPERTY: [$_A$ open]

Then this is predicated of an internal subject, giving us a first argument:

(44) [the door [V [$_A$ open]]]

If no further argument is added, the subject 'the door' is promoted to the sentence-syntactic subject-position, giving us a state:

(45) STATE: The door is [t [V [$_A$ open]]]

But we may also head-move *open* into the lower V, turning the A into a V, and merge this V with the higher V:

(46) PROCESS: The door *open-H-s.*

And finally, we may add another argument to the VP:

(47) ACCOMPLISHMENT: John [$_{VP}$ V [the door [V [$_A$ open]]]]

which, after head-movement, in sentential syntax, ends up as the structure (48), in which the internal subject, which cannot now become a sentence-subject, has become an object (internal argument or complement) of the verb:

(48) John [*open-V-s* [the door]]

With each new argument and concomitant head-movements (or head-fusions), a new lexical item is created, in another dimension. Each is an atom, and there is no question of 'lexical decomposition'. Yet, as there is a hierarchical structure in the sense above, and dimensions are recursively built, atoms can entail each other.

There cannot then be, as a matter of necessity, any such thing as an event without a state, which is as it should be, as the state is what 'measures out' the event, or is that in which it 'culminates'. The build-up of a syntactic structure does not *recapitulate*, on this picture, an independently given set of 'notional categories', as per HK (1993) or Baker (1997, 2003). The syntactic structure in question creates notional structures where none were before. The 'dimensional' solution to our problem solves the problem we started with in a non-circular way. That way may be right or wrong, but the solution proposed does not posit semantic complexity as something independently given, or as given by the structure of the real world. It is, for what it is worth, an explanatory approach to semantic theory: an attempt to explain semantics, as opposed to do it.

3.5 Conclusions

The empirical study of the analytic deserves to move to centre stage in our investigation of the mind. Generative grammar as such can be rather straightforwardly construed as a Kantian endeavour that seeks to unveil the synthetic *a priori* in naturalistic terms. It has not greatly touched the deepest and most controversial domain of the analytic, though, which consists in semantic entailments between 'atoms' that *seem* structurally driven. I have argued that in its current mainstream conception it excludes even the possibilities for such entailment, given its one-dimensional conception of structure-building or Merge, which effectively deprives the linguistic system of what I have called 'hierarchy' (and which is distinct from the hierarchy of the sort that is merely discretely infinite and that we find in the integers). As in the previous chapter, interesting metaphysical implications follow from the proposal of a recursively structured multi-dimensional syntax in the sense of Uriagereka, forthcoming: see Hinzen and Uriagereka 2006.

Most characteristic for the re-conceptualization of the analytic attempted here is that analytic entailment has nothing to do with truth. It is not a truth about the world, but our concepts, I have argued, if an activity entails a state, for example. As far as the world is concerned, the real might as well consist of events only, or particles only (or we might regard it as a 'social construction', or whatever): there are *various* ontological schemes that we can impose on the real, and mere natural language commits us to none. Our linguistic schemes make the appearances fall into certain categories, but these need not reflect the structure of the real, nor are they necessarily assumed to do so by ordinary speakers. Thus we should not be surprised to find that entailments hold between concepts even if they do not pick out anything in the external world, or if constraints on that world, as far as science has determined them, violate them (as when scientists say most of the universe's mass is 'massless mass').

Important for historical reasons is the conclusion that the traditional Quinean verdict about the impossibility of a principled distinction between the analytic and synthetic, or linguistic knowledge and world knowledge, is not relevant: rational inquiry will draw it in in the course of advancing explanatory hypotheses on the structure of the faculty of language. The distinctions in question may thus shift as progress is made, hence may have no *a priori* or principled basis. But nothing of that sort is required for an inquiry into the analytic content of the mind to make sense. Lastly, we might emphasize that on the present account each question about whether some entailment is analytic is, if positive, a purely *formal* or structural question, both at the level of complex expressions and at the level of atoms. This is to say that there is no help from the present notion of analyticity for someone asking whether *gay marriage* is a contradiction in terms, for example.[15] The answer to that question could not be a formal one, or an answer that appeals to the intrinsic linguistic structure internal to lexical items as represented in a human brain. This is all to the good, for there is no factual answer to this question. It depends on decisions and conventions, and there may be a variance of these even within the same community (the notion of 'same' community being notoriously unclear, as no healthy community is uniform).[16]

One perfectly legitimate worry is whether our highly restricted (and narrowly linguistic) notion of analyticity will ever tell us anything we deem to be of deeper philosophical interest. The history of philosophy suggests no optimism. No matter how philosophers have tried to determine the nature of *justice*, for example, by exploring their concept of justice, nothing conclusive has been brought about. But this does not show that there is no such concept, with a determinate content, as something that guides our assessment of human actions. It might be that the internal structure of that concept, if it has one, is just not transparent for a mind like ours in the present state of its evolution. Our minds have managed an analysis of the generative principle of

[15] Georges Rey (p.c.) mentions to me that a Canadian philosopher of language was commissioned by a court of law to give an expert judgement on this. An utterly wrongheaded idea if I am right.

[16] What about the analyticity of '2+2=4'? This is a slightly different case. Some suggest that mathematics and language share fundamental structures, the former being abstractions from the latter. This is speculative of course, but it would bring the example into the scope of a formal analysis, relative to a (indeed possibly the same) system of knowledge. That is, the structure of the human system of mathematical knowledge, however related to language, might be such that it entails that 2+2=4.

number—an easy case—but they fail badly in the analysis of *house*, which is already much too complex, apparently, and maybe there is not much hope that we will ever succeed for something like *justice*. Nothing in biology suggests that we *should* be able to have a cognitive access to the causes of how we apply concepts that we grasp *a priori*. *A priori* knowledge *need* not be transparent to us. That our analyses of *justice* have never yielded anything that people would have agreed really is the essence of justice is no argument then against the fact that they did analyse the concept of justice, or that their analysis was guided by the *a priori* knowledge that they had of it. Somebody analysing the concept of *number* may only succeed in providing an analysis of the integers (hence only partially grasp the content of the concept), but we would therefore not say that he did not analyse the concept of *number*, or was not guided by his grasp of it, in getting wherever he got.

For most concepts, we may have to conclude that our grasp of them only *shows* in the way we apply them: our understanding *zeigt sich*, as Wittgenstein would have put it, but we cannot much advance beyond this. This would show the importance of the study of the history of ideas as a way of unveiling human concepts.[17] The history of ideas would depict our grasp of the concept of *human rights*, say, as it has developed over the centuries, interacting contingently with historical circumstances. It would be a particularly interesting task to study seriously whether any sense can be defined in which there has been a *progress* in our understanding. In philosophy, unfortunately, there appears to be little progress over the millennia, which some would take to suggest that philosophical concepts may actually be defined as being those that we happen to grasp, but that simply do not get transparent to us, ever, as a consequence of principled cognitive limitations (McGinn 1993). There are reasons for pessimism in this domain, therefore, which there may not be in the domain of the mathematical sciences, whose central concepts and modes of understanding are easier.

We have also come back in this chapter to our earlier assumption that human thought and semantics has *two* aspects: a conceptual and an intentional (or, as I have said, a 'judgemental') one. The former has to do with configurational relations between lexical words, while the latter has to do with LF-syntax. Conceptual and intentional information seem empirically distinct and governed by independent principles. The latter depends asymmetrically on the former, as LF has no concern with the implicational relations between words, or the thematic roles that words have when figuring as arguments. Recognizing

[17] This, we might note, is a Heideggerian and hermeneutic idea: to study the concept of being (and man) by way of studying the history of its understanding (*Seinsgeschichte*).

a level of D-structure in earlier versions of the generative project was to recognize a level of linguistic representation where conceptual-thematic relations between an event and its participants are syntactically encoded, and nothing else is. This is to draw a clear boundary between language and thought, or linguistic and non-linguistic thought. We see the former constrained in ways that we do not know how to motivate in referential or 'cognitive' terms.

HK offer an explicit theory that analyses these constraints in narrowly linguistic terms, thereby giving some credibility to the linguistic-syntactic nature of human conceptual structure: this theory consists in a systematization of the constraints in question and their reduction to a small number of very basic argument structure types. The theory, we should note, depends on a richer theory of argument structure than a minimalist theory appealing to essentially Merge alone (Chomsky 2005a, 2006) allows. The latter could make no sense of restrictions to, say, a single specifier within the lexical projection of a head: any such restriction is a stipulation that diverges from how the Strongest Minimalist Thesis (SMT) is conceived. The SMT requires that we find nothing in language except Merge, which yields discrete infinity, plus what interfaces demand. A conception of phrase structure such as HK's goes far beyond this, thereby leaving many features of phrase structure as at present unexplained, hence as features special to language not following from anything else.

Minimalism comes with the hope that there will be few such features, but, of course, it is consistent with their existence, if they can be motivated by the explanatory benefits they yield and the empirical facts (e.g. impossible words) they explain. Keeping the system simple and free of the phrase-structural constraints that HK impose will leave all the restrictions unexplained that HK can derive from these constraints. I have thus here similarly opted for a richer system of phrase structure because it seems that the alternative will have to compensate for its impoverishment elsewhere; dumping the complexity in the interface systems, in particular, as argued in Section 1.4, seems straight forwardly circular. If these systems are to be syntax-free, they will not explain structural facts of syntax and their inherent constraints. Whatever semantic motivation we may make plausible as we learn more from the comparative study of cognition, we know it is likely to stop at some point. This is the point where syntactic constraints and the thoughts they encode follow from nothing other than themselves. What standard Minimalism as yet lacks is a theory of this innovative process, the process of *categorization*—which generates new kinds of ontologies with respect to pre-syntactic schemes of animal thought.

To put this differently, in a sense standard Minimalism may be as wrong as generative semantics was in erasing the boundary between language and thought: syntax is not trivially determined by semantic conditions imposed on it, once Merge is added. It is *a priori* surely more plausible that D-structure (conceptual information, in my sense, or what external Merge generates) can be motivated semantically, than that LF, or intentional information, can be so motivated. But if we see how constrained even D-structure is, and the constraints in question are specified in syntactic terms, even that conclusion may not seem too plausible.

4

Structure for Truth

4.1 The fate of truth: deflation and elimination

Neither reference nor truth-theoretic properties of a sentence or statement, I have suggested, add anything to its 'substantive' conceptual content. They rather affect the 'formal' properties of an expression. Take the lexical item *water*, which as such has a *substantive* content: that of the *concept* of water. If we find out what externally existing substance a use of the word *water* by a speaker at a time *t* and space *s* happens to pick out—a specimen of H_2O, say, or of XYZ, or of 'heavy' or 'light' water, depending on where in the universe we are—no substantive content is added to that of the word *water* as it was and must have been understood by us prior to undertaking the relevant chemical investigation. It was the actual *reference* of the English word *water*—which has a particular meaning, or which is linked to a concept in our understanding—that was determined in the investigation, not its *meaning*, or conceptual content.[1] The latter was taken as given from the start. If it hadn't been so given, no physical or chemical investigation could have yielded much insight as to what the concept in question was. The point repeats, as I argued in Chapter 2, with any reference we undertake to persons, cities, etc. Similarly, in the case of truth: evaluating a sentence as true or false does not change or determine, but presupposes, a grasp of its meaning, where, as always, we understand by a sentence a natural object analysed at different levels of description, including at particular phonetic and semantic levels. No substantive content is added to the sentence or proposition that is asserted: truth is not a quality like *red*, *morose*, or *chic*. We cannot connect truth to any sensory quality or particular appearance. As noted in Chapter 1, there is no visual image connected to it, no any particular kind of emotion or feeling—the truth does not feel like anything. Truth is wholly abstract. Yet, despite all that, truth is not meaningless or insignificant. What is added to a meaning, when a judgement of truth that involves this meaning is made, is the subject matter of this chapter.

[1] The latter, given my 'atomist' commitments, should of course not be confused with an 'identifying' description—see my defence of the rigidity of reference in the next chapter.

As noted in Section 3.4, the 'moment of truth'—a moment in the derivation where the generated sructure is evaluated for truth—is crucial to the derivational dynamics at large, and perhaps partially characterizes its very nature. Truth arises where a generated structure is placed into an ongoing discourse and acquires some intentional significance with respect to it: truth is an aspect of the expression's 'force', which on common assumptions is encoded in the upper regions of the CP-layer (Rizzi 1997). Note that evaluating a structure for truth is a point of no return: once we have done that, we cannot go back and build further structure on top of the one we had. If we wish to build such further structure, the 'moment of truth' has to be deferred to the next higher phase where truth assessment is possible. So, a proposition that is evaluable for truth, such as *she bought apples*, can only embed if it is *not* evaluated for truth: it is a condition for understanding *Milly said she bought apples* that the embedded proposition is *not* evaluated for truth, but only the matrix clause is. Truth-evaluated structures are necessarily root (or main) clauses. Now, if truth as applied to root clauses was meaningless, its predication would add nothing to the content of (1). Sentence (1) would be identical to the judgement (2). But it is obvious that it is not: we can grasp (1)—in the sense of *thinking* or *contemplating* its content—without engaging in an actual judgement of truth that makes use of the structure in (2):

(1) The Earth is flat
(2) It's true that the Earth is flat

Admittedly it is marginally possible also when using the expression (2) to merely think or contemplate its content, without actually engaging in a judgement of it that carries a force. But as long as we are using (2) ourselves (rather than contemplate its use by another person), this option is only marginally available (if we withhold judgement, the structure virtually transforms itself into a question: *is it true that the Earth is flat?* It has a fragile and uncertain status: a judgement of truth *reduces* that uncertainty. So, again, a judgement is something fundamentally different from a mere thought. If it was not, it would be hard to explain why, if we merely contemplate a thought such as (1), we can endlessly add conceptual material to it, as in (3), whereas, if we use (2) in an actual judgement of truth, no such embedding is possible at all: this is indicated in the totally ungrammatical (4), where I use exclamation marks to indicate that an actual judgement is being made (by the speaker):

(3) believes [the Earth is flat]; John believes [the Earth is flat]; after John believes [the Earth is flat]; etc.

(4) *believes [it's true that the Earth is flat!]; *John believes [it's true that the Earth is flat!]; etc.

Let us say, then, that a predication of truth carries us from a thought to a judgement, viewed as something categorially different from a (mere) thought. How might we study truth thus understood empirically? What is empirically there to be studied is the dynamics of a syntactic derivation that involves a particular lexical item, namely 'truth' (or a variant of the same lexical root, such as 'true'). Like any other lexical item, truth becomes structuralized as the derivation proceeds. As the structure-building process completes, it ends up in a particular final position. This structure-building process we can study, and we can ask for the cognitive and semantic significance of any of its steps.

We can also study occurrences of such judgements in space and time. But that appears to be a problem still beyond the scope of current scientific inquiry. Behaviourism was a failed attempt to subject verbal behaviour (i.e. uses of language on particular occasions) to this form of inquiry, regarding it as externally controlled (or conditioned) by physical parameters of the environment. On this picture my writing down this very sentence is a causal consequence of its having gained in 'strength' as a consequence of various reward and punishment schemes I was subjected to in the past. Similar such causal histories turn all of my assertions into statistically predictable events. But, as Chomsky (1959) pointed out, this account metaphorically extends the meaning of terms such as 'conditioning' or 'stimulus' to aspects of real-world verbal behaviour to which they only apply if their meaning is effectively *changed*. That is, the claim that my verbal behaviour is externally 'controlled' in effect comes to mean—or to be a misleading paraphrase of the fact—that my behaviour is the consequence of my 'deciding', by my free will, to judge true what I do.

Regarding the prospects of a Spencerism or Skinnerian 'scientific' theory of behaviour nothing much seems to have changed in the last half-century. In this sense, in a methodologically naturalistic, empirical, and explanatory inquiry into human judgements of truth, a study of the *externalization* of these judgements, in the specific sense of an inquiry into why truth judgements qua historical events take place when they do, should likely be left out. In other words, the study of truth should be restricted to its structural aspects, not unlike the way Tarski suggested.[2]

[2] As Etchemendy (1988) emphasizes, Tarski's primary goal—at a time long before our understanding of linguistic structure became more sophisticated and modern linguistics hadn't even started—was the reduction of the semantic notion of truth to independently given *syntactic*, *logical*, and

Naturally one could study truth in non-explanatory—normative or descriptive—terms as a concept figuring in our public political discourse. There we obviously see it used and misused as a powerful political tool and public metaphor, for example. But again this dimension of an inquiry into truth, crucial as it would be in a socio-political form of inquiry, cannot figure in the naturalistic undertaking we are engaged with here. The same applies to the study of assertion, argumentation, and discourse: we can descriptively structure such behaviour, lay down various norms according to which it should proceed, and describe these in formal terms. But this enterprise is very different and especially far beyond the narrow scope of the biolinguistic study of the human linguistic capacity as pursued here, which sticks to the sentence-boundary, essentially, and which the larger endeavour appears to presuppose.

It has been argued that the very *source* of our concept of truth is our concept of assertion and justifiability (Dummett 1996), but as noted, we try to assert what we deem true, and we think that asserting it as true will not make it so. So either we talk about the practice of assertion as inherently involving a grasp of the concept of truth, in which case the practice does not explicate the latter, and depends on it; or we talk about a practice of assertion *as that practice might have looked like* in the case of creatures lacking a concept of truth (see Price 2003; Hinzen 2006c). But in that case we could only guess what this 'assertoric practice' would be like. Postures of territorial defence, say, in creatures lacking truth, might be candidates to consider as non-alethic forms of 'assertiveness'. To the very extent that such a practice fell short of invoking truth, it would not contribute to the understanding of that notion either.

One might drop behaviourist constraints on how knowledge of linguistic meaning is acquired and used on occasion, and focus on an externalist *semantics* instead, but as I concluded in Section 2.3 when discussing Fodor's (1990) proposal to this effect, it does not lead us much further either. In fact, the reason for rejecting referentialist explanations of meaning—essentially, that the denotations these appeal to are not independently specifiable—translates into a reason for rejecting externalist explanations of truth: there are external correlates in this case as much as in the case of acts of reference making use of NPs; but as in that case, causal relations to these correlates

set-theoretical notions. This project deliberately left the problem of intentionality and the existence of semantics exactly where it was—it's not a *semantic theory*. It but it shows that whoever tackles this problem need not be disturbed by the problem and paradoxicality surrounding the truth predicate, since that predicate can be eliminatively defined.

do not explain why truth exists. If we posit, on analogy with the word–thing relation posited in standard models of NP-reference, some external relation between sentences and mind-external objects that is explanatory for what intentionality sentences specifically involve, the same problem of independent access arises: whether, if we didn't have any CPs in our language, we would still think that the world contained things of the category 'fact' or 'state of affairs'. Naturally, there would be a physical world out there, with various forces and particles, but the existence of such a world does not require a common-sense ontology of 'facts' and 'states of affairs'.

If I question whether our standard ontology of objects, events, facts, etc. can be viewed in language-independent terms, I am not constructing a 'sceptical argument', or denying 'realism'. It holds as it did before that the sciences in developing explanatory theories hope and expect their theoretical terms will capture an aspect of the real, and typically they do. But again, this contention does not depend on the other one that native and intuitive ways of conceptually categorizing the world must be isomorphic to some ontological structures that the world out there 'really' has. For all the progress of physics has shown us, most of these categories are hopeless in speaking of the physical domain. The question of realism as it arises in science does not arise for our intuitive modes of understanding.

The problem of a relational understanding of truth is much more acute than in the case of NP/DP reference. It is at least *prima facie* fairly intuitive in the latter case that in using the term *London* we are referring to a city, which is an 'object' in some cognitive (rather than metaphysical) sense. That a verb like 'wears' refers to any specific object out there, or that a declarative statement such as *Laura wears a hat* is 'about a fact' or 'refers to it' is much less clear. Intuitively, in fact, the statement is one about *Laura*; and the predicate the statement involves, *wears a hat*, is not intuitively or phenomenologically 'about' anything. Predication is the relation that connects the linguistic subject and the linguistic predicate, and it has been thought that it, too, has a correlate out there, a relation that connects Laura, the person, and the property of hat-wearing, which she instantiates. But predication is an operation that, quite possibly, only one kind of evolved mind is capable of, whose relation to the physical environment should be regarded as a contingent one. If we ask what meaning the posited external instantiation relation is supposed to have, predication is the only thing we know that we can appeal to: predication, which is something we can perform and study as a relation structuring a human clause, is what makes our talk about instantiation meaningful. Maybe we can argue on metaphysical grounds that predications of truth reflect the ultimate nature of the real, in a way that is independent of the specific nature of our minds and predications we perform: the same structures found in our minds can be found out there too. But if we consider how intricate and specific the structures are that have to be built up before truth can be judged—a TP embedding a VP and topped by a CP—the possibility in question may not seem likely, and we should wait for good grounds on which such an empirical hypothesis might be defended. The problem here is not only the specificity of the structures that are truth-evaluable, but also that of the operations that construct them and that give them, if I am right in the previous chapter, their specific 'unity': head-movement in particular.

These remarks against an externalist strategy in making sense of truth judgements as a natural phenomenon make good sense in light of the fact that in our ordinary understanding, truth *does* not actually seem to be understood as a relational concept. What we rate correct or incorrect, or as capable of truth, is clearly not the *world* or what is out there, but what *judgements* we make about it. If we wonder how to judge an open issue, external 'facts' feed into our judgement, but will not determine it. Truth is a question, not of the facts, but of what we *judge these to be*. We do not *depict* the world when judging the truth, or *represent* it, in some passive sense of 'mirroring'. On the contrary, in seeking to determine the truth among all the appearances that present themselves as facts, we are seeking to go beyond these appearances to how we venture things are really like, possibly *despite* their appearances.

This we can determine only in creative thought and experiment, not in passively 'representing facts'. A scientist presented with certain empirical data may as well reject the experimental or empirical facts, given a theoretical proposal inconsistent with them, seeking other data confirming the theory instead. So, judgement, as the notion is used in its ordinary sense, is importantly *free*, as opposed to externally controlled somehow, and we would ascribe no normative force to a judgement that we knew was externally or internally conditioned, caused, or controlled. Calling it a 'representation of a fact' does not as such lend any authority to it: representation is no basis for justification. Again, it is not the facts that matter to a judgement, but what we think is *right*, and that assessment will in all relevant cases be a creative act on our part, rather than a representational one. If we are being presented with several assertions, and we ask which one is true, *representing* the assertions or their contents will not help; we will have to turn to something else, a judgement, which, of necessity incurs a risk of error.

On an externalist and empiricist conception of mind, truth is *bound* to be a representational notion; coupled with a physicalist metaphysics, representation will moreover necessarily be of *physical* entities. As a consequence of that, the truth-aptitude of statements lacking these features will become the problem it has been in recent discussions. But ordinary truth-judgements do not seem to be subject to such constraints. The statement that abortion is a perfectly unproblematic device at any stage of the pregnancy is as much about abortion as the above statement was about Laura. No question of truth-aptitude arises for it for ordinary speakers, most of whom, I take it, would, upon little reflection, agree on the truth value assigned to it. The opinion cited about abortion seems as paradigmatic a falsehood as one can find. When asked to give an aesthetic judgement, too, such as 'Beethoven is a greater composer than Berlioz', we might, if asked to seriously consider this matter, weigh reasons for and against, and finally arrive at the verdict: 'Well, if I absolutely have to make a judgement, then, yes, on balance, I'd say Beethoven is greater' (see Dworkin 1996). Take, also, a philosophical judgement, such as 'Life has neither meaning nor purpose', held to be true, for example, by Dawkins (1976). Philosophers clearly debate these questions, treating them as factual, and they can get quite passionate about them.

Any account of truth should do justice to these perfectly ordinary behaviours and practices of rational judgement, rather than treating them as embarrassments that a properly enlightened philosophy—enlightened, in particular, by 'evolutionary thinking', or 'empiricism'—should subject to therapy (see Rorty 2001; Stich 1990, Churchland 1995). The human mind should be explained, not explained away, and its workings should constrain metaphysical theorizing about truth, as opposed to themselves being constrained by such theorizing. A theory that says humans should not seek truth but increased prosperity fails to see that this is not how humans work, who could as well not care less about prosperity, and strive for truth at the latter's expense. A theory that calls truth an 'ethnocentric' concept is inconsistent with the fact that humans plainly apply it as an absolute and universal concept as well, and assert it no matter whether members of their own ethnic group agree with them. Theories that say propositional truth as conceived here cannot exist because we know the mind works differently (as a connectionist net, say, with none of the inherent structures in it that I am arguing support truth judgements), or because it cannot be a product of Darwinian evolution (which favours adaptation not truth), impose *external constraints* on our empirical inquiries into that feature. Such constraints effectively prevent such inquiries to come up with features of our mentality that are inconsistent with the external constraints imposed and challenge prevalent assumptions in cognitive science or evolutionary theory. It seems advisable to reverse the assumed priorities, and constrain the adequacy of empirical models of the mind and its evolution by empirical facts about human truth and judgement.

Today the most widely acclaimed approach to truth is the 'deflationary' one. The approach pursued in this book so far and to be further pursued in this chapter has important commonalities with the deflationist approach, so I wish to comment on it (although, as it will turn out, ultimately these commonalities may be somewhat superficial). Deflationism as much as the present approach (i) neither ascribes any substantive conceptual content to the notion of truth, (ii) nor gives any explanatory role to a 'correspondence' relation, (iii) nor assumes the existence of an external 'property' of truth. As for this property, commitment to properties is part of the general predicament of referential semantics which I here reject. I generally see no evidence for the empirical claim that such properties (as opposed to the concepts that, on this view, 'refer' to them) need to exist, particularly in the case of truth. As for the correspondence relation, the present approach rejects it essentially for reasons of a lack of empirical evidence, rather than on grounds of a conceptual, functional, or metaphysical analysis of the concept of truth. As for 'is true' not being 'substantive' or a 'real property/predicate', in the way that, say, 'is bald' is, I have put this point a bit differently above: truth is, not a substantive, but a *formal* concept, which organizes the intentional structure of an expression as opposed to its conceptual content. This is as in the case of 'existence': it equally does not add anything to the substantive conceptual content of X to say that X exists, as noted in Section 1.2.

Still, of course, an NP as such differs from an expression of the form *NP exists*, as much as '*p*', as such, where *p* is any sentence or proposition, differs from *(that) S is true*—unless we simply view the former members of these pairs as containing *implicitly* what the latter make *explicit*. We thus learn nothing about this difference by studying the respective former members of these pairs. The usual dichotomy between 'descriptive/substantive/real', on the one hand, and 'non-descriptive/insubstantive/unreal', on the other, thus seems to me better captured by a distinction between 'conceptual' and 'intentional' layers of the clause, with the latter layers not adding to its lexical layers where substantive conceptual material is encoded. Functional or formal categories such as *a* or *this*, Tenses such as *-ed*, or Complementizers such as *that*, form the bare skeleton of the intentional structure of the clause, modifying the substantive lexical material of the clause, not in content, but intentional presentation. Specifically, Determiners may cross-linguistically have an *individuating function* with respect to the noun they attach to (they do not go with mass nouns, cf. **The water is in oceans*, as opposed to *Water is in oceans*; see Section 5.2), whereas the C-domain closes off the derivation of a given propositional content by supplying it with a assertoric or interrogative force. In short, the lexical/functional distinction serves us better than the descriptive/non-descriptive distinction; and having a 'formal' content does not mean having none.

I am also sympathetic to the deflationist (or 'minimalist', in the sense of Horwich (1998)) proposal that truth has no *explicit definition* (a feature it again possibly shares with existence), and lacks a substantive nature of which there can be a *theory*, in the way that there are theories of planets or chemical molecules. But in the light of the atomist commitments incurred in Chapter 3, this aspect of truth has less to do with truth than with the impossibility of defining most concepts in general. The concept of truth is a particularly good candidate for a conceptual primitive, even if words in general were not. Neither truth's being a 'formal' concept in the sense above, nor its lacking a theory or a definitional analysis prevent the concept of truth from forming a fundamental ingredient in the human conceptual scheme, irreducible in its meaning and function to any other concept.

Yet, on the present scheme, that truth is fundamental and non-redundant has nothing to do with the fact that it has a practical utility (for example, an 'expressive function'), as in so-called 'pro-sentential' theories (Grover 2001). In general, as noted in Chapter 2, we need to distinguish given structures from the uses or functions they pick up. Explaining the functioning of a concept (what it is useful for, what problem it solves) is not to explain why it *exists*, or why we *have* it—even if the prosentential analysis of truth were correct. That is not only because the function of a thing need not be intrinsic to it, but also because its function requires the structure that is able to have that function. In short, the question of the causes of the existence of the truth concept is not answered by pointing to something like a function of the truth-predicate in coordinating discourse and anaphoric relations. It is correct that the truth predicate allows us to both refer and endorse a proposition without mentioning it, as in 'That's true'. But that leaves the mystery of the origin of that concept where it was.

Another one of the current functional characterizations of the role of the truth-predicate is that it is a mere 'de-nominalizing device' (see, e.g., Künne 2003: 18, 35–6, 318). The idea here is that the complementizer *that*, when attached to a declarative sentence, has the effect of 'nominalizing' it, giving us 'That the Earth is flat', and that the addition of 'is true' at the end of this latter expression does no more than to *undo* this effect, giving us the original sentence in its pristine purity all over again. In short:

(*that* + the Earth is flat) + *is true*
<=>
the Earth is flat

One equally often finds a related intuition (see e.g. Davidson 1999: 634), that, in the schemata,

'*p*' is true iff *p* [where *p* is an expression and '*p*' a name for it]
the proposition that *p* is true iff *p*,

the expression substituting for *p* on the left-hand side is in a context where it functions as a 'singular term' and 'referential expression', due to its occurrence as the 'subject of a predication'. But the notion of a subject—a notion standardly defined in grammatical and configurational terms—does not co-vary with that of a 'referential expression' (nor with that of a 'nominal' expression). Sentences may have propositional subjects, and it does not follow from that that their subjects 'refer' to propositions or any other external object. Somewhat more plausibly, the notion of referentiality is inherently linked with a particular grammatical category (namely, the determiner phrase or DP), but the notion of a subject is not that of a category. As for the previous intuition, that an expression of the form 'that the Earth is flat' is nominal, it is no better supported. The structure of an expression of that form is that of an ('extended') projection of a Verb, which is in turn embedded in functional projections like TP and CP. This is the standard path that sentential projections take: they are extended projections of verbs.[3] Being a sentential and truth-evaluable unit, a sentence does not stop being one when it becomes the subject of a predication, or if a lexical head takes it as its complement, for example, 'believes', giving us 'believes that the Earth is flat', or 'the proposition that', as in 'the proposition that the Earth is flat'.

Since no nominals are generated in this way, then, no argument can be constructed that concludes the referentiality of sentential expressions in the relevant positions from their nominal status. But even if we granted the nominalization idea, it is unclear whether we could agree in any way that the addition of 'is true' has a 'de-nominalizing' effect, in part because it is not clear what 'de-nominalization', if taken literally or at face value, should be in the first place. Syntax is widely regarded as 'conservative' in the sense that if a structure is generated and initially characterized by certain relationships of heads and their complements, no further operation, higher up in the syntactic tree, can *undo* what was done lower in the tree, when the syntax began building it. In short, the overt Complementizer will not simply vanish into thin air as a truth-predication is added. If we invent a 'nominalization' and a 'de-nominalization' operation, then we need to check this against the grammatical reality, and the latter, if anything, points in the opposite direction. It is for this reason alone likely that *if* the left hand of equivalences like the one depicted above is indeed equivalent in some sense to its right-hand side, this

[3] In an informal sense: I am not implying any commitment here to something like Grimshaw's (1990) theory of sentences.

will have to be so because the latter *contains* in a (phonetically) inexplicit form what the former contains explicitly, a point to which I return below. Little insight is then to be gained from the equivalences above.

Denying that any of the equivalence schemata above could serve as a definition of truth, Alfred Tarski offered an *eliminative* definition of truth that has all instances of the first equivalence schema above as logical consequences. His discussion and the entire debate ensuing from it, including the deflationist one, is couched in an 'E-linguistic' paradigm. In particular, sentences are regarded as sequences of sounds or signs, which then become 'symbols' by an arbitrary act of correlating them with external objects.[4] In other words, we deprive natural language expressions of their semantic features, which on the present view are part of what individuates them as natural objects. If we deprive expressions of meaning, and stipulate that meaning accrues to them by mapping sub-sentential constituents to certain external 'objects' and 'properties', the question with regard to sentences automatically becomes the question of what objects we map true sentences to (truth values in Frege's case, arbitrary sequences in the case of Tarski, situations and facts in other approaches). The whole question does not arise on the present approach, where 'mapping' structured linguistic expressions (pairings of sounds and meanings) to anything is regarded as not helping in any way in an explanatory approach to semantics. The question of truth is not the question of what to 'map' a sentence to, or of how to do so, but of how truth as a concept internal to a mind attaches to a given complex structure in the structure-building process that gives rise to an interpretable expression with a particular intentional structure.

The very notion of an 'object-language' seems to imply an 'E-linguistic' perspective, and has an unclear empirical content. As a natural object, a language is best addressed as a generative procedure, which never crystallizes in a completed external object that we can describe by its physical properties, as noted in Section 1.2. An expression is meaningful not as a physical object but only as used in a particular way by a creature with the right kind of mind. An expression of the form *'Aristotle' refers to Aristotle* might thus as well be rated false: what the quotation marks enclose, on the view under discussion, is a physical object, a 'sign', and on common assumptions, what that sign together with the quotation marks around it names is that sign itself; but a sign does not have mysterious referential properties: referring is something a person does when using it. If so, a truth-definition for such meaningless strings lacks explanatory relevance for the study of human linguistic competence. If a meaningless string does not have any semantic properties, no question of

[4] On this also, see Frege: 'What does one call a sentence? A series of sounds' (Frege 1956: 292).

truth or reference arises for it. If it is a *statement* we have to be looking at, containing what I am calling a *judgement* of truth, then such an object intrinsically *contains* semantic properties; in particular it involves a predication of truth that the speaker performs, subject to structural constraints. Once we individuate his expression in such semantic terms, the question of whether external entities exist to which such expressions must be 'mapped' arises as an empirical issue. The evidence for positing such relations in the case of truth judgements is unclear, and I will return to it below.

Another aspect of the notion of an 'object' language (at the lowest level of the hierarchy of meta-languages) in Tarski's truth definition is that it must not itself contain predications of truth. But to ban such predications for a natural language is like banning its use in assertoric contexts; it is to ban the very algebraic nature of predication, which, once it exists in a language, can apply to any lexical item, whatever its content. The entire motivation for banning truth-predications at the lowest level of the hierarchy of meta-languages reflects an extra-linguistic concern with language as a form of logic, to which extra-linguistic constraints such as the validity of the classical logical laws must apply.

A crucial question in any explanatory approach to truth must be why we specifically evaluate CP-like structures for truth, as opposed to words, PPs, or NPs (see Section 1.2). But it is unclear how the two major constraints imposed on any theory of truth since Tarski even speak to this question. The answer given here is, firstly, that semantic and syntactic complexity correlate; secondly, that the needed complexity for an evaluation of truth is not reached prior to the point where a CP has been constructed and can be placed into an ongoing discourse; and thirdly, that a declarative statement (or judgement) inherently is a quantification over the truth that it is judged to have, in the sense of a quantification over parts or presentations of wholes to be introduced later in this section. Let us look at two concrete versions of the usual Tarskian constraints, the 'Equivalence Constraint' and the 'Disquotational Constraint' (again, in (6), *p* is to be replaced by a declarative sentence of English and '*p*' is a name for that very sentence):

(5) EC: It is true that *p* if and only if *p*
(6) DC: '*p*' is true if and only if *p*

According to deflationists and Horwich-style minimalists, (5) and (6) exhaust everything there is to be said about truth; moreover, they are often regarded as *a priori* principles. Examples (5) and (6) in essence differ in that the latter predicates truth of (named) (E-)-sentences, whereas the former is said to predicate it of 'propositions'. Now, to start with this latter difference between sentences and propositions, it seems to be a red herring with respect to the basic problem in question. Truth paradigmatically applies to expressions of a sentential form, not to words or, for example, nominals; to say that this is because sentences express propositions but words and nominals do not is irrelevant because the next question will be how it comes that we map specifically sentences to propositions. Moreover, as argued in MMD, if we can explain semantic properties of sentential expressions by appeal to their inherent structures, these explanations are not furthered by mapping these expressions to any mind-external entities whose structure usually replicates that of the expression.

It is widely held that if I believe that wine is either red, rosé, or white, there is a proposition that is the 'object' of the 'belief-relation', and the 'content' of my 'belief-state', and that, since *you* may believe the 'same thing', we *both* can stand in this very relation, 'sharing' a relation to the 'same' proposition, which therefore must be 'objective' and 'mind-independent'. But the empirical content of most of these notions involved should be questioned. Sharing beliefs requires a measure of shared cognitive structure and cognitive systems that allow us to form similar kinds of thoughts and conclusions on the same occasions. There is little reason to doubt such shared cognitive structure in the species. Frege's worry, then, that if the contents of thought are studied in psychological or mind-internal terms, these contents would all come out as 'private' and as 'subjective', can be put to rest, on the grounds that it involves mistaken empirical assumptions on the nature of mind. If we assume for empirical reasons that the mind is inherently an 'algebraic' one (*sensu* Marcus 2001) rather than a 'Cartesian theatre' of 'ideas', the motivation for anti-psychologism disappears. Thinking will involve these systematic structures, which I have here argued are intrinsic to the contents we can think, and thus these contents can be shared without there being shared mind-external 'contents' that we are 'belief-related to'.

As for (6), the notion of a 'sentence' is as noted that of an essentially non-linguistic, physical sign or sound. *Ipso facto*, it will be unclear *why* instances of the bi-conditional in (6) would hold (if they do). The sentential expression substituted on the right-hand side of (6) gives an interpretation of the expression named on the left-hand side. Now, the association of any *name* with an object is arbitrary, modulo convention, in the sense that any object can be called by any name. But the association of *structured expressions* (with inserted lexical items in particular syntactic slots) and specific interpretations, is certainly not. So the way that, in the assembly of a lexicon, names are attached to things will tell us nothing about how sentential expressions systematically determine or entail certain properties of meaning. The determination of these semantic properties is by compositional principles that we lack a conscious apprehension of and do not form conventions for. Neither do the principles of the syntax–semantics mapping depend on the *logical* syntax of a quoted expression alone. Thus, for example, the universal 'conservativity' of natural language binary quantifiers (the fact that $(Q(A))(B)=Q(A)(B\cap A)$, with A the internal and B the external argument of the quantifier Q), is a specifically *linguistic* constraint on the interpretation of binary quantifiers that logic as such does not demand. In short, (6) will have to exploit intentional aspects of the expression that follow from its inherent structure, rather than explaining these aspects.

Sentence (6) at best presents a fact—a disposition by competent speakers of English to accept instances of (6)—leaving its explanation open.[5] Explaining our uses of a truth predicate by dispositions to accept instances of (6) is simply to introduce a new explanandum. If we have the factual uses of language explain the meaning of words and constructions and their truth-conditional properties, we cannot of course appeal to the meaning of these words and constructions to explain the uses and the properties in question; but we must, since there is nothing else to non-vacuously explain them. At worst, (6) will not even be meaningful, however. For, if quotation marks were indeed to form an unstructured name of an expression (as on Tarski's or Quine's views[6]), (6) would be no more meaningful than any other truth-predication attached to a name. That is, (6) would be similar to (7):

(7) John is true iff *p*

The same point holds for *any* view on which a quotation is a referential (as opposed to a propositional) expression.[7] The problem raises its head also for the propositional version of the Tarskian T-schema: 'the proposition that *p* is true iff *p*', where there is no quotation of or reference to a linguistic expression: this is because any instance of this propositional version will state a brute association of names (singular terms, on standard assumptions) and their uses or interpretations, which has to be strictly *learned*, as in the case of any other name (although in the present instance there would be an infinity of names to be learned!). For there is no linguistic expression, in this case, whose

[5] As Etchemendy (1988) emphasizes, Tarski himself did not conceive of his truth definition as even providing the semantics of a natural language: it 'cannot possibly illuminate the semantic properties of the object language' (1988: 56), since the only facts that can follow from a Tarskian definition of truth are facts about logic, syntax, and set-theory, Tarski's project being that of an elimination of semantic notions rather than their explanation (1988: 57).

[6] As Tarski put it, a quotation name is 'a name of the same nature as the name of a man' (Tarski 1956: 159–60).

[7] Including Davidson's own view, which rejects the Tarski–Quine view.

internal structure we could appeal to in order to find out how the reference of the singular term 'the proposition that *p*' is determined.[8]

The sentential version (6) is meaningful as long as the normal view that a quotation forms an object-denoting singular term is rejected, and truth is ascribed to a proposition as opposed to an object of reference. Even in that case, however, it can only be meaningful (or an equivalence) if either the right-hand side means what the left-hand side does, or at least necessarily agrees in truth value with it. As for the former option, equivalence in meaning, we argued for the necessity of distinguishing judgements from mere thoughts (or thoughts *with* from thoughts *without* an evaluation or predication of truth). With respect to the interpretation of (6), there are then two possibilities: either the right-hand side is a judgement or assertion, too, like the left-hand side, or it is not. In the former case, the right-hand side must have the additional structure *implicitly* which the left-hand side makes *explicit*, and we have made no advance in understanding truth. The predication of truth precisely is the additional extra in question, and the right-hand side simply does not analyse the left-hand side. In the latter case, there cannot be any talk of an equivalence at all, and (6) in fact resembles (8), which is either false or meaningless:

(8) (We make the judgement that) it is true that *p*, iff *p*

Sentence (8) is false if '*p*' on the right-hand side is read as standing for a fact. It is meaningless if it is read as standing for a mere thought (without an evaluation of its truth), in which case we have something rather like (9), where the question mark indicates that the truth value of *p* is unsettled:

(9) (We make the judgement that) it is true that *p*, iff *p?*

So (8) is meaningful only if the right-hand side is effectively read as a judgement of truth. Which brings us back to the first option, that the left-hand side merely makes explicit a judgement presumed to be there on the right-hand side ('there', at a semantic rather than phonetic level of representation). A common gloss of the T-schema, to the effect that 'the right-hand side is *asserted* just in case the left-hand side is', suggests this as well.[9] Consider in fact a nice formulation in Read (1994: 31), which makes this vivid: 'The T-sentences show us that predicating the truth of a proposition is equivalent

[8] Davidson (1999) formulates this objection to Horwich's (1998) minimalist vision of truth.

[9] But that option would make questionable that we can talk about a truth-theoretic or extensional equivalence at all in the case of (6), since it is doubtful whether explicit judgements of truth are themselves evaluated for truth, an issue to which I return later in this chapter.

to asserting a proposition.' But what is asserting a proposition? It is predicating the truth of a proposition.

It has also been said that what (6) tells us is that the 'extra' that is involved in evaluating the truth of a given thought content is fully contained in the predication that *p* contains within itself already. That is, the predicate:

(10) [is white]

tells us all there is to know about the double predication

(11) (That snow) is white is true.

But, the mere thought content (12)

(12) Snow is white

involves a predication with *or without* a *further* predication of truth or falsity. It seems we can contemplate the content of snow's being white, while leaving its truth value open. It is in this way not true that the predication internal to a proposition is as such sufficient for a predication of truth. Moreover, if we add a further lexical item, truth, to the structure underlying (12), and a further predicative relation, its reduction to the former predication would imply a disappearance of lexical structure and syntactic relations that would be somewhat mysterious from a grammatical point of view; in fact, it would violate a principle widely assumed in minimalist grammar, namely that material with an interpretive significance at the conceptual–thematic interface or the discourse-interface, once added to a derivation, could not simply evaporate. Finally, as is well known, there are of course truth judgements such as *Whatever stands in the Times is true* that simply do not contain any 'primary' predications relative to which the truth predicate might be said to be 'flat', 'transparent', or 'redundant' (see Gupta 1993).

Overall I conclude that whatever resemblance (in certain respects) there may be between the present proposal and currently dominant deflationist lines of thought, it is not a deep one, and ultimately orthogonal to my present concerns: while rejecting the externalism of the correspondence theory, deflationism remains wedded to externalist, dispositionalist, and functionalist conceptions of language; the internalist avenue is not explored. Most importantly, I fail to see the explanatory scope of deflationism with respect to what is the main question here, the origin of alethic competence. One crucial aspect of the answer to that question is, if I am right, the specific structural hierarchy we find in the human clause (especially the Complementizer domain), and the duality of conceptual/thematic and intentional/discursive information. Both of these pose substantive and unresolved evolutionary puzzles, the solution to which, if again I am right, has to be sought on internalist lines. It is not clear to me how an analysis of our 'inclinations' or 'dispositions' to accept sentences *containing* the relevant concept (such as instances of (5)–(6); cf. Horwich 1998: 23) and *exploiting* the propositional syntax in question, would even speak to this goal. Our linguistic behaviours and practices of acceptance are themselves what is in need of an explanation, and that explanation will have to *appeal* to a possession of the concept of truth itself. In what follows I will pursue the alternative vision that truth, like other fundamental notions of human cognition such as 'cause' or 'object', is a cognitive primitive not reducible to anything else, whose structural aspects we can submit to empirical inquiry, regarding them as abstract and non-perceptual pre-conditions for human intentionality and language use: a species-specific way of 'being in the world'.

I will therefore leave discussion of alternative contemporary frameworks at this point and turn to my own positive proposal.

4.2 Two kinds of predication

To make sense of language and meaning, philosophers have frequently exploited the relation between language and truth.[10] The sections to follow present the beginnings of an empirical study of an aspect of this relation in the form of a study of the actual structures that sentences expressing truth judgements have. In short, I here switch from studying 'truth conditions' for sentences (determined metaphysically, or normatively) to studying the structures of expressions of the form *This sentence is true* or *This sentence has (some) truth to it* themselves. The study of these expressions, I will argue, teaches a lesson: in the way that truth figures in human cognition, it is not an externalist notion. My starting point is that recent work in grammatical theory suggests that there are two fundamentally different forms of predication. In the kind of predication I shall be specifically interested in, the predicate stands in a relation to the subject that I will call 'integral'. For example, in (13), a part (13a) and a constitution (13b) are predicated of some whole. Both the part and the constitution relate, I shall say, integrally to their respective wholes:

(13) a. John has two legs

(13) b. This ring is gold.

[10] The following theory has been strongly influenced by a long-term collaboration with Juan Uriagereka, and would have been completely impossible without his (1995) paper.

There is no such integral relation between the subject and the predicate in the other kind of predication, which I will call 'standard', as when I predicate of John that he wears a brown pullover or lives in Stockton. I will illustrate this distinction further as we go along and present some recent arguments that the distinction in question correlates with two different syntactic paradigms that structure the sentences expressing those kinds of predications. That is to say: a particular way of seeing the world—one expressed in making an integral predication—is closely linked to an intricate *structural paradigm* in human syntax, much in line with the general perspective on conceptualization adopted in this book, except that now, more controversially, we are moving into the intentional rather than the merely conceptual domain. The connection to the topic of truth arises from the fact that, as I shall argue, the way the truth-predicate is attached to sentences, as in (14), is in the form of an integral predication as well:

(14) What John says has some truth to it.

This claim, to be defended below, is meant as an entirely empirical one that, unlike its philosophical consequences, is simply either right or wrong. If right, then it is also an empirical fact that, structurally speaking, in the case of truth judgements the way *the mind relates a given proposition to truth is much the same as the way in which it relates a whole to a part or a substance to its constitution.*

Now, to illustrate the above distinction further, intuitively the way my hand relates to my arm is different from the way my hand relates to a pencil when it holds it. We expect a hand to be an integral part of a body, and our horror in tragic circumstances where that is not the case makes this clear. In such circumstances, my hand becomes related to my body rather in the way we expect a pencil to relate to my hand. There is a similar horror if that latter expectation is disappointed, and the pencil becomes to relate to my hand in the way my hand relates normally to my arm, namely as an integral part. Let us look at a concrete example. Sentence (15) allows for both an integral and a standard reading:

(15) There is a hand on my arm.

The integral reading, where the hand is a part of the arm, is natural, for example, in a situation where one explains to an extra-terrestrial on the phone how one looks. In that circumstance, one has a hand on one's arm much as one has two legs on one's trunk or a nose in one's face. By contrast, a situation in which the predication would be 'standard' could be one in which my hand has been severed from my arm and placed on it (or another person's hand has been). A passer-by, shocked by the sight, might exclaim: 'Gee, there is a hand on your arm!', and his surprise is a measure of the fact that he does not mean to predicate any integral relation between the arm and the hand in such a case. Hornstein *et al.* (2002), the paper where the present distinction originates, discuss an analogous case, using a beautiful example:

(16) There is a Ford T engine in my Saab.

They argue that (16) is *structurally ambiguous*. The two relevant readings are disambiguated in the paraphrases in (17), each of which, they argue, has a different syntax from the other entirely:

(17) a. My Saab has a Ford T engine.
(17) b. (Located) in my Saab is a Ford T engine.

Sentence (17a) primarily has an integral reading (which transpires despite the fact that world knowledge would lead us to expect Saabs not to run on Ford engines); (17b) has a standard, in this case locative, reading.[11] I will adopt Hornstein *et al.*'s analysis here, which centrally aims to account for (17) on a model also encompassing (16), and give an indication of their line of thought. On this analysis, both the derivations of (17a) and (17b) begin with a Small Clause (SC), which contains the lexico-conceptual elements entering into a predicational relationship. We might say that with the SC we have the conceptual material for a judgement (in my present terms), although not

[11] It may indeed be a general fact that, whenever you look at a functioning car, you may shift from a perspective looking at the car as a mere container for things located in it (cans of coke, cigarettes, windows, engines, etc.), to a perspective looking at the car as a functioning unit working by means of certain parts contributing to this functioning. But this observation does not in any way imply that (17b) has a *reading* on which it is integral, or that (17a) has a reading on which it is not. In other examples, such shifts are more clearly grammatically impossible. Consider the following example from Hornstein *et al*:

(i) There are ten provinces in Canada

primarily means that Canada is comprised of ten provinces, not that these are located there. This is also what *Canada has ten provinces* expresses, and (i) has no *be*-paraphrase of the sort in (ii) below, which corresponds to a non-integral reading. I claim that this is so in the same sense in which (iii) is out under the integral reading:

(ii) *Ten provinces are in Canada
(iii) *A Ford T engine is in my Saab.

Supposing that, indeed, my Saab runs by means of a Ford T engine, there is of course also a sense in which it is an *assertable truth*, in that case, that my Saab is a container in which the machine happens to be located (the non-integral reading). Similarly, it might be that a situation in which you preferentially say (17b) rather than (17a), would also be—for non-linguistic reasons—a situation in which it is an assertable truth that my Saab also runs by means of that engine. But what truth an expression can be used to convey in a context and what interpretation its grammatical forms license are radically different issues.

yet sufficient structure to encode its intentional structure. In particular, any fully articulated judgement presumably requires finite Tense, as we make judgements by placing propositions in time, or the temporal structure of an ongoing discourse. On the standard reading of (16), the SC-predicate unpacks as the PP *in my Saab* (19). That PP, by contrast, is not a constituent in (18), which reflects the predication underlying the integral reading of (16):

(18) [$_{SC}$ My Saab [a Ford T engine]].
(19) [$_{SC}$ a Ford T engine [in my Saab]].

That is, while in (17b), *a Ford T engine* is the SC-subject, of which the PP *in My Saab* is predicated to yield *a Ford T engine in my Saab* (as in *You saw [a Ford T engine in my Saab]*), in (17a) the SC-subject is actually *My Saab*. This makes us wonder what is the role for *in* to play in (18). Hornstein *et al.* (2002) propose a modified version of the syntax of possessive *has*-constructions first suggested by Szabolcsi (1984) for Hungarian, later transferred to English by Kayne (1993). Szabolcsi showed that the SC subject *My Saab* of (17a)—the *Possessor*, POSS—raises all the way up to the surface subject position before *be*, obligatorily in the case of Hungarian if there is an indefinite *Possessed*, as in (17a), optionally if the Possessed is definite. Kayne (1993) further argues for a phonologically non-overt D-position, prepositional in character, below the matrix-verb *be*. This is where Hornstein *et al.* argue the preposition *in* after relevant movements of the SC-constituents ultimately surfaces in examples such as (16). This D also projects a Spec, a movement site through which the Possessor moves on its way to the matrix verb *be*. All that leaves open how we get the overt form *has* that we have in (17a), but Kayne (1993: 7) argues, taking inspiration from Freeze (1992), that *has* is a surface form resulting from the incorporation of an abstract D-head into the verbal element *be*. The result of all this is (20), the underlying structure of (17a):

(20) [My Saab$_{POSS}$ be+D$_{has}$ [$_{DP}$ Spec D [$_{SC}$ [~~My Saab~~] a Ford T engine]]].

Szabolcsi also showed that when the Possessor raises up the syntactic tree, a functional morpheme encoding Agreement shows up:

(21) [My Saab$_{POSS}$ be+D [$_{DP}$ Spec D [$_{AgrP}$ Spec Agr [$_{SC}$ [~~My Saab~~] a Ford T engine]]]].

Taking this as a basis, Hornstein *et al.* argue that in the last step of the derivation of (17a), the SC-predicate *a Ford T engine* vacates the SC as well:

(22) [My Saab be+D$_{has}$ [$_{DP}$ a Ford T engine D [$_{AgrP}$ Spec Agr [$_{SC}$ [~~My Saab~~] [~~a Ford T engine~~]]]]].

The sentence:

(23) My Saab has a Ford T engine in it.

now falls into place: the non-overt D-position that Kayne postulated now becomes overt, through the very same *in*-preposition that transpires in the *there*-paraphrase (16). That is, *in* spells out the D-trace in (23), while the clitic *it* is in the Spec of Agr, the possessor's first landing site.[12]

The basic structure (22) now allows us to derive sentences expressing integral possession in (24) and (25) as transformationally related in their underlying structures. All the derivations of the examples in (24) and (25) start out with an SC encoding the same lexico-conceptual relation between the Possessor and the Possessed. What differs is in which syntactic positions these two items end up:[13]

(24) a. My Saab's Ford T engine
(24) b. The Ford T engine of my Saab
(24) c. My Saab has a Ford T engine (in it)
(25) a. John's sister
(25) b. The sister of John
(25) c. John has a sister

Let us now discuss some theoretical aspects of this analysis. Implicit in it is the denial that the difference between integral and non-integral possession is a *lexical* one. But why not assume what seems most natural, that integral possession *is* a lexical matter?[14] In that case, in both *John has a sister: Mary* and *Mary is a sister of John*, there would be a relational term taken from the lexicon that has two variable positions in it: *sister*(x,y), with what we can think of as a 'referential' argument (Mary) and a 'possessive' argument (John). We could then say that when the *has*-variant is used, it marks a (relational) property of the possessive argument (the property of having a sister), while

[12] Some readers have remarked that (23) is ambiguous for them. The non-integral reading is invited in (i):

(i) My Saab has a Ford T engine (located) in (side) it.

But here the *in* is not in D, but the head of a Prepositional Phrase *inside my Saab*. There is good syntactic evidence that this PP is not a syntactic constituent on the integral reading, one piece of evidence being that a Spec-PP such as *right* deprives us of the integral interpretation, witness (ii):

(ii) There is a Ford T engine right in my Saab.

This is what we expect, if on the integral interpretation there is no PP-head for *right* to relate to.

[13] Concretely, in (24a), I take the genitive *'s* to materialize in D; the Possessor *My Saab* has moved to Spec-D, and the Possessed has moved to Spec-Agr. In (24b), the Possessor remains *in situ*, the definite Possessed moves to Spec-Agr, *of* lexicalizes Agr. In (24c), the Possessor, as argued before, moves up all the way to Spec-*be*.

[14] See Keenan (1987: 305–7) for a proposal on more traditional lexicalist lines.

the *be*-variant marks a property of the referential argument (the property of being a sister). Crucially, both would involve the same *sister*-relation. But as Uriagereka (forthcoming: ch. 3) notes (and see Freeze 1992: 589), this cannot be quite right, if only because most languages lack an auxiliary *to have* as a lexeme with a similar status as *to be*, and even English expresses integral possession equally without it (as in *John's sister*, *a man with a sister*, or *the sister of John's*). If most languages lack *have* in addition to *be*, the difference in the properties *being a sister* and *having a sister* cannot be blamed on *have* and *be*.

The systematicity inherent in the fact that all languages appear to express integral relations would be expected if indeed it was a matter of syntax rather than the lexicon, on the standard assumption that the latter is the source of linguistic variation. Additional support for this is that the Kayne–Szabolcsi syntax originally developed for 'integral possession' is not lexically restricted to this paradigm and in fact extends to all kinds of reversible part–whole relations, including those between objects and their constitution (*a ring of pure gold*, *the gold of this ring*), masses and their measures (*four kilos of meat*, *a meat of four kilos*, *90 per cent of humidity*, *a humidity of 90 per cent*), countries and their provinces (*Canada's ten provinces*, *the ten provinces of Canada*), or propositions and their truth values (as I will argue). It thus becomes undesirable to see these relations as lexical ones. There is virtually nothing that would not have all sorts of parts to which it is integrally related, as Uriagereka notes. Everything—excepting God, or the transcendental Ego of the German romantics, perhaps, neither of which are conceived as being integrally related to anything else—seems to integrally relate to any number of things (although not all), say as a part. All this is hardly encoded in the human lexicon. If we ask what the respective integral relations in the examples just given have in common in lexico-conceptual terms, it is not clear what it is, and what we could make our basis for defining the lexical meaning of integral possession. As we try to define the alleged lexical relation of integral possession through paraphrases, it seems we find that possessive syntax will occur in them in one or another way, this being their identifying feature. At the same time, Uriagereka notices that the syntax of *have* is not like that of the theta-structure of a lexical verb, having nothing analogous to 'D-structure' in the sense above. So, while plausibly syntactic, the syntax in question is *sui generis*.[15]

[15] Thus, interestingly, with neither *have* nor *be* do we get 'zeugma' effects arising when verbs identical in their phonetic representation but different in their underlying thematic requirements get conjoined. Compare (i) with (ii) and (iii) (from Uriagereka forthcoming: ch. 3):

(i) *you are carrying a broad smile on your face *and* your nice lover in your arms
(ii) you normally have a broad smile on your face and your nice lover in your arms
(iii) you are lucky to be broad smiled and blessed with such a nice lover.

On the other hand, it is also interesting to note that not everything can be 'had', implying that there are restrictions to the universal availability of integral relationships. For example, a thing's standing in a *mathematically necessary* relation to another one will not necessarily imply any integrality for their relationship. Hence *extra-linguistic* (such as semantic or mathematical) considerations do *not* seem to be the basis for when something is integrally related to something else. Thus, for example, we would not normally say that a plane 'has' a line, even though it geometrically entails one, necessarily. Moreover, nothing that is integrally related as a part to some whole in the present sense is *intrinsically so related* in some trivial physical sense. Thus, for example, my heart, an integral part of my body, might be exchanged for another. Its integral relation to me is then a matter of judgement. If the heart is taken out from my body and put on a table next to me, I may still say (if I can): 'This is *my heart*', and identify with it, although I may also not, and a doctor's statement: 'You have a heart [pointing to the removed one]' might just as well be judged as being plainly false. Note that nothing changes physically in the heart that these judgements are about, when we switch from viewing it as an integral part to viewing it non-integrally.

Note next that in a judgement about some thing's 'having' some other thing, the first thing's relation to the second does not as such imply anything about which of the two terms denoting the two things in question takes on a *referential* role in the judgement in question. Again this supports the present perspective, in the way that it argues for drawing a distinction between the lexico-conceptual part of a judgement, and its logico-intentional one. Thus, for example, nothing changes *lexico-conceptually* in the relation between the university and the faculties, if we say (26a) or (26b). The changes are in the expression's intentional structure, or in what the ultimate referent of the complex expressions is:

(26) a. a university of four faculties
(26) b. the four faculties of the university.

These are both derived from the same SC at the bottom of the structure, encoding an integral relation between the university and its faculties which have an identical thematic relationship as Possessor and Possessed. Examples (26) differ, rather, in referential properties, and the point of the present proposal is that we derive those by either moving the Possessor or the Possessed to a referential site in the functional structure on top of the SC. Since overall reference in (26a) is to the university (the possessor), the syntactic position of that item in the structure encodes reference, whereas, in

(26b), it is the position of the four faculties that the university has. On the account above, this referential site is descriptively the Spec of the AgrP. Hence, just as in the case of verbs projecting certain argument roles, which remain what they are no matter where syntactic transformations carry them thereafter, the thematic roles that Possessor and Possessed play remain what they are no matter what the actual judgement turns out to be, or what it ends up being about.

On the former 'lexicalist' proposal as I have depicted it above we would by contrast posit a relational term *four faculties*(x,y) in the lexicon to express the constitution or part–whole relation between *university* and *four faculties.* But this leaves us clueless, as Uriagereka (2002: ch. 10) points out, about how to explain a gap in the paradigm of reversibility that is not predicted on the lexicalist proposal: (27a) is impossible, while (27b), along with (26), is entirely fine:

(27) a. *The/a four faculties' university
(27) b. The university's four faculties

The gap can be syntactically explained by observing the geometry of movement paths: in (27a), the SC-predicate moves to Spec-D in a situation where moving *university* would yield a shorter move:

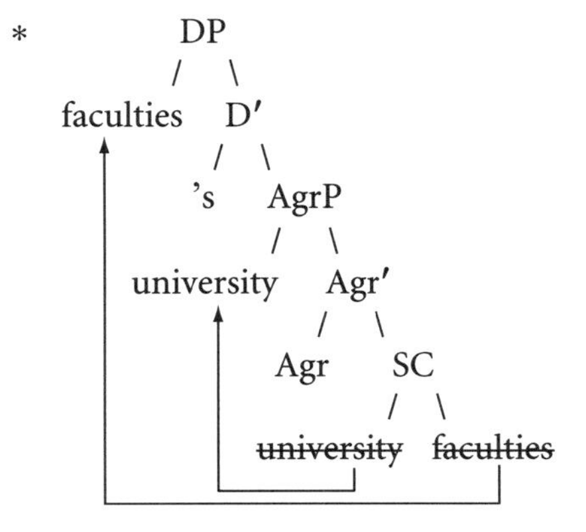

Consider in fact what happens if we suppose that (26) and (27) are not transformationally related by virtue of the same SC, or being identical in respect of their lexico-conceptual structure. We would have to posit *two* rather than one relational term, each with a referential and a possessive variable position, as a matter of lexical fact: *faculties*(x,y), which encodes the relation of a part to a whole, and *university*(y,x), which encodes the relation between a whole and its parts. Moreover, once we get down to consider a *faculty of four*

departments, we cannot re-use our previous relational term *faculties*(x,y). After all, it formalized the relation of a part to a whole rather than, as now required, a relation between a whole and its parts. That is, not only will every lexical term whose denotatum relates to something as a part have to be relational, every lexical term will have to be relational *in different ways*. The resulting view of the human lexicon does not look appealing.

I conclude that Uriagereka's case that integral possession is not lexico-conceptual in nature, but inherently syntactic, is a strong one. The fundamental idea here, that part of where formal ontological notions such as part and whole come from is syntax, is intriguing indeed. With all this in mind, let us turn to truth judgements and the question of whether the paradigm of integral relations transfers to this instance or not.

4.3 Predicating truth

Consider the judgements in (28), which are interestingly different and stronger forms of truth judgement than those with a possessive syntax in (29a, 29b), as well as other instances of the possessive paradigm in (30) and (31):

(28) a. that the Earth is flat is true
(28) b. the truth is that the Earth is flat
(29) a. That the Earth is flat has (some) truth to it[16]
(29) b. There is some truth to the Earth's being flat
(30) the truth of the Earth's being flat
(31) the truth is that of the Earth's being flat

In this section I will suggest that the right derivation of these structures is on the lines of (21), above. Before we come to that, let us first digress to (32), below, however, in which a possessive construction involving truth configures the complement of an attitude attribution:

(32) a. You will realize [the truth of the Earth's being flat]
(32) b. You will realize [the truth (of) that the Earth is flat]

As Torrego and Uriagereka (2002) argue, the complements of the above attitude attributions are not simply complex NPs of a standard sort, as in (33):

(33) John heard [the rumour that the Earth is flat].

[16] Some readers have found (29a) only 'marginally grammatical', but I am very surprised by such a claim. Would the then-pope not have feared, at some point, that there might be some truth after all to what Galileo said? I constantly say in discussions, pondering a view that someone proposed: 'It is not *absurd*. There *is* something to it!' 'It has *some* truth (to it), though not much!' And sometimes I strengthen this: 'It *is* (completely and entirely) true!'

The way a proposition may be true is very different, it turns out, from the way in which it may be a rumour. A contrast like the one between *That the Earth is flat has some truth to it* and **That the Earth is flat has some rumour to it* suggests a divergence between these two paradigms in fact rather immediately. Consider further the contrast in (34a, 34b), brought nicely into focus upon adding *only*:

(34) a. That the Earth is flat is (only) a rumour
(34) b. That the Earth is flat is (only) a truth

While (34a) is perfect colloquially, it is hard to imagine a situation in normal speech where (34b) would seem natural, except maybe for a logic class. These judgements *reverse* in (35):

(35) a. That the Earth is flat is only the rumour
(35) b. That the Earth is flat is only the truth

If (35a) is good at all, it requires an addition like 'that I told you about'. Such an addition is not only entirely unnecessary for (35b); but the sentence that would result, *That the Earth is flat is only the truth that I told you about*, is entirely different from (35b) in ordinary speech, where (35b) means something like: 'I emphatically assert that the Earth is flat'.[17] Sentence (35a), by contrast, does *not* mean what it would mean if it were parallel with (35b), namely: 'I doubt that the Earth is flat'. In short, while *the rumour* in (35a) is short for a possibly longer definite description, *the truth* in (35b), crucially without the relative clause, is not at all used for such identification purposes. Torrego and Uriagereka (2002) suggest that while *rumour* is a head that projects in standard ways upon merging with a complement, *truth* in (32) is an SC-predicate predicated of a propositional constituent in a small-clausal ('base-adjoined') fashion. Indeed, the Kayne/Szabolcsi/Hornstein *et al.* paradigm, which bottoms out with a SC-predication of this very sort, makes good sense of the paradigm in (28)–(31) above, repeated here:

(28) a. that the Earth is flat is true
(28) b. the truth is that the Earth is flat
(29) a. That the Earth is flat has (some) truth (to it)
(29) b. There is some truth to the Earth's being flat
(30) the truth of the Earth's being flat
(31) the truth is that of the Earth's being flat

[17] Or: 'That the Earth is flat is only the truth! Why should I not say it?'

The suggestion is that all of the above expressions in their underlying structures bottom out with the same SC encoding an integral relation between a propositional constituent and its truth. I shall call the latter a 'presentation' of the former: a judgement presents a particular proposition under a certain aspect, like the aspect of its truth (see (36)). The derivation, for example, of (29a), is entirely parallel to that in (22) (see (37), where the propositional constituent *that the Earth is flat* is abbreviated as 'prop' and *be*+D+T is spelled out as *has*):

(36) $[_{SC}$ [proposition] truth]

(37)

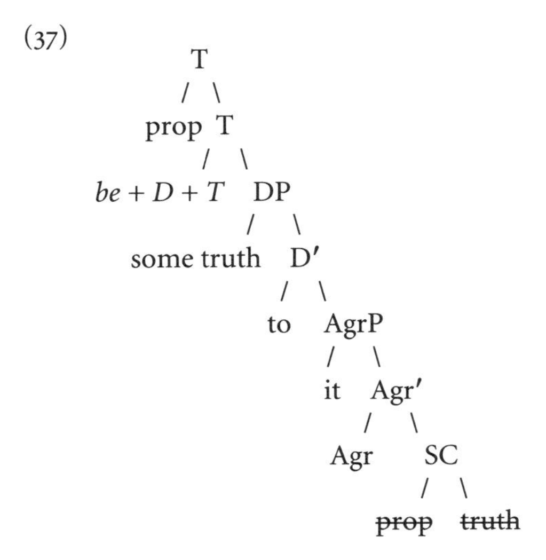

If this is the right structure, we predict the same interplay between *lexico-conceptual* relations encoded in the SC, on the one hand, and how the whole expression's referentiality or *intentional* structure eventually pans out. Thus, for example, we may be talking primarily about the truth, as in *the truth of the Earth's being flat* or *the truth is that the Earth is flat*, or about the proposition, as in *that the Earth is flat is true*. Indeed, if we compare the paradigm in (28)–(31) with the integral paradigm in (38), below, interesting parallelisms can be observed, having to do with similar definiteness and indefiniteness effects:

(38) a. this large Ego of mine
(38) b. this large Ego is mine
(38) c. I have a large Ego

Example (38a) corresponds to something like (30), (38b) to (31), (38c) to (29a). As for the definiteness and indefiniteness effects, notice how in (39)–(40), below, similar oddities and contrasts arise under the integral interpretation:

(39) a. *a truth is that the Earth is flat
(39) b. ??an Ego is mine
(40) a. *that the Earth is flat has the truth to it
(40) b. *I have the/this large Ego.

Example (39) illustrates a constraint, that if the SC-predicate is promoted to sentence-subject position, it *has* to be definite, whereas, if the SC-subject is, the SC-predicate *must not* be definite. As one reader has pointed out to me, (40b) may seem somewhat odd, but it is not entirely out, at least with *this* in the place of *the*. But observe that the *integral* reading is at stake. It seems that on the reading where (40b) is marginally fine, it has a wide-scope paraphrase: it means that there is this large Ego that I have. This makes good sense of a general verdict against wide-scope paraphrases of integral predications. Thus, observe that in (17a) *My Saab has a Ford T engine*, the indefinite cannot have wide scope if the sentence is integrally interpreted: it cannot mean, on that reading, that there is a Ford T engine such that it is in the Saab. This same phenomenon transpires with the integral (41), which clearly does not allow (42), in which *some truth* scopes out from under the matrix verb:

(41) There is some truth to what this author says,
(42) *Some truth is to what this author says.

The same happens if we replace *to* by *in*. Sentence (41) will in that case be ambiguous between the integral and the non-integral reading, but scoping out *some truth* forces the non-integral one, witness (43), which is ungrammatical under the integral reading, and which I claim is parallel with (43b), which also is ungrammatical under the integral reading:

(43a) *Some truth is in what this author says.
(43b) *A Ford T engine is in my Saab.

We predict the ungrammaticality of (43), if we assume that *some truth* is not a *subject* in its underlying predicational structure, but a predicate, as I argued. There is, finally, also the parallelism between the ungrammaticality, on the integral reading, of (44) and the ungrammaticality, on the same reading, of (45):

(44) There is a Ford T engine in(*side) My Saab.
(45) There is some truth in(*side) what you say.[18]

[18] Here one objection suggests itself: (45) is ungrammatical for *semantic* reasons—namely, just because *in* disambiguated as *inside* lexically selects a non-abstract object. Note however that I am only claiming that (45) is ungrammatical on the integral reading, and that those semantic reasons cannot be that decisive: (45) may be (marginally) meaningful by forcing a purely locative reading, where the idea

In sum, the proposal is that *the truth of the Earth's being flat* or *the truth that the Earth is flat* are structured by the possessive Kayne/Szabolcsi/Hornstein *et al.* syntax, and that a form like (46)

(46) The truth is that the Earth is flat

is derived by predicate raising, as in (47), leaving the Possessor in place:

(47) [the truth BE [$_{\text{SC}}$ that the Earth is flat ~~the truth~~]].

This is what we expect in terms of the Kayne/Szabolcsi/Hornstein *et al.* structure, where, if the Possess*ed* is definite, it raises up to the matrix and the auxiliary *be* shows up. Thus we have (48):

(48) This sister is John's

In turn, if the Possess*or* raises, the D-element undergoes the incorporation into AUX that we have taken from Kayne's and Freeze's work, yielding *has*, so that we get *That the Earth is flat has some truth to it.* Consider finally a very interesting *semantic* parallel between the possessive constructions in (49) and (50), below. There is a contrast between the a-examples and the b-examples which is relevantly similar:

(49) a. Tyson has two big fists and a large Ego
(49) b. Tyson is two big fists and a large Ego

(cf.: *Two big fists and a large Ego is all Tyson is [is all of Tyson]*; *Tyson is nothing but two big fists and a large Ego*)

(50) a. That the earth is flat has some truth to it
(50) b. That the earth is flat is true.

The contrast of course is that the (a)-examples are each weaker than the (b)-examples: in the former, no matter whether we talk of the big fists or the truth, these are just *aspects* under which we view Tyson, or the proposition that the Earth is flat, but it is not the whole of these. Tyson is also something else, aside from his fists and his Ego: regarding big fists (one part or aspect of his over which we quantify), Tyson *has those*—but we invite or at least do not

is to locate some truth in what you say (say, *on p. 476 of your book*, or *in the first half* of your speech). This is evidently non-integral and not the reading I intend. One reader worries about *There is some truth (to be found) in what you say.* In this example, *some truth* is the subject of the predication, and there is a prepositional phrase *in what you say*, which is inexistent on the integral reading (or so I claim). Being the subject, it also can raise, as in *Some truth is (there) in what you say (namely, on p. 476)*, which we do not observe in integral predications.

preclude the thought that there are also other aspects that he has. In the same way, in (50a) the relevant proposition is only partially true: we seem to imply that it is not quite right, and may also have some false aspects to it. In the (b)-examples, by contrast, it is as if the object reduces to those very aspects (they *stand* for the whole, so to speak, or make it up entirely). The point of the assertion (in this sort of dismissive verdict) is: *regardless* of how we look at Tyson, he is just that and nothing but that: two big fists and a large Ego. In the case of predications of truth, we could paraphrase these two versions, as in (51):

(51) a. Regarding truth, (the proposition) that the Earth is flat has *that*
(51) b. Regarding (the proposition) that the Earth is flat, *it* is true.

In both cases, once again, nothing changes *lexically*: we have a proposition, and its truth, standing in the same integral relation in both cases. What the above paraphrases indicate is that what changes is our *perspective*, what we *refer* to, and *what we consider in the context of what*, which is a change in the derivationally later *intentional* structure of the sentence. In (51a), we consider the proposition in the light of its aspect of truth: it comes into view in the *context* of this one of its aspects, and we leave open under what other, if not opposite, aspects it may come into view as well. Nothing like this happens in (51b). The proposition as such is just that: true. The proposition *itself* is the context with respect to which we consider truth. Thus *the truth* takes wide scope in (51a), while the proposition scopes out in (51b). If scope is derived by movement, the relevant difference is intrinsically one relating to the transformationally derived aspects of the clause. This essentially seems to be the explanation for the difference in strength we observed in (50a, 50b): the scopes of quantified NPs are *nested* within one another.

More generally speaking, quantification and reference in natural languages are *contextually confined*. If I say *The murderer (whoever he is) is insane*, I do not quantify over all murderers, but just contextually relevant ones. For concreteness, let this contextual confinement that a speaker assumes in an utterance be expressed through second-order context variables, X, which specify, for a first-order individual variable x, over what kinds of things x is to range (cf. Higginbotham 1988: 39–40). Assume, secondly, that if there are several expressions of generality in a sentence, the context variables associated with them nest and take *scope* over one another. Assume, thirdly, that when we predicate truth of a proposition in SC-fashion, the two NP-constituents of the SC move out of the SC into positions where they are specified for their referential and quantificational information, in the context of a third, single-event quantification (recall that all root clauses on the view of Chapter 3 correspond to single events, or are centred around verbal heads with a single event position). Then just as in a case like Tyson and big fists, where we make a judgement about a particular (single) event and the larger-scope quantification can be over either Tyson or the fists, in a judgement of truth (call it a 'truth-event', *t*) we can have the larger quantification being over either the truth or the proposition, resulting in (51a) or (51b) respectively. Finally, assume, in the spirit of the Minimalist Program, that Movement occurs only when forced by the need to check certain features. We have seen that one of the terms in an integral predication plays the role of the referential one, the one that determines what the expression as a whole is about; assume then that there is a *referential* feature [ref] to be checked in the checking domain of Agr, given that this appears to be the place where the item that we make reference to moves. Assume also, to code context confinement as demanded in the first assumption above, that there is a *contextual* feature [c] to be checked in Spec-D, the site of the event-quantification. Then there will be one thing, *x*, which plays the role of the proposition that the Earth is flat at *t* (the Possessor-role), and there will be a thing, *y*, which plays the role of the truth (the Possessed) at *t*. We can now suggest, with Uriagereka (2002), that the semantic difference noted in (50–51) follows from the syntactic fact that either the context variable determining the range of *y* scopes over the context variable associated with *x*, or *vice versa*.

In any utterance of (50a), then, a speaker will assume that for some truth-event *t*, there is some *truth* (the Possessed) ranging over things *y* confined to a context *Y*, for some thing *x* (the Possessor), confined to a context *X* set *into Y*: the proposition is considered or quantified under the aspect of, and in the context of, a quantification over its truth. In an utterance of (50b), by contrast, a speaker will assume that for some proposition which ranges over things *x* confined to a context *X*, there is a thing *y*, its truth, confined to a context *Y* now set *into the context X*. As before, the SC fixes the 'quasi-thematic' or conceptual structure of the predication. Contextual confinement is regulated via the Spec-D position. Although reference is to the Possessor in (50a), which checks the [ref] feature in Spec of Agr, the *context* within which we view the integral relation in which it stands to its truth is fixed by the Possessed which is LF-moved to Spec-D (yielding the reading (51a)). By contrast, in (50b), the *Possessor* moves through the Spec-D site to the matrix position before *be*, thereby checking the contextual feature, while the Possessed remains *in situ* in its original SC-position: the Possessor is thus not only what determines reference, but is at the same time what does the other job too, namely confining the context in which truth matters (yielding the reading (51b)). Reference-fixing and context confinement fall together. As a consequence, the truth comes into view in the context set up by the Possessor, not vice versa, which is the desired result. The proposition is true in a non-contextual (or non-partial) way.

In this section, I have collected some evidence that if we ask how humans cognitively structure the relation between a sentence and the truth we may judge it to have, integral syntax holds the key. Note that this is an empirical claim, right or wrong. If right, the relation between a sentence and its truth is an integral one. The question is now: what does this mean, and what is the philosophical significance of this observation? Before we turn to that, we extend the current claims to the complements of attitude attributions.

4.4 Alethic attitudes

While I have mainly talked about non-embedded integral predications, the analysis of an attitude attribution like (32) suggests that they occur embedded as well. This means that so-called 'propositional' attitudes apparently *need* not have *propositions* as their contents, in the philosophical sense of abstract objects relating non-integrally to a truth value in each possible world—but small-clausal predicational structures as well, which, as I put it, *present* propositions in a particular way. Now, if the content of the complement clause of an attitude attribution to a speaker has an inherent relation with the content of a sincere assertion of that sentence by that speaker, then in cases where the content of an attitude attribution is a small-clausal predicational structure, the content of the corresponding assertion should be a judgement based on that predicational relation as well. That is independently plausible, for someone saying:

(52) The Earth is flat,

does not say just *that*. He does more than uttering a sequence of words with a certain structural meaning, but also *presents* them as true (conveys this *stance* towards them). If we make this explicit, he is really saying something along the lines of (50), above: *That the earth is flat is true*, or, perhaps, the weaker *That the earth is flat has some truth to it*. What if not something like this (which, exactly, being a matter of context) is somebody asserting if s/he asserts (52)? What else could s/he be interpreted to *say*?

I am not suggesting here that somebody asserting (52) is 'disposed to *infer*' one of these other assertions, or anything like that, but that an assertion of (52) really *has* the underlying structure of one of a truth-predication. This structure is *there* in an assertion of (52), if only at the level of its underlying syntactic representation. It does not follow from this contention that the meaning of (52) and the SCs in (32) would have to be the same. It generally makes a difference if an element covertly present in the underlying structure is made overt, a situation in which we see certain specific discourse effects arising, a form of 'surface-semantics' not unlike the cases of *do*-support: *I do want an ice-cream* is different from *I want an ice-cream* as regards its discursive function. Making the parts marking the judgemental character of (52)/(50) overt equally serves a particular discourse purpose: if one asserted (52) and met some resistance on the side of one's interlocutor, one may not only reaffirm, but explicitly indicate one's commitment to (52) by asserting one of (50), with this choice depending on which strength in one's endorsement of veridicality one wishes to convey.

If there is such hidden structure in an assertion of (50), we have to say that someone who were to *report* on the content of an assertion of (52), say in one of the guises of (53),

(53) a. John said that the Earth is flat
(53) b. John believes that the Earth is flat

would really mean, if we made it fully explicit, something like the expressions in (54), below. There the *that*-clause is the associate of a referential pronoun 'it', and '(is) true', the predicate of a small-clausal complement of the declarative or epistemic (or factive) attitude verb, marks the attitude taken by John towards the veridicality of the proposition cataphorically referred to by *it*:

(54) a. John said that it_i is true [that the Earth is $flat]_i$.
(54) b. John believes it_i true [that the Earth is $flat]_i$.

The reason is that if an assertion of (52) really is an assertion of one of (50), *reports* of an assertion of (52), as in (53), are really reports of things like those in (50), and thus themselves like the reports in (54). We may therefore conjecture that contents of complements of declarative/epistemic attitude attributions (such as *(that) it (is) true that the Earth is flat* in (54)) are *generally*, and not just in the special case of (32), integral truth predications. In this case, we could also derive the fully general philosophical conclusions that attitude contents are, (i) *not* abstract (since judgements are not, which are hypothesized to be concrete structures in a human mind/brain)[19], (ii) *not* language-independent (for it is essential to them that they have a certain linguo-syntactic structure)[20], and (iii) *not* supplied with external

[19] Syntactic structures remain abstract, of course, in the different sense that we are not talking about cells.

[20] Note that they not do not 'refer to' syntactic logical forms, but have them, in the same sense in which they have phonetic forms. It would also not seem wrong to say they *are*, or *consist in* those structures.

'reference'- and 'truth-conditions', in the standard sense, as I have already argued and will support further below. Indeed, Uriagereka and Torrego (2002) argue that (32), as well as structures like (55), below, with null complementizers, are *paratactic* constructions, hence contain root clauses, as the present approach would predict:[21] their 'complements' are not propositions qua arguments of the matrix verb, but structures which are assembled *separately*, and then put together via a generalized transformation (data from Uriagereka 2002: 264):

(55) a. Dijeron habian llegado ayer
'They said/thought they had arrived yesterday'

(55) b. Lamento no estés contento con tu trabajo
'I regret you are not happy with your work.'

The authors interestingly distinguish this paradigm, which involves declarative, factive, and epistemic verbs—verbs taking an alethic complement—from another one, where also an overt complementizer appears to be missing, and which involves volitionals and desideratives (recall Section 1.5):

(56) a. Deseo lleguen bien
'I wish you arrive well'

(56) b. Quiere no les falte de nada
'He wants they miss nothing'

They demonstrate that the degree of connectivity between the matrix verb and the propositional dependent is weaker in the former paradigm (55). This for example shows in processes of *wh*-extraction, in which the null-complementizer cannot be crossed:

(57) *Qué libro dijeron/pensaron/creyeron no habían leído?
'What book did they saw/think/believe they hadn't read?'

(58) Qué libro quieres/deseas/espera hayan leído?
'What book do you want/wish/expect they may have read?'

Similarly, predicate raising is an illegitimate operation when the complementizer is null, as is neg-raising and the licensing of negative polarity items, and bound variable binding. Upon making the complementizer overt, all of these become possible. We may also recall the interesting contrast in (59), below:

(59) a. (That) we are going to the movies, I believe.
(59) b. *(That) we go to the movies, I want.

[21] This does not imply that there are not genuinely hypotactic forms of embedding, too. But I am committed to say that full truth judgements could not be argumental dependents. Davidson (2001) argues that all attitude reports are paratactic.

That we can drop the complementizer in (59a), but not in (59b), attests to the latter's hypotactic character, and that in the former, alethic, case, something else, of a paratactic nature, is going on. The way I am tempted to interpret this is that when truth is involved, the system has two different options: first to subordinate a clause and go on with structure-building, and secondly to invoke a paratactic dependent that is both syntactically and semantically more independent.

4.5 Implications for the metaphysics of truth

The primary concern of this book has been cognition, not metaphysics nor ontology. Integral relations—notions such as part and whole, or substance and constitution—have since Aristotle been interpreted as *metaphysical* notions. Not so here, where they have been treated as categories of our *cognition*, in a Kantian sense. Put differently, objects are wholes if *conceived* or conceptualized as objects-together-with a certain quantifiable structure of parts or aspects to which they may relate integrally: the aspects or parts are not cognitively speaking objects in their own right, but have a specific inherent *connection* with the objects of which they are the aspects. If I am right, this connection is a matter of human syntax—a specific structural paradigm in human conceptualization. It is not independent of the latter, or a matter of metaphysical fact. Accordingly the integrality of truth predication isn't a fact about the metaphysics of truth either. It is a fact about how truth figures in our cognition.

Sometimes we *cannot* conceive an object as an integrated whole. We are apparently wired so as not to be able to do so, for example, in the famous Russellian case of the cow's four legs, an 'object' that simply does not appear to have, for a creature with a cognition like ours, the right connectivity to be integrated into a whole. Four legs are, in this context, not an object in their own right for us (although other contexts are conceivable, in which we would judge them to be such an object). But even if viewing an object as a whole of parts, we *need* not view objects as wholes comprised of parts: we need not engage in any such quantification over parts, and this is precisely where the issue of proper name reference becomes relevant: cognitively speaking, we may have, conceptually, just simple objects around us—Tyson, say, plain and simply, without considering or conceiving him as a whole comprised of various parts. It requires a step of cognitively analysing objects to view them as inherently structured in a particular way. Note that even though we need not conceive of Tyson as a whole comprised of parts, after we *have* done so, it is not arbitrary any more how Tyson and his parts relate. They will relate integrally to him, and not, say, as Tyson will relate to the fists of his manager.

Tyson's fists will relate integrally to him even if they are, say, cut off and put in a museum. As long as they will be known or exhibited there as *Tyson's*, that will be essential to them: they will not be objects in their own right, but essentially *belong* to another object, Tyson. That again shows that nothing as trivial as mere physical connectivity is involved in relating to things integrally. If we view Tyson as an integrated whole consisting of such and such parts, we will say things like *Tyson has big fists*, and if the above evidence suggests correctly that this expression is structurally identical to a truth judgement like *That the Earth is flat has truth to it*, what this sentence expresses is an integral relation between a 'whole' and a presentation of it as well.

So, the claim, to repeat, is: a sentence has truth integrally: this is what a human being takes a truth judgement to suggest. The truth that it predicates of the sentence is not an object in its own right, it is the truth-*of* a particular sentence. Even if that is a claim about cognition, it may well tell us something about the metaphysics of truth, however. What we can say, firstly, is that a proposition does not relate to its truth in the way a formal symbolic structure relates to semantic values (designated denotational objects in the domain of a semantic model), through an interpretation function that arbitrarily connects them. If we are interested in how the human mind configures a judgement of truth, then truth does not attach to sentences in the way standard model-theoretic semantics suggests. Mapping sentences to such denotational objects is useful to various purposes, of course, but, if I am right, no contribution to an understanding of truth *predication* as a mental act that happens internally to a syntactic derivation, in an integral fashion.

We may now also be better equipped to assess the question of whether truth judgements as such have a 'correspondence' to anything in 'reality'. To start with, the integral character of the relation between a proposition and its truth, I argued, is a fact in the eye of the beholder. It is not a matter of truth and falsehood, in some absolute or non-human sense. Indeed, if the question is what in the world corresponds to a whole-of-which-a-certain-part-or-aspect-is-predicated, I suppose this question has no answer. I would not know what to look for. Parts of objects (in the sense encompassing other integral aspects such as truth) are certainly not individuals out there, in any standard sense, nor are constituents or amounts of things, which can equally stand in integral relations to these things. Moreover, as noted, objects *need* not be viewed as wholes comprised of parts, and they are not wholes by nature. They are not *found* to be wholes, but are wholes when cognitively configured in a special way. For example, there is nothing *in the world* (outside our heads) that changes when we switch from looking at the Ford T engine as a *part* of a whole to looking at it as an *object* in its own right. The worldly scene may be exactly the same; yet in the one case we have a part–whole predication, in the other we do not. The same reasoning may be applied to human truth-judgement, which I have analysed analogously. What worldly thing does the *judgement that something is true* 'correspond to'? Again, I would not know what to look for, emphasizing once more however that no 'anti-realism' is implied here: it is as true as it always was that explanatory constructs that scientists creatively come up with in their heads seem to be sufficiently tuned to what is out there so as not in general to pick out nothing at all.

Suppose by contrast and for the sake of argument that the standard picture of semantic theory was right and that in (28a) or (29a), say, repeated here as (60a, 60b):

(60a) that the Earth is flat is true
(60a) That the Earth is flat has (some) truth to it,

that the Earth is flat 'denotes a proposition', in the substantive philosophical sense in which a proposition is a mind- and language-independent metaphysical entity that has its truth conditions or denotation essentially. On this picture, a proposition is of its *nature* something that is true or false, relative to possible worlds, irrespective of human judgement. It is true or false as a matter of metaphysical fact. How would one analyse on this view what somebody asserting *That the Earth is flat* is doing? Somebody asserting this would, on this view, assert that a certain proposition that is true or false relative to any given context or possible world, in particular the given one, is true, or has truth to it.

Note that there is a sense in which a proponent of this classical picture, as well, basically says that an assertion of *That the Earth is flat* is really an assertion of one of the forms of (60). What we have on the analysis now under discussion is merely an *additional* assumption that, (i) *That the Earth is flat* inside the respective expressions of (60) 'denotes (or expresses) a proposition', and (ii) that proposition is true or false (or denotes the relevant truth values), in a sense independent of human truth judgement. Now, if so, (60a) either is an assertion, of a true proposition, that it is true, or of a false proposition, that it is true. But it is unclear why either of these options would adequately describe the meaning of (60a). To be sure, an external observer might be independently convinced that the Earth is flat, and comment on a person's asserting (60a) in the following way: she asserts, of a true proposition, that it is true. But this seems to tell us nothing about how the speaker configures or structures a judgement expressed in (60a). We certainly cannot paraphrase the content of an assertion of (60a) as conceived in the mind of the person asserting it, by saying:

(61) Either a certain true proposition is true, or a certain false proposition is true.

Why bring in 'propositions', and make the additional assumption that *that the Earth is flat* in (60a) 'refers' to one such thing? Note that once this assumption is brought in, it is only consequential that not merely *That the Earth is flat* 'denotes a proposition', but the whole of (60a) as well. But how do we then state the truth conditions of *that* whole proposition? State *in English*, I should say. Example (62), below, would be too weak a candidate for the statement of this condition, since that would also be the official truth condition for an assertion of *the Earth is flat* (without the truth predicate). Hence it does not capture the surface-semantic effect *added* by the overt truth-predication. But the relevant statement is also not (63), which sounds weird:

(62) The Earth is flat.
(63) That the Earth is flat is true is true.[22]

That might be due to its lacking a second Complementizer, as Uriagereka (p.c.) objects. If so, a more appropriate version of an attempt to state truth conditions for (60a) is (64):

(64) That that the Earth is flat is true is true.

But the grammaticality of (64) seems to me uncertain. Importantly, it sounds best if we actually construe the first complementizer, not as a subordinating complementizer, but as a cataphoric referential expression co-indexed with a judgement following it in the form of an 'appositive' insertion:

(65) That: that the Earth is flat is true, is true.

If we really had two complementizers in (64), the construction would be somewhat similar to (66) (cf. (67), construed on analogy with (66)):

(66) That for John to win should impress me made me sad
(67) That for the Earth to be flat should be true is true.

But these are very weird. However generous we are with their grammaticality, the basic problem we are hitting upon here again seems to be that assertoric force simply does not iterate or recursively embed. Judgements do not embed

[22] Things get worse with the other instances of (28–29), e.g. (28b), which results in something like the following statement of its truth condition: cf.

(i) that the truth is that the Earth is flat is true
(ii) that the truth is that the truth is that the Earth is flat

in other judgements. That is why the paratactic insertion in (65) improves the situation so much.

Going back to the problem of stating the truth condition for (60a), I do not *know* whether or not there are really 'facts' or 'conditions' out there which 'correspond' to things like *The Earth is round*. However, I find my credulity stretched beyond measure if for (60a), too, there would have to be a 'corresponding' *judgement*, an act of presenting something as true, out there, as well, in order for it to correspond to anything. This problem aggravates further with (60b), and a search for such external correlates makes no sense at all in the case of a judgement like (68):

(68) That the Earth is flat has no truth to it.

For what would somebody asserting (68) assert? That something that is true has no truth to it? That something that is false has no truth to it? These options exhaust the possibilities, on the standard picture, but none is adequate. The former is contradictory, the latter tautological, but (68) is perfectly informative.[23] There is no difficulty at all, on the other hand, if we accept that (68), as a whole, is a judgement, rather than 'expressing or denoting a proposition' that non-integrally (or as a matter of metaphysical fact) 'bears' a truth value, and is composed of other such propositions with similar such truth values. If these metaphysical assumptions cause the above difficulties, we might as well abandon them. A judgement relates the propositional (but not proposition-denoting) expression *that the Earth is flat* to its truth, but there are no external and non-integral truth conditions that judgements have, and there are no 'facts' in the world 'corresponding' to them.[24]

4.6 Conclusions

As in a piece of 'ordinary language philosophy', I have here analysed the meaning of *true* by studying our uses of this word and the specific structures in which this particular lexical concept appears. These structures are subject to an inquiry that makes no metaphysical presuppositions while having

[23] Thanks to Juan Uriagereka for the example. One should note also that in English usage (68) has nothing 'paradoxical' to it at all, in the sense of the logical paradoxes.

[24] It is noteworthy that one formal semantic theory comes to something like these conclusions on purely logical grounds, that is, not on the empirical/grammatical path I pursued here: Martin-Löf's Intuitionistic Theory of Types, which distinguishes judgements from propositions and prioritizes the former over the latter. For discussion and references see Hinzen (2000). The major difference is that Type Theory employs essentially a technical notion of proposition, which may indeed be essential for the logical purposes that Type Theory is designed for.

implications for our metaphysical thinking about truth. Just as Wittgenstein, when inspecting uses of a word, would have looked for mechanisms that generate these uses, I have too. These mechanisms do not lead to a judgement's *being made*, but this, or human action in general, is not the issue. They also tell us nothing about how 'language relates to the world', but only about how thoughts relate to the truth that we predicate of them. It seems we cannot even *try* to really think what it would be for truth to relate externally to our thoughts. For if we thought this, syntax would tune in, and make this relation integral again. Maybe there is a non-integral truth-relation between mind and world, holding as a matter of metaphysical fact. But then we should be able to analyse it. And if we do that, my argument that this relation is an integral one, with no external correlate, tunes in.

How it happens that our minds, with whatever structures are inherent to them, relate to the world in intentional terms of course here remains the mystery that it has always been: the account given has only been a syntactic one; however, the contention here has been that syntax is an essential part of its solution. Before there can be talk of any such intentional relations and their potential 'representational success' in enterprises such as science, there has, to start with, to be a build-up of structure in the mind that at first accesses purely conceptual resources, and then, without modifying these conceptual structures in further compositional ways by adding more conceptual material, takes a constructed proposition so as to *present* it as being true or false. It is as if the process of constructing a certain mental object suddenly stops, and we objectify or represent it, so as to consider it together with a certain presentation of it. This very process is a part of the origin of truth.

With respect to the overall aim of this book, as described in the Prologue, we may at this point conclude this: if there is a threat to the 'internalism' that structures the present overall inquiry, it will *not* come from the fact that this one species on Earth is capable of building 'intentional' structures in which truth uniquely figures.

5

Structure for Names

5.1 Explaining rigidity

It remains to demonstrate that paradigmatic forms of nominal 'reference', rather than being a threat to an internalist research programme, presuppose it. The specific forms of intentionality we see in the case of name reference will in this chapter be argued to be systematically conditioned syntactically, a desirable conclusion under assumptions of a 'transparent' and compositional syntax–semantics mapping as well as learnability considerations. In particular, I will argue the so-called 'rigid' interpretations of nominals have an explanation in the linguistic form of these nominals, and in this sense a wholly internalist one. Particular referential modes, with which lexical atoms finally come to figure in referential acts, are manufactured in the derivational dynamics. Rigidity is one particular such mode of reference of nominals, contrasting with more flexible such modes. I want to begin by illustrating this mode with some familiar examples.

An object referred to as (or picked out by the identifying description) *the brightest celestial object regularly seen near the western horizon after sunset* might be Mars rather than Hesperus: all it takes to make this a fact is a cosmic reshuffling due to, say, a slight shift in the cosmic constant. In that circumstance, however, it would still be true that by using the name *Hesperus* we would refer to the very planet we did before, namely Venus, even though that planet, in our current world, and not Mars, is the brightest celestial object regularly seen near the western horizon after sunset. In other words, while names like *Hesperus* refer in a way that their referent survives even a major cosmic reshuffling, descriptions need not so refer, being more flexible in their meaning.

Similarly, in the world of the Olympics, *the greatest of all times* might not be Maurice Green, but might, in principle, be someone different every four years. On the other hand, it is *not* possible that Maurice Green might be someone else, say Carl Lewis, or that George W. Bush might be his brother Jeb. Still, come to think of it, might George W. Bush not *be* his brother Jeb? How much do we really know? Nor do I have a problem imagining me to be Maurice Green, as I do when saying: *If I was Maurice Green, the world's fastest man would be a philosopher.* So is proper name reference really as rigid as we thought?[1] In sum, the data suggest that in some cases of the uses of names, rigidity is for real, while in others, reference seems to follow different and apparently more descriptive modes.

My central question here will be to explain these modes of reference, and rigidity in particular. If semantics is to be explained—or provides *data*—what provides the explanation must be something different than semantics. Now, a name like *Green* seems syntactically simple or atomic, while a description like *the greatest of all times* is, if anything, syntactically complex, as well as compositionally interpreted (as an existential quantification, I will assume, whose existential quantifier is probably coded syntactically in the position of the determiner *the*, a point to which I return). In other words, there is an obvious syntactic difference between names and definite descriptions. One can regard this fact as either irrelevant or not, with regard to the explanatory problem posed. But the former option clearly is not the null hypothesis, if only again for reasons of acquisition: the assumption of a tight mapping between syntax and semantics will importantly reduce the otherwise indefinite number of possibilities that the child will have to consider. In short, from a linguistic point of view, any stab at an explanation of the fact we seek to explain should depart from the obvious difference in the overt syntactic forms of the kinds of expressions involved. It is simply unlikely that expressions so radically different in syntactic form would be interpreted in semantically identical ways.

To generalize this point, absent good evidence to the contrary, something of the atomic syntactic form *X* should not, *ceteris paribus*, be able to mean what the non-atomic *the X* does. On the same grounds, a proper semantic representation of *X* should not be ιX, where the 'iota'-operator (cf. Chierchia 1998), is a mapping from a set (or the extension of a predicate) to an individual, turning the predicate into an expression with a referential import. Iota is effectively defined as equivalent to the definite determiner *the*: the X = ιX (see Chierchia, 1998: 346). However, in the absence of any such determiner in the structure of an expression, it is not clear what in the linguistic form iota should follow from. Moreover, given compositionality, the meaning of 'the X' *presupposes* that of 'X'; hence, plainly, 'X' itself should not itself have

[1] One might avoid a negative answer to this question by saying that while epistemically possible, it is not *really* possible that George W. is in fact Jeb: we might contend that there is no conceivable possible world in which the former is the latter. But that conclusion is too ungenerous. For all we know, our actual world might be one where George W. is Jeb, and our world is *surely* possible. In this case, when referring to George W., we always really refer to Jeb, although in his 'guise' as George W., which he took on (to extend his power and influence the voters?).

the form 'ιX', given that 'ιX' essentially means what 'the X' does. To illustrate the same methodology of 'transparency' with another example mentioned in Section 2.3, we should wonder why the meaning of the English word *dog*, which denotes a kind, should be given by appeal to the meaning of the morphologically *more* complex word *dogs*, which denotes a set of individuals. Again, things should in some plain sense be the other way around: individuality should become relevant only once kinds are there, and not be a presupposition for the definition of kinds. Before kinds can be chunked into, or be presented as, individuals, the kinds must be there. The meaning of 'dog+s' *presupposes* that of 'dog', and for this reason the meaning of the former should not be invoked in the explanation of the meaning of the latter.[2]

Again, if we take syntactic form seriously as a hint towards underlying semantic complexity, this suggestion is a natural one. But it means that the meaning of *dog* should *not* be thought of as a set of individuals, or depend on the existence of such a set. On the contrary, to identify a set of individual *dogs*, we need the concept of a *dog*. I return to this issue in the end; let us, for now, simply insist that the meaning of *dog* is not usefully described as a set of individual dogs. Let us describe it instead as a *concept*, assuming these to figure essentially in our understanding somehow, as they must, and to be distinct from the *extensions* (sets of individual objects) that they determine.

The methodological assumption of a transparent syntax–semantics mapping, in the case of names, means that if we formally have an atom, X, in a syntactic representation, we should have, formally, an atom in the corresponding semantic representation, too, as we assumed in Chapter 3. A definite description like *the X*, in being syntactically complex, must then be regarded as posterior to what exists prior to and independent of syntactic processes, namely the lexicon. Getting an expression of the form *the X*, which is semantically a description, requires a syntactic derivation (the projection of a DP), and, idioms aside, there is no such thing *in* the lexicon. If names *are* in the lexicon, as they intuitively seem to be, they *cannot*, contra Russell, be syntactically complex in the way that descriptions are.

What then could some such philosophical claim as that 'names really are descriptions', semantically, mean? It could be a claim about how a name should be formally *represented* in the notation of some formal language

[2] Consider Chierchia's (1998: 345) following sentence: 'Singular common count nouns like *dog* are (characteristic functions) true of individual dogs.' It is strange that to explain the meaning of an item X, one must exploit the meaning of another item, Y, that *contains* X as a proper part. Chierchia also explains mass reference via the notion of individuals, but this is not consistent with the fact that languages precisely mark individual presentations of nominal spaces: if Chierchia is right, these should be the linguistically simpler notion, with mass presentations constructed from them and thus linguistically marked.

designed for purposes of semantic representation. But that would not be particularly interesting, as it would leave entirely open *why* a particular linguistic item should be mapped onto that semantic representation, rather than another one. If we wish not only to *represent* the meanings of expressions but to *explain* why they have the meanings they do, we should be pointing to the *linguistic form* of the expression, and say it has *that* interpretation because of *that* linguistic form. On this conception, a claim that names are really descriptions is an *empirical* and *structural* claim about the syntax of the expression in question. As such, few philosophers who have spoken of the 'semantic equivalence of names and definite descriptions' have defended it, apparently assuming a much looser syntax–semantics interface, on which one syntactic object can be mapped to whatever our semantic intuitions suggest. If the syntax–semantics interface is tighter, as it should be, the reason we give for a structural assumption should be something other than the need to make a certain semantics come out right; we should not be left in the dark about why a particular semantics is the one it is, for a given expression.

My guiding intuition will therefore be that when something is *inflexible* or *rigid* in its denotation, the reason is that it is, in its syntactic form, maximally simple or atomic too.[3] Only something that has *parts* can have *variable* parts, and hence

[3] I won't take this to mean that names cannot be internally complex, but that they lack an internal syntactic complexity that is compositionally interpreted. Obviously, that they are totally unstructured is not true, e.g., of surnames of some Irish and Scottish chiefs of clans:

(i) the O'Donoghue of the Glens
(ii) the MacNab

Complex names can be like idioms, having a status intermediate between semantically compositional phrases and semantically atomic lexical expressions. Note in this connection that the 'saxon genitive' in Dutch is found only after names or namelike entities, as in (iii)–(iv), although not after common nouns that are not namelike, as in (v)–(vi):

(iii) mijn Opa's fiets
'my grandfather's bicycle'
(iv) Gerard's fiets
'Gerard's bicycle'
(v) *mijn buurman's fiets
'my neighbour's bicycle'
(vi) *het schip's kapitein
'the ship's captain'

However, it *is* possible after complex names, as in (vii)

(vii) Burgermeester Foortman's voorstellen
'Mayor Foortman's suggestions'

This indicates that complex names indeed *are* names rather than complex phrases of a standard sort, with a systematic and compositional semantics. Thanks to Ben Shaer and Hans den Besten for discussion of this issue.

change (or have a different denotation/referent in different possible worlds). Hence we need, to start with, a *variable* in the underlying syntactic form: but the way a variable is licensed in natural language is through an operator that gets into its position through a movement. Hence we need an operator-variable structure to get a descriptive reading with the variability in interpretation that the letter entails. I will assume the interpretation of definite descriptions as quantificational DPs, on which the definite determiner denotes a generalized quantifier. Thus, in *the king of Moldavia*, *the* expresses a second-order property of the property of being the king of Moldavia: the fact that it applies to exactly one individual.[4]

Let us begin our inquiry into the origins of reference from the by-now familiar observation that all names *can* in fact take determiners in essentially the same way as *nouns*, hence can function as *predicates* in much the same way that nouns (like *man*, or *king of Moldavia*) paradigmatically can:

(1) a. The early Russell
(1) b. The Russell of 1902
(1) c. Yesterday's Tyson was a disappointment
(1) d. This Tyson is a sad memory of his former self
(1) e. All of Green was joy and relief
(1) f. Tysons are rare in the history of sport
(1) g. Much Tyson remains to be re-discovered.
(1) h. During my stay in Vegas, I met Tysons all over the place.

Note in particular the possibility of mass-quantifying a name, as in (1g), and the capability of a name like *Tyson* to be used as a noun denoting a set of different people with certain identical characteristics (1f, 1h), or the same person under different temporary circumstances or stages (1c, 1d). As another manifestation of the predicative status of names, consider that they incorporate into other nouns:

(2) a. Russell-lovers abhor Wittgenstein.
(2) b. Every Napoleon-admirer owns a hat.

Tyler Burge in the early 1970s concluded on the basis of examples similar to the ones in (1) that all names really *are* nouns, or function as predicates rather than referential expressions or singular terms (which is what Quine held as well, or Russell, at a time; see also Elugardo 2002), hence that they are simply not special. Burge accounted for their apparent rigidity, which he assumed them to have as well, through an element that he posited *externally*

[4] It is the function f from entities to truth values such that there is exactly one x such that f(x)=1.

to them, a 'rigidifier', which he thought of as an attached demonstrative determiner, although for some reason that determiner does not show up overtly in the phonetic form. The proposal was thus that rigidity is not a feature of names, but a feature of the attached demonstratives, viewed as the only 'logically proper names'. In short, the underlying structure of an overtly 'bare' (determinerless) occurrence of *Napoleon* is really something like the more complex *[$_{DP}$ this [$_{NP}$ Napoleon]]*.

A major problem with this proposal, as Higginbotham (1988) observed, is that the *non-restrictive* readings of names, on which their rigidity depends, precisely arises in the *absence* of a determiner—at least if this determiner is overt. Thus in all of the cases in (1), what we are talking about is not Russell, Green, or Tyson *tout court*, but *a specific* ('restricted') Russell, Green, or Tyson, hence individuals *falling under some description* that is explicitly or contextually given. By contrast, a non-restrictive reading arises where the determiner is *dropped*: cf. (2), above, where the name is read non-restrictively, or (3a, 3b):

(3a) Happy Tyson won in five rounds.
(3b) Tyson was rediscovered.[5]

Similarly, if we wish to maintain a contrasting reading of *Tyson* in (4a), which depends on a contextually given description, we cannot drop the determiner. If by contrast, we abolish a restrictive reading, as in (4b), and use an appositive

[5] This generalization is not true for what we may call the 'affective' determiner, which is a different case, and leads to non-restrictive readings:

(i) That Thatcher was a pain for Britain
(ii) This Tyson is a hell of a boxer.

In these cases the noun clearly does not act as a restriction to the determiner/quantifier. Interestingly, the affective reading is impossible with stage-level predications, as in (iii), which is good only when the determiner is read restrictively:

(iii) That Tyson (here) is fighting like he never did before.

On the other hand, a Tyson-stage picked out by a restrictive DP-construction can be the subject of an individual-level predication:

(iv) This Tyson (here) is a genius.

What explains this asymmetry between affective and non-affective determiners? If the stage-level/individual level distinction has a rationale in scope relations between generalized quantifiers associated to nominals in a clause, as Raposo and Uriagereka (2002) argue, then the affective DP in (i) would obligatorily seem to demand a wide-scope position in LF over the event variable; it acts as a *topic*. So, on Raposo and Uriagereka's Neo-Davidsonian semantics, there is a topical event of *Thatcher* here, such that *being a pain* is true of it. On the other hand, in (iii) there is a fighting, which is topical, and a certain Tyson-stage merely takes part in it (it occurs only as part of that event, or in a context: it is a contextual individual). What (iv) then shows is that a Tyson-stage picked out by a DP/NP-construction can also be de-contextualized and become the topic of an individual-level predication.

version of the characterization of Tyson in question, the determiner can be dropped:

(4a) *Tyson who kissed Foreman yesterday was a happy fellow.
(4b) Tyson—who kissed Foreman yesterday—is a happy fellow.

The meaning of (4b) is different from that in (4a), being non-contrastive. Tyson is not 'contextualized' in the sense of allowing comparisons with different versions of the same Tyson on different occasions. He is referred to as an individual that as such and irrespective of the events in which it participates, has a standing characteristic, that of being a happy fellow.

Burge might reply to this that he posits *covert* rather than overt determiners, but that naturally raises the question why the semantic effect of an overt determiner should be so diametrically opposed to that of a covert one. In any case, if a name was introduced by an empty determiner, then we would expect it not to incorporate into another noun. But just this happens unproblematically, as we saw in (2). In short, while there seem to be good reasons to stick to Burge's insight that names can grammatically function as predicates, his explanation of rigidity—a paradigmatically externalist explanation by virtue of its appeal to the direct referentiality of demonstratives—seems doomed.

Now, there *are* cases where it seems we *may* assume, this time on purely syntactic and cross-linguistic distributional grounds, empty determiner ($[_{DP}$ Ø$[_{NP}$N$]]$-) structures for surface-bare NPs. However, as is well-known, this option is severely restricted. In particular, singular mass nouns and plurals allow it, which are certainly *not* interpreted in the way that names are:

(5) Boys met with girls.
(6) Cats eat mice.
(7) I drink wine.
(8) I ate lion.

The interpretation in (5) is indefinite-existential; (6) and (7) have generic readings, and the nominals refer to kinds; and (8) involves an indefinite-existential quantification over a mass noun: it is interpreted as *I ate an indefinite amount of lion-meat.* Note that if that mass-reading is to give way to an individual-specific count-reading, the determiner must become overt—*more* syntactic structure must be present—as in (9), where a fully individualized lion is eaten:

(9) I ate a lion.

Again, then, it seems that empty determiner constructions are not the correct analysis of the underlying syntax of names. Positing an empty determiner in cases such as (5) to (8) is licensed on the traditional assumption (Stowell 1989; Szabolcsi 1994; Longobardi 1994) that bare NPs cannot function as referential arguments in the absence of a determiner that 'turns' them into arguments. The more general idea here is that determiners have a 'singularizing' or 'individualizing' function: they allow a given 'nominal space', the denotation of the noun in question, to be referred to under either a *mass* or an *individual* (count) *presentation.* In languages that lack determiners, like Chinese, this task has been argued to have been taken over by noun classifiers (Cheng and Sybesma 1999). Only once the noun is either 'massified' or 'individualized',[6] reference to it under these modes of presentation becomes possible, as does quantification, hence definite description.[7]

To give some standard examples from Italian providing evidence for the empty determiner analysis, in (10–11) bare NPs occur in a non-argument position, while in (12–13) they occur in an argument-position:

(10) Gianni e [$_{NP}$ amico di Maria]
John is friend of Maria

(11) [$_{NP}$ Amico di Maria] sembra essere Gianni
friend of Maria seems to be John

(12) *Amico di Maria mi ha telefonato
friend of Maria me has phoned

(13) *Ho incontrato amico di Maria ieri
I have met friend of Maria yesterday

Secondly, if empty categories must be properly governed, then the ungrammaticality of

(14) *Aqua viene giu dalla colline
water comes down from the hill

is naturally explained as a proper government violation. Compare by contrast,

(15) Viene giu acqua dalla colline
comes down water from the hill

[6] I follow Cheng and Sybesma (1999: 516, 519–20) in their claim, directed against Chierchia (1998), that Chinese *makes* a mass/count distinction, although this is expressed not at the level of the noun but at the level of the classifier, which speaks against the need for a semantic parameterization (see further Longobardi 2001).

[7] Chomsky (1995: 292) refers to D as the 'locus of reference' in the grammar; in a similar way, Szabolcsi (1994) spoke of a deictic and 'subordinating' function of D, comparable on her view to the relation between T and VP, or C and IP in the human clause.

where proper government is respected. Let us assume, then, that Romance surface bare-NPs are really (at least) DPs, and that when the empty determiner is present, it correlates either with an indefinite-existential or with a generic interpretation. Indeed, as Neale (1990: 45) argues (cf. also Longobardi 1994: fn.29), in an expression like 'the F is G', the former (indefinitely existential) interpretation is the contribution of the empty determiner position as such, while the definiteness aspect of the article is contributed by this particular determiner's specific lexical content. That is, on a conjunctive analysis 'the F is G' decomposes into (16–17), where (16) is the default contribution by the determiner position ('there is one x that is F'), and (17) is that of the specific determiner which fills this position:

(16) $\exists$x F x
(17) for all x, if x is F, it is G.

Chierchia (1998) assumes the existential quantifier to be a type-shifter, which transforms what is, by its nature, a predicate, into an argument. A perhaps more plausible assumption is that $\exists$ merely serves to bind off a given variable that is created through a syntactic transformation. That is, the indefinite existential reading does not have to be *created* through some special operation; it simply *is* the semantic contribution of the D-head.

We are now ready to state a paradox: let us take it that bare NPs cannot function referentially or as arguments in the absence of a Determiner in their underlying structure. But structures of the form D-NP at least with empty D do not have a referential interpretation in the way that names have. And Names, which are bare NPs, function paradigmatically referentially and figure in argument positions. In brief:

(18) THE PARADOX OF NAMES
Proper names are bare NPs, and they are paradigmatically referential. But bare NPs are paradigmatically not referential.

Longobardi (1994) resolves this paradox through the natural conclusion that names simply *are* not NPs but DPs. This makes immediate empirical sense of the fact that names can be syntactically found even in positions where languages like Italian forbid all other bare NPs, such as pre-verbal argument positions. For if the name fills the D-head position (has moved to it), no lexical government requirement on empty categories would rule such examples out.[8] More importantly for our present project, however, the fact that names *lack* the kind of interpretation that bare nouns

[8] Cases like *Il Gianni mi ha telephonato* may be handled quite straightforwardly, by means of an analysis of *Il* as an expletive determiner, and an associated expletive replacement analysis of that determiner at LF.

in argument positions generally receive, and have a different interpretation, can *also* be explained under the movement analysis. For the head movement from N to D—by *substitution* for D, not *adjunction* to it, as Longobardi (1994: 640) crucially assumes—will plausibly have rigidity as its semantic reflex. The reason is that if the empty determiner-position is *filled*, there is no operator-variable construction that can trigger the default-existential reading that we have associated with it. A descriptive reading of the whole DP is not possible because there *is* no head-noun any more in N_0 that could define a range (i.e. a restriction) for a variable bound by a quantifying operator hosted by the D-head.[9] The descriptive reading would thus correspond to the interpretational schema (19), while N-to-D movement gives rise to an entirely different, referential interpretational process:

(19) 'Denotational Interpretation'
[D [N]]: Dx, such that x belongs to the class of Ns

After N-to-D movement, no operator-variable structure (A′-chain) is input to the semantic interpretation, and quantification is blocked. If there is no quantification, no descriptive head-noun is quantified over; hence the referent cannot change; and hence the reference cannot be but rigid.[10] This is the first syntactic and wholly internalist derivation of the rigidity effect that I consider in this chapter. Before I criticize it, consider its transfer to Chinese, as suggested recently by Cheng and Sybesma (1999), assuming for the moment their proposal, adopted from Tang (1990), that classifiers project full phrases (ClPs) that have NP complements. In Chinese, if a bare NP is to have a definite

[9] One objection that might be formulated here is that on one current view of movement in the Chomskyan tradition, the tail (base position) of the chain formed in a movement transformation is simply one copy of the moved item. Hence the position of the noun in the launching site of the movement wouldn't be empty. However, the crucial point seems to be that through N-to-D movement, there is no operator-variable structure and hence no quantification forms. I later return to other objections to the Longobardian view under discussion.

[10] Chierchia (1998: 399) severely misrepresents this argument, assuming the proposal is that 'the semantic character of proper names somehow endows them with a syntactic feature [+r] (something like 'rigidly referential') that needs to be checked by raising it to D.' But while it is true that reference is configured in D (in different ways), rigidity is not featural. It is a consequence of syntactic position; and there is no interpretational or semantic property of 'names' to which I assume the syntactic process is sensitive, or which 'drives' the syntactic process. Indeed, rigidity is not a property of names only and can affect all nominals. Rigidity is a side-effect of a grammatical process, not a feature. Chierchia (1998) asks why grammar 'should project syntactically what is already taken care of by something we surely need anyhow, namely the way in which syntactic categories are mapped onto their meaning?' But how exactly a given lexical item such as *Russell* or *Tyson*, as we have seen, is 'mapped to their meaning' is an open issue, and at least in part a consequence of the syntactic context in which they appear!

interpretation, this can happen in two ways: either an overt classifier is inserted, which is the Cantonese option; or no classifier is inserted, and then according to Cheng and Sybesma a Longobardi-style movement of N to an *empty* Classifier position takes place, accounting for the definiteness effect; this is the Mandarin option. Sentence (20) is a Mandarin example, (21) a Cantonese one (all Chinese examples to follow are from Cheng and Sybesma 1999):

(20) Gou jintian tebie tinghua
dog today very obedient
'The dog was very obedient today'

(21) Wufei yam jyun *(wun) tong la
Wufei drink-finish CL soup
'Wufei finished drinking the soup'

At this point in Cheng and Sybesma's story, something surprising happens, however. They assume that the meaning of D, hence of Cl, is essentially equivalent to that of Chierchia's (1998) iota-operator that we have encountered in the beginning of this section: both shift semantic type from predicate to individual. In other words, they assume that D or Cl do in the syntax what iota does in the semantics: they create referential arguments, and yield the definite interpretation. This is the basis for the proposal of Chierchia (1998), that D and iota can and do *compete* with one another, in an optimality-theoretic sense (see also Gärtner 2004). If a determiner is present, the application of iota is blocked. This, of course, is only plausible once a 'global' organization of human grammar is assumed, in which something in the syntax can compete with something in the semantics, to which it has no access in the 'T'-model at work in the Principles and Parameters framework and in Minimalism. On the latter model, iota is not there in a syntactic derivation, being not there even in any human lexicon. Hence two derivations, one of which contains a lexical determiner, and the other one of which does not, cannot compete with one another or rule one another out. On these assumptions, the explanation of the definiteness effect in Cantonese, that because classifiers are inserted iota cannot be used and applied to a bare NP, is dubious.

In fact, however, it seems that *independently* of the specific grammar model we assume, iota is not needed, since it seems that classifiers in Cantonese simply do the work that iota does; and in the case of Mandarin, the explanation of the definiteness effect in bare NPs—that because classifiers are not present, iota can and must operate—makes it unclear how iota can be triggered by something like the *absence* of a syntactic formative. In any case, iota seems *again* here unneeded, since for Mandarin the authors precisely assume that the head-noun moves into the head-Cl position. But that *is* the derivation of the definiteness effect in the Longobardi-style account that these authors themselves assume, who attribute to both D and Cl an 'individualizing' and 'type-shifting' function (Cheng and Sybesma 1999: 520, 524). So the iota-operator in the Mandarin case does, again, no more than duplicate an action that has taken place in the syntax already. Although the authors claim (1999: 522) that N-to-Cl movement is a 'necessary step' for iota to operate, it makes the operation of iota redundant.[11] Iota follows from nothing in the syntactic form, and in the explanations above it seems it need not enter at all. I will revisit this conclusion later on.

Consider now *proper* nouns in Chinese, when these occur in demonstrative-classifier combinations that yield restrictive or predicative readings:

(22) Nei-ge Hufei zhen bu xianghua
that-Cl Hufei truly not decent
'that Hufei is really not reasonable!'

This again suggests that names—although movable to Cl—are like all other nouns in being base-generated in N and undergoing head-raising from there, like other definite bare nouns. Once again, however, Cheng and Sybesma (1999: 523) follow Chierchia (1998) in suggesting that name-movement, if it happens, is *semantically conditioned*, by a 'type-mismatch' between the type of the name generated in N, namely <e> (the type of individuals), and the type of entities that 'should' be in N, namely <e, t> (the type of predicates). In other words, movement is thought to be necessary in order to shift semantic type. But this account implies that it is an *intrinsic* property of names that they are names; for it is that property that is meant to drive the syntactic derivation. This seems theoretically highly questionable. As noted, a name is plainly a noun, hence if a name is not a predicate, why is it base-generated in N in the first place? Moreover, the proposal has a teleological flavour: the idea that a semantic fact sets the syntactic machine into motion is a bit like the idea of telling one's body to get sick. Syntactic processes do not run for a reason, and they do not run just because a nice semantic result would ensue if they did. So much autonomy of syntax, I think, we should uphold.

While these are only theoretical considerations, there are empirical ones as well. It is demonstrably only a matter of *convention* when a common noun is

[11] Cheng and Sybesma concretely suggest (1999: 522) that there are two options: either iota changes a predicate type to the entity/argument type, and then there is a type-mismatch of the item in N and the type it should have when being in N. Therefore N-to-Cl movement takes place. But this is to motivate movement semantically, which is a non-standard account of movement. *Or*, they suggest, N moves to Cl because otherwise iota cannot operate; but this is again to motivate movement semantically. And it is precisely because Cl does the type-shifting work that iota is supposed to do, that iota seems unneeded.

used as a name, and when not. That is to say, it has nothing to do with the workings of the language system as such. Thus it is an arbitrary convention in German, which could have been otherwise, that the noun *Wolf* (meaning *wolf*) is also a personal proper name, while the noun *Hund* (meaning *dog*) is not. That the operations of the syntax are not only independent of such facts but ignore them is shown by the fact that it can override them. Thus if convention dictated the semantic interpretation of an expression with a structure like (23),

(23) Dog came in

it would be ill-formed, in the way that **dog came in* clearly is. But, in fact, it *is* well-formed under the interpretation where a person called 'dog' came in, hence where the nominal acts as a proper name rather than as a descriptive condition on some object of reference. That may be so in the idiolect of a speaker who knows someone of that name, or in my own idiolect, if I cannot for the life of me find another interpretation of (23). In this sense the example *forces* that interpretation, as no other one is available (see further examples from Hebrew and Chinese below in (24–26)). This would be explained under the assumption that proper names move to Cl/D: for it would be because of that move that the noun loses its descriptive content in (23).[12] In sum, it is not that we have got a proper name here, base-generated in N, which then waits to be promoted on the ground that it is, semantically, a proper name, and a type-mismatch occurs. No, it is because of the promotion to D that it *is*, or rather *becomes*, a proper name. Proper names are the creatures of the syntax, which, despite all conventions that there may be, can rule what to make a proper name and what not.

There is thus only a conventional difference between names and nouns, which the syntax ignores when promoting head nouns to different positions in the clause.[13] Borer (2005) reaches a similar conclusion, offering the example (24), from Hebrew:

(24) Ze'eb radap axrey ha.yeled
'Ze'ev chased after the boy.'
(not: 'a wolf chased after the boy', although *Ze'eb* denotes both 'wolf' and is a proper name).

[12] We should and need not expect that it will lose its descriptive content *entirely*—as has happened with German *wolf*, used as a proper name—since grammatical form determines linguistic interpretation only modulo convention: knowledge about the latter may interfere with grammatically conditioned facts and create interaction effects.

[13] The conventionality of the name–noun distinction is supported by eponyms, i.e. names that have become nouns historically (e.g. *Caesar* in Latin).

Similarly, consider (25) from Cantonese (taken again from Cheng and Sybesma 1999: 523), where bare nouns in sentence-initial position yield a proper name interpretation,

(25) Sin-saang mou lei
teacher not-have come
'Teacher/*the teacher did not come.'

or (26), from Mandarin, where the same is true:

(26) Linju bu lai le
neighbour not come SFP
'Neighbour won't come any more.'

Cheng and Sybesma here comment that 'some common nouns' (like *neighbour, teacher*) 'can' also refer rigidly to individuals, but the right conclusion seems to be that, modulo convention, *all* can. Very paradoxically, but interestingly in the light of my previous discussion, they also suggest that N-to-Cl movement in such cases is 'without the ι operator' (1999: 523), which is effectively to *concede* that the iota operator is unneeded for the referentiality, confirming my earlier point that it is a descriptive device that denotes the result of a process that, in the authors' own model, takes place in the syntax through a transformation already. It also confirms my earlier contention that the N-movement is *not* driven by 'the nature of proper names instead of the ι operator' (ibid.), since there *are* no proper names in the numeration underlying the derivation of (25).

This completes my presentation and defence of what I take to be a first, conceptually and empirically motivated way of deriving the rigidity effect, essentially by appeal to N-to-D movement and its inherent semantic consequences. On this particular view, before relevant transformations have applied, no noun refers rigidly; and without functional projections, no noun functions referentially as opposed to predicatively. In this explanation, we have not appealed to beliefs, world knowledge, or pragmatics: it has been a wholly internalist one. Let us add to this account what I said in Chapter 2 about the atomic conceptual content of names. The conceptual content of names is what remains *stable* or constant across radical shifts in the *physical* referent of the name in question. Specifically, as illustrated in (1), we can make individual-level reference to *Tyson*, as in *Tyson is guilty*; or refer to different individual Tysons on different occasions ('Tyson-stages'), as in *This Tyson (here) is a disappointment*; or to a Tyson-kind, as in (1f); or even to non-individual Tyson-masses, as in (1g). But in all these cases, we can only do so if we *have* the lexical item *Tyson* with its idiosyncratic sound and meaning in the first place, which illustrates once more our distinction between intentional and conceptual information. Different Tyson-stages are *different*, and Tyson-masses are different from individual Tyson-stages, but they are all instances *of Tyson*. Thus there must be a sense in which the latter's lexical meaning is as such independent of whether we refer to him as an individual, as an individual stage, or as a mass, using specific correlating syntactic paradigms in each of these cases, all more complex than the mere atom *Tyson*.

We are therefore forced to say that as a lexical item, both the referent of Tyson and its mode of reference are not yet settled: they depend on a particular syntactic configuration into which they enter. For example, if, in the course of the derivation, *Tyson* gets plural morphology and surfaces as a bare NP in an argument position, it is bound to be interpreted either as kind-referring (cf. 1f), or indefinitely existentially, as in (cf. (1h), similar to (5) or (8)). If the indefinite existential reading of *Tyson* correlates with an empty determiner position, and the individual-level reference arises when the determiner becomes overt, as in *Yesterday I met a Tyson that was mild*, or as in *I ate a lion* (9), this suggests the conclusion that the specific mode of the referential act—everything except his pure lexical content—and in particular the formal ontology of the referent, are computed syntactically in the course of a derivation: reference crucially is an inherently syntactic phenomenon. If we ask, again, what *is* that same Tyson-thing, this 'pure lexical content', that remains constant across possible worlds and acts of referring to it, we can only circularly specify it: it is Tyson. Attempts to non-circularly specify this individual by appeal to a *relation* that the word *Tyson* has to a particular external object, Mike Tyson, as physically described, seems hopeless: there is no conceptual necessity, even, that Mike Tyson, our object of reference, *has* physical properties, as noted. The opposite position would be that the reference to the individual, concrete, physical Tyson (as opposed to individual stages of this object, mass-presentations, or disembodied version of it) is coded into the *lexical meaning* of the word. But that Tyson has this physical existence is a matter of belief, inquiry, and experiment, not meaning or conceptual understanding.[14] We may *lose* the belief, while the meaning, for all we can tell, stays the same, as, for example, when we utter (27):

[14] Collapsing belief and meaning remains a pervasive feature of philosophical discussions on names. Consider Braun and Saul's (2002) 'resistance to substitution in simple sentences' puzzle, that (i) seems true to many, while (ii) seems wrong, and should lead to the falsehood of (i) too, given the identity of Superman and Kent:

(i) Superman leaps more tall buildings than Clark Kent
(ii) Superman leaps more tall buildings than Superman.

(27) Tyson, who died and now lives in heaven, will always remain the one he was.

No human language, as far as I know, morphologically marks the difference that existence makes. Whether some entity really exists, or exists in a particular form, according to current physics or common world knowledge (say, whether water is H_2O or XYZ, or maybe a visual illusion), is *a posteriori* information that the linguistic system does not know about. This rightly predicts that there is no evidence that the linguistic system computes compositional semantic interpretations for sentences containing *Hamlet* in any different way than it computes such interpretations for expressions containing *Tyson*. As Longobardi (1994: 638, fn 32) notes, wide-scope (*de re*) and rigidity effects for names for fictions and for actually existing individuals are the same. If it turned out, contrary to received wisdom, that Hamlet actually *was* a historically real entity, and that, by contrast, Tyson *never* existed, nothing in our *concepts* would change. The next day we might find two headlines in the newspaper, *Tyson proved to never have lived*, or *Hamlet proved to really have lived*, whose compositional understanding by us depends on the

It strikes me that the explanation of this puzzle is entirely straightforward, from a linguistic point of view. Thus there is a constraint operative in the human linguistic system according to which if there are two referential expressions in one clause, they are by default interpreted as not referring to the same thing (reference is obviative). The mechanism is a dump one: two nominals, two interpretations. This constraint exerts its influence even if the formative used for both nominals is the same: thus (iii)

(iii) John killed John

strikingly cannot mean that John killed himself, an interpretation for which the system uses a new and special formative, *-self*; if (iii) can be interpreted at all, it is interpreted so there are two different persons both called John. This is even true in a language like Afrikaans, where there *is* an option for a co-referential interpretation, but only in the quite different case of 'appelative' nominal forms interpreted as second person (data courtesy Hans den Besten, p.c.):

(iv) Oom moet Oom gedra
uncle must uncle behave
'you have to behave yourself'

We see the same influence in our interpretation of (ii), which sounds 'strange' to us, as we would predict, and is not relevantly different in this respect from (iii). Like (iii), (ii) makes us look for different referents where the formatives involved indicate there is only one, which is what puzzles us. There *are* examples where this severe constraint can be overridden, as in small clause constructions like (v), in which the two referential nominals do refer to the same thing:

(v) We called [$_{\text{Small Clause}}$ him John].

But these are rather special cases. In short, the first judgement above is unproblematic and expected. The second is explained as an interface effect: the language system interfaces with others, notably human belief systems. Thus, while the former system demands two referents in (iii), the latter comes in telling us that both referents are the same. This is a contingent truth; the former, that the two referents are distinct, is an analytic one, following from the rules and workings of the linguistic system itself. This entire explanation has no need for the notion of a language-external and mind-external 'referent', and the puzzle arises only on the latter's assumption.

fact that the names occurring in them mean exactly what they do now. A specification as part of the lexical meaning of the relevant names, according to which Tyson is embodied and Hamlet is not and was not, would positively hinder the way language is actually and compositionally understood in such counterfactual cases. In short, in explaining namehood, or rigidity, existence makes *no* difference. Our materialist belief that Tyson reduces to an actual external individual in flesh and blood should not enter into the analysis of the lexical meaning of *Tyson*. It should not, because embodiment is no constraint on this item to function compositionally in language in the way it does. Hence neither the rigidity of names, nor an analysis of the pure conceptual content of Tyson, viewed apart from its mode of reference on an occasion, forces any externalist conclusions.

5.2 Atomicity and reference

Although the analysis of the previous section fits our internalist purposes in this chapter, it faces some objections. To begin with, as Juan Uriagereka notes (in personal communciation), it seems unsafe to assume that argument-NPs must necessarily be DPs, a crucial presupposition to the above analysis (or that of Longobardi 1994, 2001; Cheng and Sybesma 1999; and Borer 2005). Thus, (28) appears to mean the same as (29), where the NP has been incorporated into the verb.

(28) I hunt partridges every fall
(29) I go partridge-hunting every fall,

But if *partridge* is a DP in (28), this incorporation should be impossible, on the assumption that DPs do not incorporate. This doubt about the arguments-as-DP analysis does not mean that D is not the 'locus of referentiality', or a 'subordinator', as proposed above, but only that some syntactic arguments can be purely 'conceptual' rather than more complex referential arguments.

The second complication is that the above N-to-D proposal tells us virtually nothing about how to handle cases mentioned initially in this chapter, like (30)–(31), below (see Uriagereka 2002: ch. 12 on these sorts of examples):

(30) If I was Maurice Green, the world's fastest man would be a philosopher.
(31) This Tyson is a sad memory of his former self.

Note that, in (31), a *particular* Tyson is referred to, say the one I am just witnessing in a fight, and it is distinguished from Tyson *as such*, since it does not follow from (31) that Tyson, on the individual-level, is a sad memory of his former self. Similarly, what cases like (30) demand is not the impossible thing that I be someone else, but that a (standard) version (individual guise) *of me* changes into another (non-standard) version *of me*: one that has more of Green (say, his running power) in it than the current one. In other words, the point of the fantasy in question is that relevant *parts* or aspects of me are swapped for relevant parts of another person: what we are creating, in the words of Uriagereka (2002), is a *chimera*. But note again, as in the end of the previous section, that, although both (30) and (31) involve a restrictive reading of the proper names involved, at the same time they exploit the *rigidity* of these very names, whose reference must stay *constant* across the whole swapping of parts. The paraphrase:

(32) If some relevant parts of me were swapped with some relevant parts of Green

as such suggests this: for this fantasy is only coherent if, no matter all that swapping of parts of me and him, I remain myself and Green remains Green. Otherwise an absurdity ensues, since I must become someone else. In short, no matter how we syntactically construct complex modes of presentations of individuals, partition them and quantify over their parts, as in (32), there is a sense in which rigidity is preserved, and apparently just because the same lexical concept occurs in our derivation, whatever structure we derive in it syntactically. That suggests against the Longobardian derivation of the rigidity effect that *rigidity cannot be the effect of a syntactic process* after all; rather, it is best conceptualized as what *survives* the transformational process. Since what survives the syntactic process is in effect the *lexical items* it contains, namehood as such *is* a matter of the lexicon after all. A Longobardi-style head-movement analysis seems powerless to explain the rigidity effect as manifest in such examples.

This suggests the conclusion that Longobardi-style analyses are *right* in the assumption that namehood resides in the *absence* of a DP-internal operator-variable or quantificational structure. But rigidity is what a noun has *before* the nominal space it denotes is partitioned into a number of parts that can be swapped for others. That partition requires syntactic complexity: if I am to refer to myself under a *description*, as in *some (relevant) parts of me* (or the song *All of me*), the structural resources I use are *more* rather than less: for in *rigidly* referring to me, I just use *me*. Rigidity, in other words, should reside in the *syntactic simplicity* of a mental representation, which, due to its simplicity, cannot support descriptions and quantifications that have a variable reference. Let us then drop the requirement that NPs in argument positions are quantificational by default, with namehood and rigidity arising from *overriding* this default, as in a Longobardi-style analysis. Instead, let us pursue the intuition that rigidity is an inherent property of *the noun itself*, as a lexical item, or as denoting a primitive nominal space, unspecified for its ontological character. What the formation of DP-internal quantificational structure does is to *override rigidity* by allowing a richer and more flexible mode of reference. Consider again (25), repeated here as (33), and compare it with (34):

(33) Sin-saang mou lei
teacher not-have come
'Teacher/*the teacher did not come.'

(34) Go sin-saang mou lei.
CL teacher not-have come
'The teacher (*Teacher) didn't come.'

Example (33), *lacking* an overt noun classifier of the sort that shows up in (34), forces a proper name interpretation. Example (34), having this classifier, crucially forbids it. In this sense, in classifier languages like Chinese, a proper name interpretation and a syntactic structure involving a classifier are *inherently inimical*. What follows from this observation, that *names do not take classifiers*, and are interpreted restrictively otherwise? Cheng and Sybesma comment on their example (34) as follows:

> We attribute this to the individualizing function of classifiers. The [Cl+N] phrase with an overt classifier yields an interpretation in which the classifier picks out a particular instance of the kind denoted by the common noun. This yields the definite interpretation and not a proper name interpretation. (Cherg and Sybesma 1999: 524)

But then it follows analytically that *prior* to the attachment of the classifier to the noun, it is *not yet* individualized, which is precisely my stance here. The nominal is, as it were, a *pure or abstract concept*, which is not classified for individuality or mass, and hence not (yet) quantifiable—which derives the conceptual–intentional distinction one more time. If we take this together with the observation that proper names do not take classifiers, we arrive at the striking conclusion that nouns that act as names and denote rigidly do *not* as such denote concrete individuals. An individual or a mass presentation (which proper names can also get, as we saw) must be *computed* in the course of the syntactic derivation, and depends on the attachment of an appropriate classifier or quantifier. As we do that and quantify a name thus understood, restrictive and descriptive readings, with particular associated ontologies, arise.

This account does again not entail that names are not predicates. It rather entails that predicates (nouns) as such can refer rigidly, a conclusion that validates an idea philosophers have argued for on independent grounds

(Putnam 1975; Kripke 1972). To mentally represent individuals and sets of them, we *presuppose* what is in my terms a pure concept, hence do not explain it, something the syntax of these mental representations mirrors by making a word denoting a set of individuals more complex than a word denoting a concept, and making a construction denoting one individual more complex than a construction denoting a mass (empty determiners give us mass readings, and to get count readings, there must be an overt determiner).[15] If we wish to take seriously the idea that countable individuals require an overt lexical determiner, but masses not, mass presentations should not be seen to depend on concrete individual presentations. They do not, on the account now defended, where nouns taken from the lexicon are simply concepts, and are as such neither referred to as masses nor as countable individuals.

Our final explanation of rigidity, then, is that a 'mental space' that has no parts, stages or instances that one could count or quantify, *could* not refer other than rigidly. It is nothing that could change from world to world. A classifier, by introducing a partition into a nominal space, makes rigidity disappear. Once we have parts/stages, these parts can be referred to, such as the stage referred to in *this Tyson-stage is a disappointment*, and they can be swapped for others, creating chimeras. Rigidity, by contrast, is the trivial effect of syntactic atomicity, and it cannot be lost once the atom is there and inserted into the derivation, no matter what descriptions are computed. We have drawn this conclusion by departing from Cheng and Sybesma's quote above, which precisely does not, I think, support what they otherwise defend, namely that rigidity is an effect of N-do-Cl movement.

That leaves the obvious question of what we do with English, which does not have classifiers. But, as we noted, Cheng and Sybesma argue classifiers to be functionally equivalent to English determiners. But this would not seem right in the light of Tang's (1990) view on the structure of a DP like (35), namely (36):

15 That conclusion is directly inconsistent with Chierchia's proposal on Chinese nouns, according to which they are mass nouns, their semantics is given in terms of individuals, and they are of the type <e>. But Cheng and Sybesma (1999: 519–20) provide evidence that Chinese makes a count/mass distinction. They do this at the classifier level, which immediately suggests that individuality does not exist yet at the level of the noun. Chinese nouns can also be interpreted as bearing number specifications, despite their lack of plural marking, which makes it problematic to interpret them uniformly as masses. Theoretical considerations in Borer (2005: ch. 3) also argue against Chierchia's proposal regarding a semantic parameter distinguishing Chinese noun interpretation from the English one. See also Longobardi (2001).

(35) Zhe san ben shu
DEM three CL book
'These three units of (the kind) book'

(36)
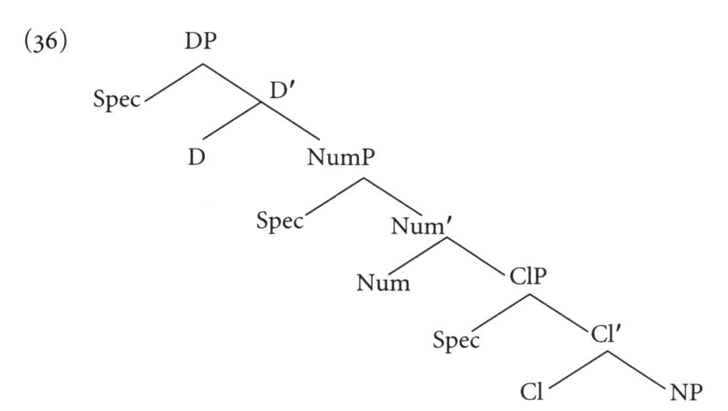

On this analysis, we get a definite description with a quantification over 'units' of the nominal space 'book' only if we have, over and above a classifier that enables quantification in the first place, also a quantifier in the numeration, presumably hosted by the D-position. This raises the possibility that the analogon in English to Chinese 'individualizing' classifiers are not determiners, but *covert classifiers* that exist at the level of the *noun*, rather than at the level of the syntax, as in Chinese. This would be to assume a *sub-lexical* syntax much as we have assumed in Chapter 2.

Although covert, the Classifiers do show up here and there, even in English, in the form of measure phrases, say, or the partitive syntax that we used in our paraphrases above, for example *all-parts-of-me.* We would have to assume, then, that when we quantify a nominal such as *Tyson* in (1d), what we quantify over is a *classified* nominal space, partitioned in a number of temporary and individual Tyson-stages (a space with an ontology introduced into it). Thus the underlying structure of a DP like 'this Tyson' is like that of 'this *stage-of-*Tyson', where what we quantify over is one particular *individual presentation* of the underlying Tyson-space. Equally, when I quantify me, as in *all of me*, there is a classified nominal space, a me-space partitioned into me-modes (modes of presentations/parts of me), where the modes in question may relate to this space much as truth relates to the small-clausal propositional subjects in the analysis of truth in Chapter 4, as depicted in (37) below. The constituents of the SC would provide for the substantive *conceptual* content of the judgement in question, and on top of this SC we would have a DP-structure with a quantifier quantifying a referential variable in between the DP and the SC:

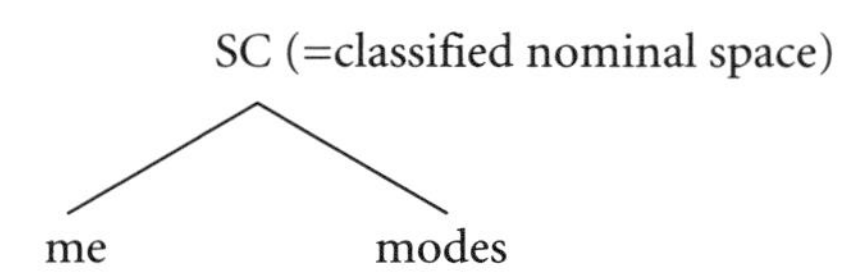

On this structural model, one can 'present' me in a certain mode, much as one can present a given proposition as having truth. At the level of the lexicon, on the other hand, 'I' is a pure concept, and 'I' has no parts or presentations to speak of, parts that could change from context to context, or from world to world, so as to preclude rigidity. Moreover, there are different modes of presenting a person: there can be a mass presentation, and there can be an individual presentation. Finally, there are entailment relations between these ontological modes, which suggest a recursive structure of the sort I argued for in Chapter 3 when explaining lexical entailments in terms of a multi-dimensional syntax. Stacking small-clausal predications yields this result (Uriagereka 1995):

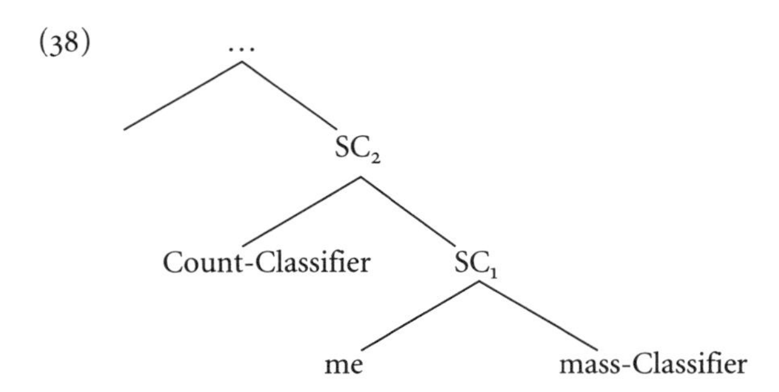

It is thus an intriguing hypothesis that we find the same, or at least an abstractly and formally similar space-predication semantics, no matter whether we look predicational and hierarchical structures in the nominal spaces or 'propositional' ones:

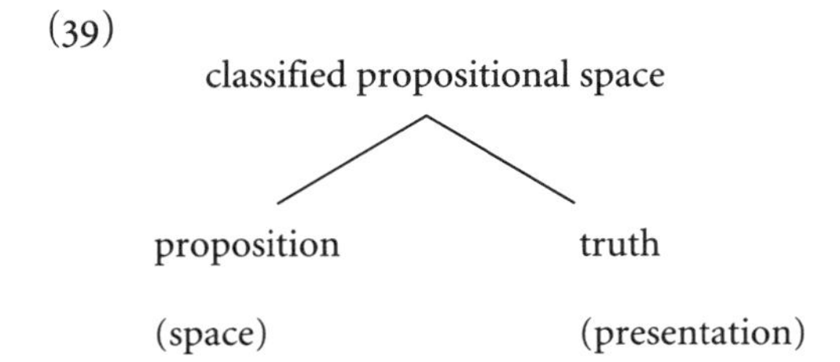

As noted, however, there is in this latter propositional instance no recursive structure-building beyond this point: when it has reached the truth, the mind reaches the end of the structural domains that language can open up for it. The road is from the conceptual to the intentional, and no further.

5.3 Conclusions

We may summarize the structure-driven referential possibilities for a given lexical name as follows:

(i) reference to an indefinite amount of a mass (cf. *Much Tyson remains to be re-discovered*)
(ii) reference to an indefinite number of individual instances of a kind (cf.: *I met Marias all over the place*),
(iii) direct reference to this kind itself (cf. *Marias are usually good girls*),
(iv) a definite number of individual instances of this kind (cf. *I met a Maria/the two Marias*)
(v) a version of one particular instance of a kind denoted by the name by contrast to another such version (cf. *Yesterday's Tyson was a disappointment*),
(vi) a 'style' or 'kind' (cf. *A Maria is usually a good girl*)
(vii) individual-specific and non-contrastive reference to an individual (cf. *Maria is a good girl*).

In each of the cases (i)–(vii), the mode of reference depends on specific preconditions in the syntactic structure of which the 'name' is a part. The range of referents always involves the same atomic lexical concept, but it would be a mistake to tie that concept to a particular kind of referent in the world: our reference to things in the world is always perspectivally configured on occasion. If we refer to it as an individual, in particular, that requires syntactic specification which goes beyond the mere conceptual-atomic content of the lexical item as such.

If we like, we may say that names are distinct from nouns in being 'tagged' in the lexicon as names; but this does not preclude them from acting as nouns in a suitable syntactic context. As for nouns not tagged as names in the lexicon, they also can be forced into being names, in which case their relation to their referent is semantically arbitrary (conventional); they can also, in that case, rigidly denote a kind, as in the case of *man* in *man is the curse of this planet.*

To repeat, under strict compositionality, the reference of complex expressions *must* be built from that of its maximally simple or atomic parts: at the bottom of human reference lies that of non-structured human concepts, but their modes of reference are not yet fixed there. There is, moreover, a sequence of increasing orders of conceptual complexity correlating with the way in which the linguistic system gradually builds up mass and individual presentations of something that conceptually retains its identity (remains the 'same thing') in these various changes in presentation. These are presentations that a given nominal space may have and which need to be structurally fabricated—which again is not to say that a given item listed in the lexicon may not be conventionally associated with a noun or a mass-reading.

Rigid reference of a lexical concept shows up at LF/SEM if, and only if, a given nominal space taken from the lexicon, after entering the derivation, is not classified, hence not presented in a particular guise. For Kripke and most philosophers who have followed him, by contrast, rigidity as a semantic phenomenon has pointed in a radically externalist direction, such as a 'causal theory of reference', or a social-normative theory. Again, the explanation for rigidity does not lie here. Causal relations between acoustic tokens and the world do not as such begin to explain either that there is intentional reference in the human lineage or that it is rigid. Causal relations between my physical surfaces and a (dead) person, Gödel, do not explain, for example, why and how I refer to him as a person using a name. Nor is there anything physical about Gödel or causal relations that my body has to his (now disintegrated) body that would explain why my reference to him as a person is rigid. In this same philosophical tradition, referring rigidly to things like Hamlet or Pegasus will be a non-issue (that is, entirely unacceptable). But from a linguistic point of view, there is no asymmetry at all between using names of fictional entities and using names of 'real' ones, as suggested in Section 5.1: language is not sensitive to this metaphysical difference. The linguistic form and the grammatical mechanisms are the same in the two cases, and only an independent metaphysical and epistemological agenda would treat them differently. Rigidity is also independent of systems of belief. It finds its origin within the linguistic system. There is no such linguistic issue as the issue of negative existentials, or 'Plato's beard', in the sense described in Chapter 1. Treating it as one is to miss out on what makes language as a species-property most distinctive: the fact that it is free, and unconstrained to refer to whatever we can think, as opposed to merely what is physically real or prevalent in the here and now.

Overall, what this chapter has suggested amounts, if I may be allowed to be fundamentally immodest and pretentious as this book draws to a close, to a sort of 'Copernican turn' in the theory of names. In Kant's case, this turn consisted in the contention that it is not the mind that is organized by its outer experience, but that our experience is organized by the inherent (categorial) structure of the mind. Similarly here, it is not our names that revolve around the world and change together with it, but the world that changes according to what our names suggest. To make this point again in the way I made it before, on the Kripkean conception, it is a fact about Gödel, this external object, that he might not have been another person, hence would not be someone else if we found that he did not do what, if anything, we think he did: discover the Incompleteness Theorems. But this external thing, Gödel, clearly does not as such tell us about how we will regard it to change or not in possible circumstances. Again, for all that its *physical properties*, as an external object, tell us and allow us to conclude, he could as well be a *different* thing, if, say, his hairstyle changed. That we think he relevantly remains *the person* he was (although not the physical object he was), depends on adopting a perspective that our human concept of a person affords. If we looked at it as an entity, or a physical object, he would be relevantly different. Hence it is not properties of the external object—or causal relations between it and us—which tell us when it changes and when it is the same. As Hume noted, personal identity is not a matter of physical appearance, a point that perfectly generalizes to other referential domains, be it cities or cars, river or pens. If anything, I want to have made plausible that the specific interpretation of names—traditionally a stronghold of externalist views of language—is plausibly regarded as having internalist ingredients.

Conclusions

Both truth and reference are within the scope of the internalist research programme here entertained. Our mind gives us these ideas in the first place: we do not find truth independently of it, as it were, as a mind-independent relation in the world. Or, if it is such a relation, we need truth as a concept to detect it. A first step I have made here is to re-conceptualize and shift the problem of truth from the metaphysical to the cognitive domain. If anything, truth is a human concept. If it is something more, like a relation between mind and world, we need evidence that we do not need when we say: it is a human concept, a cognitive universal. As that universal we can study its remarkable features, as well as the structures into which it enters, and which do seem intrinsic to it, in a way that they do not to a general and cross-species notion of adaptation or representation.

That truth is not a relation is no proclamation of 'anti-realism' at all. When theorizing about the world we generate explanatory constructs that make sense of the real: we hope our theoretical terms will resonate somehow and to some extent with what the world is like. As far as I can see, there is no reason not to believe that they do; and in particular, that the explanatory constructs of theoretical linguistics, when characterizing the structural edifice that the mind is, do capture as aspect of the mind's properties. Yet, it does not follow from this statement of 'scientific realism' that an ordinary judgement of truth will have to be viewed as anything other than a mental object in which a propositional structure is presented in a particular guise (the guise of truth), or that it will be 'representational' of some external and mind-independent entity that somehow exists out there and whose structure it 'mirrors'.

Indeed I have defended the idea that, likely, with the evolution of a structured human language, the categories of thought changed as well: language was ontologically innovative, yet not necessarily in a way that these new categories depict any structure out there that pre-existed language, and can be identified in language-independent terms.

The study and explanation of reference allows related conclusions. There are, for all it seems, no external objects whose mind-independent properties would explain why and how we refer to them. Rigidity, in particular, almost certainly has a purely internalist explanation and may be a straightforward consequence of the nature of lexical concepts and their lack of syntactic complexity. The nature of the real does not predict that we will refer to it rigidly, nor that we will use to this purpose a relatively narrow range of human concepts and the perspectives they engender. What stabilizes, fixes, and rigidifies reference is not the world, but the mind: the concepts in terms of which we think.

References

Abler, W. (1989). 'On the particulate principle of self-diversifying systems', *Journal of Social and Biological Structures* 12: 1–13.

Amundson, R. (1998). 'Typology reconsidered', *Biology and Philosophy* 13: 153–77.

—— and Lauder, G. V. (1994). 'Function without purpose', in Hull and Ruse (eds.) (1998), 227–57.

Anderson, S. R. and Lightfoot, D. (2002). *The Language Organ. Linguistics as cognitive physiology* (Cambridge: Cambridge University Press).

Antony, L. and Hornstein, N. (eds.) (2003). *Chomsky and his Critics* (Oxford: Blackwell).

Arbib, M. (2005). 'From monkey-like action recognition to human language: An evolutionary framework for neurolinguistics', *Behavioral and Brain Sciences* 28: 105–67.

Astington, J. W. and Baird, J. A. (eds.) (2005). *Why Language Matters for Theory of Mind* (Oxford: Oxford University Press).

Baker, M. (1988). *Incorporation* (Chicago: University of Chicago Press).

—— (1996). 'On the structural positions of themes and goals', in J. Rooryck and L. Zaring (eds.) *Phrase Structure and the Lexicon* (Dordrecht: Kluwer), 7–34.

—— (1997). 'Thematic roles and syntactic structure', in L. Haegeman (ed.) *Elements of Grammar* (Kluwer: Dordrecht), 73–137.

—— (2001). *The Atoms of Language* (New York: Basic Books).

Baker, M. C. (2003). *Lexical Categories* (Cambridge: Cambridge University Press).

Borer, H. (2005). *In Name Only* (Oxford: Oxford University Press).

Bowers, J. (1993). 'The syntax of predication', *Linguistic Inquiry* 24: 591–656.

Brandom, R. (1994). *Making it Explicit* (Harvard: Harvard University Press).

Braun, D. and Saul, J. (2002). 'Simple sentences, substitution, and mistaken evaluations', *Philosophical Studies*: 1–41.

Burge, T. (1973). 'Reference and proper names', *The Journal of Philosophy* 70: 425–39.

Carey, S. (2004). 'Bootstrapping and the origin of concepts', *Daedalus*: 59–68.

Carstairs-McCarthy, A. (1999). *The Origins of Complex Language: An Inquiry into the Evolutionary Beginnings of Sentences, Syllables, and Truth* (Oxford: Oxford University Press).

Chametzky, R. A. (2003). 'Phrase structure', in Hendrick (ed.), 192–225.

Cheng, L.-S. and Sybesma, R. (1999). 'Bare and not-so-bare nouns and the structure of NP', *Linguistic Inquiry* 30(4): 509–42.

Chierchia, G. (1998). 'Reference to kinds across languages', *Natural Language Semantics* 6: 339–405.

Chomsky, N. (1959). 'A Review of B. F. Skinner's *Verbal Behavior*', *Language* 35, (1): 26–58.
—— (1966). *Cartesian Linguistics* (New York and London: Harper and Row).
—— (1995). *The Minimalist Program*, MIT Press.
—— (2000). *New Horizons in the Study of Language and Mind* (Cambridge: Cambridge University Press).
—— (2001). 'Derivation by phase', in M. Kenstowicz (ed.) *Ken Hale: A life in language* (Cambridge MA: MIT Press), 1–52.
—— (2002). *On Nature and Language*, eds. A. Belletti and L. Rizzi (Cambridge: Cambridge University Press).
—— (2003). 'Replies to critics', in Antony and Hornstein (eds.), 255–328.
—— (2004). 'Beyond explanatory adequacy', in A. Belletti (ed.), *Structures and Beyond* (Oxford: Oxford University Press), 104–31.
—— (2005a). 'On Phases'. Ms.
—— (2005b). 'Three factors in language design', *Linguistic Inquiry* 36(1): 1–22.
—— (2006). 'Approaching UG from below', Ms., MIT.
—— and Lasnik (1993). 'The theory of principles and parameters', in Chomsky (1995): ch. 1.
Churchland, P. (1995), *The Engine of Reason, The Seat of the Soul* (Cambridge, MA: MIT Press).
—— (1998). 'Conceptual similarity across sensory and neural diversity', *Journal of Philosophy* 95(1): 5–32.
Collins, C. (2002). 'Eliminating labels', in Epstein and Seely (eds.), 42–64.
Davidson, D. (1968). 'On saying that', *Synthese* 19; reprinted in Davidson (2001). *Inquiries into Truth and Interpretation* (Oxford: Clarendon).
—— (1999). 'The folly of defining truth', *Journal of Philosophy* 93(6): 263–79; cited after the reprint in M. Lynch (ed.) (2001), 623–40.
—— (2001). *Inquiries into Truth and Interpretation*, 2nd edn (New York: Oxford University Press).
Dawkins, R. (1976). *The Selfish Gene*, 2nd edn (1989) (New York and Oxford: Oxford University Press).
—— (1983). 'Universal Darwinism', in Hull and Ruse (eds.) (1998), 15–37.
Den Dikken, M. (2006). *Predicators and Linkers* (Cambridge, MA: MIT Press).
Dennett, D. C. (1995). *Darwin's Dangerous Idea* (Harmondsworth: Penguin).
—— (2003). *Freedom Evolves.* (Harmondsworth: Penguin).
Descartes, R. (1637). *Discours de la Méthode*, Introduction and notes by Et. Gilson, (Paris: Vrin, 1984).
De Villiers, J. (2005). 'Can language acquisition give children a point of view?', in J. W. Astington and J. A. Baird (eds.), *Why language matters for theory of mind* (Oxford: Oxford University Press), 186–219.
De Villiers, P. (2005). 'The role of language in theory-of-mind development: What deaf children tell us', in J. W. Astington and J. A. Baird (eds.), 266–97.

De Villiers, P. and de Villiers, J. (2003). 'Language for thought: Coming to understand false beliefs', in Gentner, and Goldin-Meadow (eds.), 335–84.
Devitt, M. and Sterelny, K. (1999). *Language and Reality*, 2nd edn (Cambridge, MA: MIT Press).
Dienes, Z. and Perner, J. (1999). 'A theory of implicit and explicit knowledge', *Behavioral and Brain Sciences* 22: 735–808.
Dretske, F. (1988). *Explaining Behavior* (Cambridge, MA: MIT Press).
—— (1994). 'Fred Dretske', in S. Guttenplan (ed.), *Companion to the Philosophy of Mind* (Oxford: Blackwell), 259–65.
—— (2006). 'Minimal rationality', in Hurley and Nudds (eds.), 107–15.
Dummett, M. (1996). 'The source of our concept of truth', in M. Dummett, *The Seas of Language* (New York: Oxford University Press).
Dworkin, R. (1996). 'Objectivity and truth: You'd better believe it', in *Philosophy and Public Affairs* 25(2): 87–139.
Elugardo, R. (2002). 'The predicate view of proper names', in G. Peter and G. Preyer (eds.) *Logical Form and Language* (Oxford: Oxford University Press), 467–503.
Epstein, S. and Seely, D. (eds.) (2002). *Derivation and Explanation in the Minimalist Program* (Oxford: Blackwell).
Etchemendy, J. (1988). 'Tarski on truth and logical consequence', *The Journal of Symbolic Logic*, 53(1): 51–79.
Fernandez, K. J., Marcus, G. F., DiNubila, J. A., and Vouloumanos, A. (2006). 'From semantics to syntax and back again: argument structure in the third year of life', *Cognition* 100: B10–20.
Field, H. (1972). 'Tarski's theory of truth', *Journal of Philosophy* 69(13): 347–75.
Fisher, R. A. (1930). *The Genetical Theory of Natural Selection* (Oxford: Oxford University Press).
Fodor, J. (1990). *A Theory of Content and Other Essays* (Cambridge, MA: MIT Press).
—— (1998). *Concepts. Where cognitive science went wrong* (Oxford: Clarendon).
—— (2001). 'Doing without what's within: Fiona Cowie's critique of nativism', *Mind* 110: 99–148.
—— (2003). *Hume Variations* (Oxford: Clarendon).
—— (2004). 'Having concepts: A brief refutation of the twentieth century', *Mind and Language* 19(1): 29–47.
—— and Lepore, E. (no date). 'Morphemes matter: The continuing case against lexical decomposition (Or: Please don't play that again, Sam)'. Rutgers University Center for Cognitive Science.
—— and —— (1998). 'The emptiness of the lexicon', *Linguistic Inquiry* 1: 429–38.
—— and —— (1999). 'Impossible words?', *Linguistic Inquiry* 30(3): 445–52.
—— and —— (2002). *The Compositionality Papers* (Oxford: Oxford University Press).
—— and Pylyshyn, Z. (1988). 'Connectionism and cognitive architecture: A critical analysis', *Cognition* 28: 3–71.
Freeze, R. (1992). 'Existential and other locatives', *Language* 68(3): 553–95.

Frege, G. (1956). 'The thought', *Mind* 65(259): 289–311.

Gärtner, H.-M. (2004). 'Naming and Economy', Ms., ZAS, Berlin.

Gallistel, C. R. (1990). *The Organization of Learning* (Cambridge, MA: MIT Press).

—— (1998). 'Brains as symbol processors: The case of insect navigation', in S. Sternberg and D. Starborough (eds.), *Conceptual and Methodological Foundations.* Vol. 4 of *An Invitation to Cognitive Science* (D. Osherson, series editor) (Cambridge, MA: MIT Press).

—— and Gelman, R. (1992). 'Preverbal and verbal counting and computation', *Cognition* 44: 43–74.

—— and Gibbon, J. (2001). 'Computational versus associative models of simple conditioning', *Current Directions in Psychological Science* (10): 146–50.

Genter, T. Q., Fenn, K. M., Margoliash, D., and Nusbaum, H. C. (2006). *Nature* 440: 1204–7.

Gentner, D. and Goldin-Meadow, S. (eds.) (2003). *Language in Mind* (Cambridge, MA: MIT Press).

Gleitman, L., Cassidy, K., Nappa, R., Papafragou, A., and Trueswell, J. C. (2005). 'Hard words', *Language Learning and Development* (1): 23–64.

Godfrey-Smith, P. (1996). *Complexity and the Function of Mind in Nature*, (Cambridge: Cambridge University Press).

Goldin-Meadow, S. (2003). *The Resilience of Language: What gesture creation in deaf children can tell us about how all children learn language*, (New York: Psychology Press).

Gould, S. J. (2002). *The Structure of Evolutionary Theory*, (Cambridge, MA: Belknap Press of Harvard University Press).

Greenberg, J. H. (2005). *Language Universals* (Berlin: de Gruyter).

Grimshaw, J. (1990). *Argument Structure* (Cambridge, MA: MIT Press).

Grover, D. (2001). 'The prosentential theory: Further reflections on locating our interest in truth', in Lynch (ed.), 504–26.

Gupta, A. (1993). 'A critique of deflationism', *Philosophical Topics* 21(2): 57–81.

Haack, S. (1978). *Philosophy of Logics*, (Cambridge: Cambridge University Press).

Hadley, R. F. (2004). 'On the proper treatment of systematicity', *Mind and Machines* 14: 145–72.

Haegeman, L. (1994). *Introduction to Government and Binding Theory* (Oxford: Blackwell).

Hale, C. M. and Tager-Flusberg, H. (2003). 'The influence of language on theory of mind: A training study', *Developmental Science* 6: 346–59.

Hale, K. and Keyser, S. J. (eds.) (1993). 'On argument structure and the lexical expressions of syntactic relations', in *The View from Building 20: Essays in Linguistics in Honor of Sylvain Bromberger* (Cambridge, MA: MIT Press).

—— and —— (1997). 'On the complex nature of simple predicators', in A. Alsina, J. Bresnan, and P. Sells (eds.) *Complex Predicates*, CSLI Lecture Notes 64: 29–65, (Stanford: CSLI Publications).

Hale, K. and Keyser, S. J. (2002). *Prolegomenon to a Theory of Argument Structure* (Cambridge, MA: MIT Press).

Hauser, M. D. (1999). 'Primate representation and expectations: Mental tools for navigation in a social world', in P. D. Zelazo, J. W. Astington, and D. R. Olson (eds.), *Developing Theories of Intention* (Mahwah, NJ: Erlbaum).

—— and Fitch, T. (2003). 'What are the uniquely human components of the language faculty?', in M. H. Christiansen and S. Kirby (eds.), *Language Evolution* (Oxford: Oxford University Press), 158–81.

—— , Chomsky, N., and Fitch, W. T. (2002). 'The faculty of language: What is it, who has it, and how did it evolve?', *Science* 298: 1569–79.

Hendrick, R. (ed.) (2003). *Minimalist Syntax* (Oxford: Blackwell).

Hespos, S. J. and Spelke, E. S. (2004). 'Conceptual precursors to spatial language', *Nature*, 430: 453–6.

Higginbotham, J. (1988). 'Contexts, models, and meaning', in R. Kempson (ed.), *Mental Representations* (Cambridge: Cambridge University Press), 29–48.

Hinzen, W. (2000). 'Anti-realist semantics', *Erkenntnis* 52(3): 281–311.

—— (2003). 'Truth's fabric', *Mind and Language* 18(2): 194–219.

—— (2006a). *Mind Design and Minimal Syntax* (Oxford: Oxford University Press).

—— (2006b). 'Dualism and the atoms of thought', *Journal of Consciousness Studies* 13(9): 25–55.

—— (2006c). 'Internalism about truth', *Mind & Society* 5(2): 139–166.

—— (2007). 'Hierarchy, merge and truth', forthcoming in M. Piattelli-Palmarini, Salaburu, P., and Uriagereka, J. (eds.), *Of minds and languages. The San Sebastian Encounter with Noam Chomsky* (Oxford: Oxford University Press).

—— and Uriagereka, J. (2006). 'On the metaphysics of linguistics', *Erkenntnis* 65(1): 71–96.

Hornstein, N. (1984). *Logic as Grammar* (Cambridge, MA: MIT Press).

—— , Rosen, S., and Uriagereka, J. (2002). 'Integrals'. In J. Uriagereka, (2002). *Derivations* (London: Routledge), 179–91.

—— , Grohmann, K., and Nunez, J. (2005). *Understanding Minimalism* (Cambridge: Cambridge University Press).

Horwich, P. (1998). *Truth* 2nd edn (Oxford: Clarendon Press).

Hull, D. L. and Ruse, M. (eds.) (1998). *The Philosophy of Biology* (Oxford: Oxford University Press).

Hurley, S. and Nudds, M. (eds.) (2006). *Rational Animals?* (Oxford: Oxford University Press).

Jackendoff, R. (2002). *Foundations of Language* (Oxford: Oxford University Press).

James, W. (1880). 'Great men and their environment', in *The Works of William James*, vol. 6 (Cambridge, MA, 1975), 163–89.

Jenkins, L. (2000). *Biolinguistics* (Cambridge: Cambridge University Press).

Kayne, R. (1993). 'Toward a modular theory of auxiliary selection', *Studia Linguistica* 47: 3–31.

—— (1994). 'The antisymmetry of syntax', (Cambridge, MA: MIT Press).

Keenan, E. L. (1987). 'A semantic definition of "Indefinite NP"', in E. J. Reuland and A. ter Meulen (eds.), *The Representation of (In)definiteness* (Cambridge, MA: MIT Press), 286–318.

Koch, C. (2004). *The Quest for Consciousness* (Englewood Cliffs, NJ: Norton).

Koopman, H. and al Sportiche, D. (1991). 'The position of subjects', *Lingua* 85(1): 211–58.

Koslow, A. (1992). *A Structuralist Theory of Logic* (Cambridge: Cambridge University Press).

Kripke, S. (1980). *Naming and Necessity* (Cambridge, MA: Harvard University Press).

Künne, W. (2003). *Conceptions of Truth* (Oxford: Oxford University Press).

Langacker, R. (1998). 'Conceptualization, symbolization, and grammar', in M. Tomasello (ed.), *The New Psychology of Language* (Hillsdale, NJ: Erlbaum), 1–37.

Langendoen, T. and Postal, P. M. (1984). *The Vastness of Natural Language*, (Chicago, NJ: University of Chicago Press).

Larson, R. (1988). 'On the double object construction', *Linguistic Inquiry* 18: 335–91.

—— and Segal, G. (1995). *Knowledge of Meaning* (Cambridge, MA: MIT Press).

Lebeaux, D. (1988). Language acquisition and the form of grammar. PhD dissertation, Amherst, MA: University of Massachusetts.

Lenneberg, E. (1967). *Biological Foundations of Language* (New York: Wiley).

Leslie, A. (2000). 'How to acquire a "representational theory of mind"', in D. Sperber (ed.), *Metarepresentations* (Oxford: Oxford University Press), 197–224.

Lidz, J. and Gleitman, L. (2004). 'Argument structure and the child's contribution to language learning', *Trends in Cognitive Sciences* 8(4): 151–61.

Longobardi, G. (1994). 'Reference and proper names. A theory of N-movement in syntax and logical form', *Linguistic Inquiry* 25(4): 609–65.

—— (2001). 'How comparative is semantics?', *Natural Language Semantics* 9: 335–69.

—— (2005). 'Towards a unified grammar of reference', *Zeitschrift für Sprachwissenschaft* 24: 5–44.

Lycan, W. (2000). *Philosophy of Language. A Contemporary Introduction* (Oxford and New York: Routledge).

Lynch, M. (ed.) (2001). *The Nature of Truth* (Cambridge, MA: MIT Press).

McGinn, C. (1993). *Problems in Philosophy: the Limits of Inquiry* (Oxford: Blackwell).

McGonigle, B. O. and Chalmers, M. (1992). 'Monkeys are rational!' *Quarterly Journal of Experimental Psychology* 45B(3): 189–228.

—— and —— (2007). 'Ordering and executive functioning as a window on the evolution and development of cognitive systems', *International Journal of Comparative Psychology*, in press.

MacPhail, E. (1998), *The Evolution of Consciousness* (Oxford: Oxford University Press).

Marcus, G. (2001) *The Algebraic Mind: Integrating Connectionism and Cognitive Science* (Cambridge, MA: MIT Press).

Mausfeld, R. (2002). 'The physicalist trap in perception theory', in D. Heyer and R. Mausfeld (eds.), *Perception and the Physical World* (Chichester: Wiley).

Mehler, J. and Dupoux, E. (1994). *What Infants Know* (Oxford: Blackwell).

Moro, A. (2000). *Dynamic Antisymmetry* (Cambridge, MA: MIT Press).

Mufwene, S. (2001). *The Ecology of Language Evolution*, Cambridge Approaches to Language Contact (Cambridge: Cambridge University Press).
Mukherji, N. (2007). 'The primacy of grammar', Ms., University of New Delhi.
Müller, G. B. and Newman, S. A. (2005). 'The innovation triad: An EvoDevo agenda', *Journal of Experimental Zoology*, MDE 304: 487–503.
Neale, S. (1990), *Descriptions* (Cambridge, MA: MIT Press).
Neander, K. (1995), 'Explaining complex adaptations', *British Journal of the Philosophy of Science* 46: 583–7.
—— (1997). 'The function of cognition', *Biology and Philosophy* 12: 567–80.
Newman S. A., Forgacs, G., and Müller, G. B. (2006). 'Before programs: The physical origination of multicellular forms', *International Journal of Developmental Biology* 50: 289–99.
Penrose, R. (1994). *Shadows of the Mind* (Oxford: Oxford University Press).
Perner, J. (1991). *Understanding the Representational Mind* (Cambridge, MA: MIT Press).
—— , Zauner, P., and Sprung, M. (2005). 'What does "that" have to do with point of view?', in Astington and Baird (eds.), 220–44.
Pietroski, P. (2002). 'Function and concatenation', in Preyer and Peter (eds.), 91–117.
Pinker, S. and Jackendoff, R. (2005). 'What's special about the human language faculty?', *Cognition* 95: 201–63.
Potts, C. and Roeper, T. (2006). 'The narrowing acquisition path', Ms.
Povinelli, D. and Vonk, J. (2004). 'We don't need a microscope to explore the chimpanzee's mind', *Mind and Language* 19(1): 1–28.
Preyer, G. and Peter, G. (eds.) (2002). *Logical Form and Language* (Oxford: Oxford University Press).
Price, H. (2003). 'Truth as convenient friction', *Journal of Philosophy* C4: 167–90.
Putnam, H. (1975). 'The meaning of "meaning"', in *Philosophical Papers Vol. 2, Mind, Language and Reality* (Cambridge: Cambridge University Press), 215–71.
Quine, W. V. O. (1968), *Ontological Relativity and Other Essays* (New York: Columbia University Press).
Radford, A. (1997). *Syntactic Theory and the Structure of English*, Cambridge Textbooks in Linguistics (Cambridge: Cambridge University Press).
Ramsey, F. P. (1927). 'The nature of truth', in Lynch, (ed.), 433–46.
Raposo, E. and Uriagereka, J. (2002). 'Two types of small clauses'. In J. Uriagereka, *Derivations* (London: Routledge), 212–34.
Read, S. (1994). *Thinking about Logic. An introduction to the philosophy of logic* (Oxford: Oxford University Press).
Rips, L. J., Asmuth, J., and Bloomfield, A. (2006). 'Giving the boot to the bootstrap: How not to learn the natural numbers', *Cognition* (in press).
Rizzi, L. (1997). 'The fine-structure of the left periphery', in L. Haegemann (ed.), *Elements of Grammar* (Dordrecht: Kluwer), 281–337.
Roeper, T. (2003). 'Watching nounphrases emerge. Seeking compositionality', Ms.

Rorty, R. (2001). 'The decline of redemptive truth and the rise of a literary culture', *European Studies* 1/2001: 19–36.

Russell, B. (1912). *The Problems of Philosophy* (Oxford: Oxford University Press).

Segal, G. (2001). 'Two theories of names', *Mind and Language* 16(5): 547–63.

Skinner, B. F. (1957). *Verbal Behavior* (New York: Appleton Century Cross Inc).

—— (1969). *Contingencies of Reinforcement*, Appleton-Century-Croft.

Smith, K., Brighton, H., and Kirby, S. (2003). 'Complex systems in language evolution: The cultural emergence of compositional structure', *Advances in Complex Systems* 6(4): 537–58.

Smith, N. and Tsimpli, I.-M. (1995). *The Mind of a Savant* (London: Blackwell).

Spelke, E. S. (1994). 'Initial knowledge: Six suggestions', *Cognition* 50: 431–45.

—— (2003). 'What makes us smart? Core knowledge and natural language', in Gentner and Goldin-Meadow (eds.), 277–312.

Spencer, H. (1855). *The Principles of Psychology* (Westmead: Gregg, 1970).

Stapp, H. P. (2005). 'Quantum interactive dualism: An alternative to materialism', *Journal of Consciousness Studies* 12(11): 43–58.

Steiner, M. (1998), *The Application of Mathematics as a Philosophical Problem* (Cambridge, MA: Harvard University Press).

Stich, S. (1990), *The Fragmentation of Reason* (Cambridge, MA: MIT Press).

Stowell, T. (1989). 'Subjects, specifiers and X-bar theory', in M. Baltin and A. S. Kroch (eds.), *Alternative Conceptions of Phrase Structure* (Chicago, NJ: University of Chicago Press), 232–62.

Szabolcsi, A. (1984). 'The possessor that ran away from home', *The Linguistic Review* 3: 89–102.

—— (1994). 'The noun phrase', in F. Kiefer and K. Kiss (eds.), *Syntax and Semantics 27: The syntactic structure of Hungarian* (San Diego: Academic Press), 179–274.

Tang, C.-C. J. (1990). 'Chinese phrase structure and the extended X'-theory', Doctoral dissertation, Cornell University.

Tarski, A. (1944). 'The semantic conception of truth and the foundations of semantics', *Philosophy and Phenomenological Research* 4: 341–76.

—— (1956). 'The concept of truth in formalized languages', in A. Tarski, *Logic, Semantics, Metamathematics* (New York: Oxford University Press).

Terrace, H. (2005), 'Metacognition and the evolution of language', in H. Terrace and Metcalfe (eds.), *The Missing Link in Cognition* (Oxford: Oxford University Press), 84–115.

Torrego, E. and Uriagereka, J. (2002). 'Parataxis', in J. Uriagereka, *Derivations* (London: Routledge), 253–65.

Tschudin, A. J.-P. C. (2006). 'Belief attribution tasks with dolphins: What social minds can reveal about animal rationality', in Hurley and Nudds (eds.), 413–38.

Uriagereka, J. (1995). 'Warps' (UMD: Working Papers in Linguistics).

—— (1998). *Rhyme and Reason* (Cambridge, MA: MIT Press).

—— (2002). *Derivations* (London: Routledge).

—— (2007). *Syntactic Anchors* (Cambridge: Cambridge University Press), in press.

Walsh, D. M., Lewens, T., and Ariew, A. (2002). 'The trials of life: Natural selection and random drift', *Philosophy of Science* 69: 452–73.

Webelhuth, G. (ed.) (1995). *Government and Binding Theory and the Minimalist Program* (Oxford: Blackwell).

Williams, B. (1992), *Truth and Truthfulness*, (Cambridge: Cambridge University Press).

Wittgenstein, L. (1984). *Philosophische Untersuchungen* (Suhrkamp: Frankfurt).

Yang, C. (2002). *Knowledge and Learning in Natural Language*, (Oxford: Oxford University Press).

Yolton, J. W. (1983). *Thinking Matter. Materialism in eighteenth century Britain* (Minnesota: University of Minnesota Press).

Index